DRESSING THE MAN

RESSING THE MAN

MASTERING THE ART OF PERMANENT FASHION

Alan Flusser

!t

itbooks

AN IMPRINT OF HARPERCOLLINS PUBLISHERS

A continuation of this copyright appears on page 308.

DESIGNED BY JOEL AVIROM
DESIGN ASSISTANTS: JASON SNYDER AND MEGHAN DAY HEALEY
ILLUSTRATOR: DAVID CROLAND

Library of Congress Cataloging-in-Publication Data
Flusser, Alan J.
Dressing the man: mastering the art of permanent fashion / Alan Flusser.—1st ed.
p. cm.
ISBN 978-0-06-019144-3
1. Men's clothing. 2. Fashion. I. Title.
TT617.F5796 2001
391'.1—dc21   2001051937

11 / 12

I dedicate this book to my mentor and Buddhist teacher,
Daisaku Ikeda
Thank you for your lifelong dedication to world peace and the happiness of mankind.
You have taught me how to help others, and by doing so, appreciate the potential inherent
in each person's life. Yours is the most stylish way of all.

In loving memory of Saul Cantor and my father, Martin Flusser,
two men whose lives made a profound difference in my own.

And finally, to my all-weather, all-court women, my cheerleaders, my bench,
Piper, Skye, Marilise, Janet, Bobba Jean, Maybelle, and especially Hope,
brightening me up in sunshine or showers.

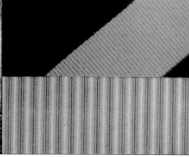

C O N T

E   N   T   S

DRESSING THE MAN

During the last quarter of the twentieth century, men lavished more money on their attire than in any other period of modern history. A stroll down any upscale shopping street would take you past a host of seductive men's emporiums brimming with clothes for every occasion, mood, or taste. Top men's designers became publicly traded global conglomerates. Men's fashion now competed with women's as big business. With entrepreneurs and self-made millionaires in prodigious supply, the time had never been more propitious for the emergence of a standing army of well-heeled swells.

1
___
PERMANENT

FASHION

Male adornment has blossomed, in part, because of the cultural shift toward personal expression and individuality that took place in the latter third of the twentieth century. During the 1950s, the typical businessman literally hid behind his gray flannel suit. The era's political climate mandated fashion conservatism and uniformity. In some circles, men who dared to dress differently were viewed with derision, as outsiders. Fortunately for men's fashion, the tradition-toppling sixties provided the jump start for males to shed their stereotyped personas. By the dawn of the new millennium, a peacock had stepped out of the gray flannel cocoon.

One positive outgrowth of the sixties turbulence was the legitimacy that the period gave to clothes as badges of communication. Masculine attire was swept up in the quest for broader social freedoms; conformity came to be regarded as almost an infringement of personal liberty. In the image-oriented eighties, men dressed to look wealthy and powerful. By the nineties, sophisticated men looked upon fashion as another means of discourse in an information-driven world.

However, in one of fashion's less fortunate ironies, when asked to name those public figures who now exemplify this newfound interest in male decor, American style gurus and menswear professionals come up relatively empty-handed. Likewise, fashion journalists from other Westernized countries are equally baffled, unable to produce even a foursome of domes-

J. GORDON DOUGLAS
Society Man

WILLIAM GOADBY LOEW
Broker

ANTHONY J. DREXEL BIDDLE, JR.
Society Man

FRED ASTAIRE
Theatre

F. AMBROSE CLARK
Sportsman

MILTON HOLDEN
Society Man

JOSEPH P. WIDENER
Sportsman

DOUGLAS FAIRBANKS, SR.
Motion Picture Actor

T. MARKOE ROBERTSON
Architect

MARSHALL FIELD
Financier

LEFT:
*Men of style,
circa 1930s, captured
head-to-toe.*

OPPOSITE:
*Men of style,
circa 2000, pictured in
celebrity headshots.*

tic male fashion exemplars under the age of sixty. And no one is trying to come up with such iconic *elegantes* as film legend Cary Grant or Italian industrialist Gianni Agnelli; just a couple of high-flying social or business magnates or even the odd Hollywood leading man with an affinity for the random sartorial flourish would do.

How is it that after almost three decades of unprecedented fashion consumption, so few capable practitioners of this masculine art form have been bred? If dressing well were simply a matter of donning the latest designer duds or owning an expensive wardrobe, fashion nabobs should be in abundance. My quick response is that learning how to dress well is much like trying to build a classically beautiful place to live. No amount of professional decoration or priceless furnishings will ultimately make much of a difference if the floors or walls that they are to adorn rest on a shaky foundation. In trying to survive in an increasingly competitive arena, the men's retailer decided to ride on the coattails of the high-profile designer brand, leaving the customer little choice but to base his dressing style on the shifting sands of fashion. Unfortunately, when the style winds change, and they always do, the trend-captive man found himself standing somewhere other than terra firma.

Learning how to dress well is not as difficult as it may seem. Much like the newly fashionable pastime of golf, stylish dressing is an acquired skill that can be honed and improved with correct practice. As a former low-handicap golfer, I am often struck by the fact that the vast majority of participants in both activities spend an inordinate amount of time repeating the wrong techniques, further ingraining the same faults into their swings, or in this case, into their closets.

While the golfing enthusiast can engage a recognized professional for instruction, the fashion follower lacks a body of objective experts to call upon for individual guidance. Any golf pro will confirm that without the proper grip, stance, and balance—the fundamentals—all the practice in the world will not enable the most dedicated golfer to fulfill his potential. Developing a flattering mode of dress is no different: without a working knowledge of the basics, a man cannot achieve true stylishness.

George Clooney   Kenneth Branagh   Nicolas Cage   Gabriel Byrne

Harry Connick Jr.   Matt Dillon   David Duchovny   Ralph Fiennes

John Cusack   Vincent Gallo   Richard Gere   Lyle Lovett

Dressing well rests on two pillars—color and proportion. Once you learn which colors enhance your complexion and why specific proportions flatter your physique, you are halfway home. And what does it take for a man to grasp these two critical aesthetics? Not nearly as much aptitude or savoir faire as you might think. Consider this: the classic male tuxedo confers instantaneous élan on all comers, yet this old-world regime is composed of only two colors, black and white. If such a simple color scenario can help any man appear debonair, you don't need to be some kind of Kandinsky to look your best.

As for proportion, here's the kind of mind-set responsible for the current state of sartorial confusion. Men, as well as women, invariably inquire whether tie widths will become larger or smaller. However, the answer lies not in the world of fashion but in the realm of personal architecture. The width of a man's necktie should relate to that of his jacket's lapels, which, in turn, are governed by the size of the coat's shoulders. (See chapter 3, "Proportion: The Foundation of Style.") Should a man be broad-shouldered, a slightly wider necktie will harmonize better with the jacket's fuller proportions; if small-shouldered, a narrower necktie would be the more flattering choice. Fashion should be accountable to a specific set of physical trademarks and not to some random, seasonally served-up set of fashion flashes.

With this individualized approach, learning how to dress well begins to take on a certain logic, if not clarity. However, men intent upon improving their dressing skills are often stymied by the lack of access to intelligent and personalized instruction. Unfortunately, no matter how sophisticated a store's merchandise, without a knowledgeable and experienced sales staff, the right clothes have little chance of ending up on the right back in the right way.

Due to unstable financing, debt-ridden balance sheets, or stockholder pressures, many larger retailers have been discouraged from thinking about the long term. And with profits squeezed by increasing overheads, sales training and service are the first to suffer. Most retailers are reluctant to invest much in educating a new hire. Although the exceptional retailer or individual sales executive might take the initiative to learn about the history and traditions underlying fine menswear, he or she is not the norm. Nowadays, the distinguished salesperson is either promoted up to management or hired away by a competitor.

Particularly at the top end, where expectations for professionalism and superior service are justifiably higher, retail expertise has sunk to an all-time low. Most better-quality retailers have traded up to more expensive merchandise, ceding almost all responsibility for the education

OPPOSITE & LEFT:
*Two paragons of "seasoned
simplicity": Signor Agnelli and
Doug Fairbanks Jr. blanketed in
the quiet assertiveness of a
two-color ensemble.*

of its sales staff to their suppliers, which is like letting the fox loose in the henhouse. As experienced veterans retire or are pushed out to make way for a more youthful and cost-efficient selling staff, men's clothing floors become increasingly bereft of those qualified to instruct anyone interested in the finer points of this masculine art form.

With most sellers' incomes derived primarily from commission, fashion advice is too frequently prejudiced by the prospect of a sale. It's rare to find a salesperson inclined to dissuade a customer from buying an ill-fitting or unflattering garment, because of the pressure to sustain or increase his figures. Too often, personal opinion and a friendly smile are responsible for the fashion-challenged's shrinking closet space. And with the economic realities currently operating in men's fashion retailing, there is not much reason to expect immediate improvement.

Whereas this might sound like chapter and verse from any period in twentieth-century menswear, such was not always the case. The twenty-year span bookended by the two world wars marked the high point of American men's retailing and fashion. This was the last time that the manufacturing, retailing, and editorial sectors of the menswear industry worked together to ensure the delivery of what it promised: authentic style and correct taste. Even though the 1920s and 1930s were decades of considerable economic tumult for America, they produced the best-dressed generation in the twentieth century. But the lesson from that bygone time was not how well kitted-out the well-to-do were, but rather that the average man's dressing tastes were not that far behind.

The Prince of Wales: The Beau of the Twentieth Century.

During that period, the American male was the beneficiary of some very favorable sartorial circumstances. The period began by catapulting the most important single force in modern men's fashion onto the world stage. While still not yet King of England, David Windsor was regarded in America as the undisputed King of Fashion. The yellow-haired heir to the throne, variously known as the Prince of Wales and later as the Duke of Windsor, visited the United States in 1924 and made front-page news. Photographers trailed him from the Long Island estates of America's wealthiest families to lunch with President Calvin Coolidge, with detours to the races at Belmont Park and the polo matches at Meadowbrook.

As British menswear's greatest traveling salesman, the young Prince of Wales and what he wore were matters of deep interest wherever he went. On September 10, 1924, *Men's Wear* magazine reported, "The average young man in America is more interested in the clothes of the Prince of Wales than in any other individual on earth." The travels of this sartorial Pied Piper elevated the new men's order to center stage. When the stock market crash came, which one would have expected to sweep fashion away, it had the opposite effect.

Wall Street might have laid an egg but fashion didn't. The Great Depression returned style supremacy to the hands of the lucky few who could still afford to dress well. General business conditions did the work of the thresher by eliminating the chaff, or those followers of fashion, leaving the kernels, those men of influential positions in finance and society, to do the leading. The new café society's dressing habits, watering holes, and social activities monopolized the attentions of the fashion press. Their intact fortunes and inbred sense of security emboldened these men to improvise and break the fashion rules. Ironically, despite the Depression, or rather, because of it, the next decade proved to be the most important period in twentieth-century menswear.

The interwar period signaled the last time that the introduction of a new men's fashion (or a different way of rigging out an old one) gravitated down from the upper brackets to the lower. In other words, before the hoi polloi could sign up for it, the high-class had to sign off on it. Any fashion innovation first required the approval of those men considered reliable arbiters of popular taste. Only when a new wearable was adopted by a sufficient number of these style setters would fashion bibles such as *Apparel Arts* or *Esquire* magazine recommend it to the greater buying public. Much like the French vinegrower's Appellation Contrôlée, each new item of apparel faced a rite of passage before it could be certified as "authentic fashion."

If this system did not foster a high enough level of consumer trust, the retailer was in turn expected to assume final responsibility for his establishment's fashion credibility. As *Apparel Arts* advised, "No merchant can devote his time to better use than to employ it in a constant effort to distinguish between real and bogus fashion. A man who cannot buy with confidence will not buy at all." This point of view became a regular theme of the periodical's monthly tidings in the 1930s. Stores selling men's apparel that lacked the correct pedigree or that ended up prematurely out of fashion

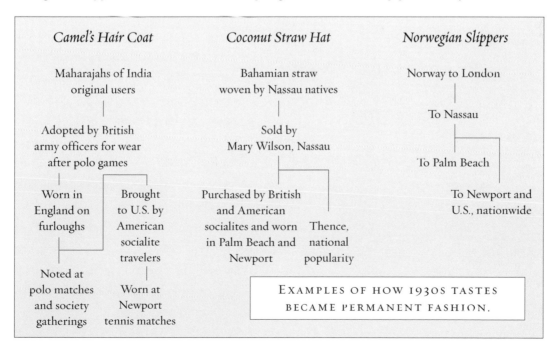

Camel's Hair Coat	Coconut Straw Hat	Norwegian Slippers
Maharajahs of India original users	Bahamian straw woven by Nassau natives	Norway to London
Adopted by British army officers for wear after polo games	Sold by Mary Wilson, Nassau	To Nassau
Worn in England on furloughs — Brought to U.S. by American socialite travelers	Purchased by British and American socialites and worn in Palm Beach and Newport — Thence, national popularity	To Palm Beach — To Newport and U.S., nationwide
Noted at polo matches and society gatherings — Worn at Newport tennis matches		

EXAMPLES OF HOW 1930S TASTES BECAME PERMANENT FASHION.

favor could expect the victim to promptly transfer his loyalty elsewhere.

By the thirties, new men's fashions appeared fast and furious. Formal evening and day attire were supplanted by more casual garments, such as the dinner jacket, the three-piece lounge suit, and the dress shirt with attached soft collar. With the advent of increased leisure time, the odd jacket and slacks ensemble, active and spectator sportswear, and all types of lightweight resort garb pressed their way into vogue. The thirties fashion-conscious male desperately needed both informed and individual advice. And amazingly, that is exactly what he got!

For all America's sartorial shortcomings to follow and for all the legend of England's supremacy in the field of men's clothes, during those interwar years, America evolved in large part through a process of cultural mimesis into the best-dressed nation in the world. Pictures of gents attending sporting events or simply en route to work corroborate this. Old newsreels and periodicals reveal a surprising number of well-dressed chaps, with the average Joe very much a part of the equation.

The question arises: How did the so-called hapless American male end up on top of the style-leader board? And how was the ideal of masculine elegance so widely disseminated during this decade? Three factors helped the American male step out from uninformed mediocrity and up the proverbial ladder toward style superiority—the prevalence of credible role models, "bespoke" fashion, and generally accepted standards of taste.

From the early twenties through the late thirties, that elusive but convenient character, "the average man," was exposed to more visual "aids" in the form of smartly attired public figures than he could shake a stick at. Well-dressed socialites, such as the Biddles and the Rhinelanders, and fashion-savvy business leaders, such as Charlie Munn and Milton Holden, formed just two of the

many strata of society helping to lift the taste level of the masses. The silver screen presented scores of male stars winging about glamorous environs. Fred Astaire, Humphrey Bogart, Gary Cooper, Douglas Fairbanks, Clark Gable, Cary Grant, Adolphe Menjou, Ray Milland, Tyrone Power, George Raft, Jimmy Stewart, and Robert Taylor were regularly profiled at work and home upholstered in all sorts of decorous finery. There was even a British contingent called the "Hollywood Raj," composed of such English gallants as David Niven, Ronald Coleman, Errol Flynn, and Basil Rathbone, who paraded around town like peacocks from Piccadilly. While Hollywood's leading men occupied center stage, England's aristocracy, consistently ranked among the swankier sahibs in the civilized world, had the tradition and the time to flaunt the Empire's influence over male habiliment. Daily tidings of the Prince of Wales were broadcast worldwide along with the social and sartorial escapades of his club-elegant confreres. Much like today's omnipresent billboards, the landscape furnished extensive opportunity to observe and imitate the goings-on.

*Basil Rathbone, part of the "Hollywood Raj,"
showing his high style.*

The second factor responsible for the emergence of so many domestic swells was the influence of "bespoke" taste, which was to say, the "London Look." *Tailor and Cutter*, Britain's weekly trade gazette, trumpeted that "a man can't make love with conviction unless he is wearing a coat cut within a half a mile of Piccadilly." With the world's economies depressed, men's style took its lead from those well-starched stalwarts with sufficient cash to have their clothes tailored on London's legendary Savile Row. The English "drape" suit and all raiment "Briddish" were regarded as the quintessence of masculine sophistication.

The thirties represented the last epoch in which a gentleman's ideal was to be attired in "bespoke fashions." Men's dress still represented a form of class-consciousness, and tailor-made clothes ranked as another of those vessels of distinction among the classes. With men's modes molded by the elite palates of the international businessman, Europe's titled aristocracy, and Hollywood's cinematic royalty, the general taste level had nowhere to go but up, and up it went.

Even today, seven decades later, were one to convene the world's best-dressed men under one roof, the majority would still show up mantled in some form of custom-made clothing. Despite the culture's need for immediate gratification, the most sophisticated dressers, past or present, continue to go to the effort and expense of bespoke tailoring. Unlike today, when fashion is something formulated by a designer or a store, back in the thirties, the style seeker learned that genuine stylishness was an extension of himself, not the other way around.

The third catalyst serving to heighten the American male's receptivity to fashion was the medium of established taste. Historically, taste in masculine attire tended to reflect that of the community's social leaders. In the nineteenth century, male decorum was largely determined by the sons of the landed gentry, while that of the new royalty and the upper class dominated the early 1920s and 1930s.

During the thirties, personal taste and expression had comfortable limits within which to operate. It was still right or wrong to wear certain clothes for certain occasions. Once a garment was classified as such, there was no need to question its legitimacy or appropriateness. "Authentic fashion" involved little speculation or potential hazard; in principle, it was nothing more than adopting apparel that had already been deemed correct and socially acceptable.

Up through the late 1950s, pivotal variations in male attire were relatively few, making it far easier to recognize and follow the dictates of fashion. Men knew roughly what to wear for most occasions. In fact, at least in the United States prior to the Peacock Revolution, there was an unspoken consensus among the well-bred as to what constituted good taste in masculine decor. It was part Brooks Brothers and part Savile Row, a dictum forged by the land's New England heritage, with gentlemanly etiquette presided over by Boston's Brahmins.

But by the late sixties, the rebellious offspring of the middle class had forced upper-class taste to take a backseat to the newly licensed freedoms of youth and the street. "Down with the Ritz, up with the street," proclaimed Paris couturier Yves St. Laurent. With the continuity of established taste broken and social customs no longer offering strong guidance for appropriate dress, the concept of objective standards for sartorial taste was abandoned. Today, one man's good taste is another man's "pizza tie" (a term from novelist Tom Wolfe).

We have now arrived at that point where the book's subtitle, "Mastering the Art of Permanent Fashion," needs some explanation. The linking of *per-*

ENGLAND'S ARISTOCRACY:
The Duke of Westminster (above) and Mayor "Fruity" Metcalfe (accompanied by his wife), one of the King's foremost savants of style.

manent with *fashion* may well strike many as an oxymoron. Particularly today, when fashion is taken to mean a commitment to risk and change, mating it with the idea of permanence is bound to cause confusion, if not downright controversy. This is not an oversight but rather an attempt to provoke the inquiring mind.

The idea of permanent fashion operates on two levels. First, it symbolizes the current paradox of modern men's fashion, which is that menswear has enjoyed three decades of unprecedented growth and freedom to configure and reconfigure the sartorial tastes of several generations, yet there are fewer genuinely well-dressed men now than before. There has been nothing permanent about recent fashion. And second, permanent fashion is the book's prospectus, its mission to its readers. For those men hoping to find sartorial fulfillment somewhere down the road, tethering their journey to the mind-set of permanent fashion will deliver them there earlier rather than later in life.

Moving toward such a state requires the creation of a classically stylish wardrobe and the knowledge of how to wear it to best personal advantage. For a wearable to qualify as fashionable year in and year out, it must possess inherent merit, usefulness, and all-around good taste. And while the evolution of one's personal look is a work-in-progress, understanding which colors and proportions suit you the best and why fertilizes the sartorial soil in which one's permanent fashionability can blossom.

Some may feel that establishing rules for good taste may inhibit self-expression. It's my opinion that they provide the only chance for genuine individuality. Real innovation has always taken place with an awareness of, rather than an ignorance of, the rules. After all, how can you push the envelope if there is no envelope to push? Knowing the basics of setting a proper table or writing a decent letter prevents getting bogged down in the small stuff. Finally, good form makes for a level playing field on which excellence has real meaning.

Therefore, for men to develop the confidence and skills to take a new look out for a spin on their own, they need visual reinforcements. Less inclined than the opposite sex to risk victimization by the caprices of fashion, men feel more style-secure when surrounded by like-attired numbers. Whereas the thirties provided an uninterrupted vista of well-clad coves, the paucity of such male paragons nowadays is perhaps the principal cause for the species's current conundrum. In an attempt to redress this Catch-22, *Dressing the Man* has pressed into service the largest and most

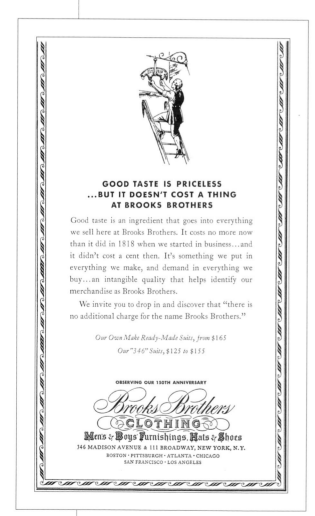

diverse collection of stylishly mantled men ever to be assembled between two covers. Hopefully, the sheer magnitude of options presented here will enable the reader, regardless of his sartorial persuasion, to expand both the grammar and range of his permanent fashion vocabulary.

However, one small caveat before we proceed. Though these pages are filled with men who demonstrate an exceptional feel for clothes, I am not trying to turn the proverbial "ape-man into an Adolphe Menjou." The best-dressed men consistently demonstrate the greatest degree of self-knowledge, which, for our purposes, means a superior understanding of their physical manner and appearance. Their style derives from an evolved inward eye that guides them toward those cuts and colors that best articulate their physiques. At such a rarefied level, an individual's bodily awareness becomes an almost unconscious dynamic, much like multiplication for a mathematician. While *Dressing the Man*'s visual content goes a long way toward preparing the reader to take that next step, teaching such a high level of style consciousness is not its primary goal.

The great dressers of the past can be a pleasure to look at, but they should be regarded as sources of inspiration, a means to an end. They developed a working knowledge of the basics, freeing their fashion intelligence to experiment and shape these fundamentals into a more personal rendering of the art form. Stretching a fundamental here, bending a rule there, the sophisticated dresser aspires to a more poetic, less studied expression. As art critic Kathleen Campbell has stated, "The perfect art is that which conceals art."

In my thirty-odd years of designing and writing about men's style, I have come to realize that men possess more natural talent for personal decor than generally given credit for. When afforded the opportunity to get firsthand advice, they turn out to be surprisingly quick studies. Having created custom clothes for a diverse audience of men, I have yet to meet one who, in the privacy of the fitting room, will not express an interest in wanting to look better. I believe that men not only want to expand their capacity for self-adornment but that they have never been more ready.

Daisaku Ikeda, third president of the Soka Gakkai, a Buddhist world-peace organization, states, "Our lives are ruled by impermanence. The challenge is how to create something of enduring value within the context of our impermanent lives." *Dressing the Man: Mastering the Art of Permanent Fashion* aspires to do just that. Although the responsibility for its realization lies squarely within, permanent fashionability is within the reach of any interested man.

*S*ome time ago, while accompanying my teenage daughter on her quest for the perfect prom dress, I was reminded of the fundamental difference between the way men and women select clothes. As her mother had shown her from their first bonding in that dressing room of life, she would dutifully hold each dress under her chin to see how it looked next to her face. Ever see a man stick a suit jacket or a necktie under his mug to judge its appeal? As my kids used to say, "Not!"

One of the most important—but least understood—functions of male attire is to lead the viewer's eye toward the face. Understanding the subtle interplay that should

2

THE POWER OF

COLOR

exist between a man's most visible and expressive body part, his face, and the clothes surrounding it is a prerequisite of fine dressing. Oscar Schoeffler, *Esquire* magazine's legendary fashion editor, once warned, "Never underestimate the power of what you wear. After all, there is just a small bit of you sticking out at the neck and cuff. The rest of what the world sees is what's draped on your frame." And which colors end up framing this "small bit of you" can make the difference between this cynosure of expression being brought to life or not.

Color influences first impressions more than any other aspect of attire. It can establish an emotional link between object and observer. When the face is surrounded by tonalities that invigorate and illuminate its presence, its ability to provoke immediate and marked reactions is amplified. Most women learn early on of the role of the face in the dressing game. The prettiest woman's face is usually a canvas to which both nature and art have contributed. Unfortunately for the man, "feminine" artifices such as cosmetics are not realistic options, leaving the male countenance more vulnerable to outside siege than those fortified facades of the fairer sex. However, men need to know how to wear color not so much for its beauty or allure but in order to heighten the face's expressive capacity in the communication process.

Although a lot is known about the effect of certain colors on the heartbeat and rate of respiration, little has been taught of late about the transforming effect of clothing colors on a man's appearance. The only time in this century that men had ready access to such information was during the heyday of men's elegance, the 1920s and 1930s. This was a period in which the drab stiffness of the Victorian costume was being replaced by the colorful informality of the evolving lounge suit and fledgling sportswear fashions.

Among the century's early fashion periodicals, *Esquire* magazine established itself as the leading arbiter of American men's style. Beginning in the fall of 1933, its editorial department would dispatch style scouts to the far corners of the globe in search of those dress innovations and style cues most likely to develop into long-term fashion trends. But before *Esquire* rolled out its fashion findings to the public at large, *Apparel Arts*, its sibling publication, would first present their commercial prospects to its professional audience, the menswear industry.

When a new color became important, *Apparel Arts* would introduce it by inventing sobriquets like "sandune" or "brownstone" to romanticize its appeal. Leading illustrators would be commissioned to portray the new color's style currency and wardrobe possibilities. Sample point-of-sale and window display layouts would follow so that retailers could learn how best to present, promote, and sell it.

As suppliers solicited wholesalers and manufacturers geared up production, *Apparel Arts* announced which upcoming *Esquire* issues would feature the new color "story." Depending on its perceived importance in the larger fashion firmament, *Esquire* would sometimes devote an entire season's coverage to promulgating the color story. Style histories discussed which celebrity and what watering hole pioneered the tony new shade. Newspaper ads linking the new color to, say, one's complexion would appear, such as the one on the following page. "Color wheels" including the new shade were devised to coordinate men's complexions with the latest suiting fabrics and furnishings. By the time the heralded new colors finally hit the shelves, both the merchants and the masses were appropriately primed.

The sheer pace of change in fashion between the wars compelled the editorial world to exalt the how-to aspect of masculine style as in no other period in menswear before or after. As a result, a man's complexion and his choice of clothes became an ongoing theme in each season's style presentation. Men were instructed on how to incorporate colors such as town browns and rustic greens into their city wardrobes and encouraged to take personal advantage of less popular shades like pink, lavender, and gold. Not surprisingly, the period turned out the most colorfully clad male in the twentieth century, not to mention the best dressed.

Unfortunately, World War II sidetracked the exuberance of the wealthy fashions of the thirties. This, followed by the gray flannel conformity of the fifties and the social upheavals of the sixties, left later generations of style-conscious males pretty much on their own in divining an individual clothing palette. In the early eighties, offshoots of several commercially successful color books for women were broached for men. Unfortunately, their methodology was so tortuous in detail and demanding in time that most men decided to ignore their entreaties of sartorial enlightenment, resigning themselves to the predictable sanctuary of the dark blue or gray business mantle.

Magazines keyed fashion color stories to different complexions.

THE ABC'S OF A PERSONAL
COLOR STRATEGY

K eeping in mind that the face is the destination to which one's attire should escort the beholder's attention, if too much or too little repartee occurs between it and the surrounding colors, the viewer's eye is diverted and one's personal presentation is weakened. Two color techniques must be learned if the male's communication center is to be assured of optimal animation and influence. The first involves the relationship between the complexion and an outfit's level of contrast. The colors of any given ensemble should exhibit the same degree of contrast as that manifested by one's skin and hair tones, a person's two primary color signposts.

Bold stripes lighting up Tyrone Power's high-contrast complexion (left), and monotone shadings dampening it (right).

The second approach revolves around highlighting each face by repeating one or more of its natural pigments in the colors worn below.

Starting with the first principle—while the rainbow of men's complexions encompasses a great variety of shadings, the field can be scaled down into two basic formats: contrast or muted. If your hair is dark and your skin light, you have a contrast complexion. If your hair and skin tone are similar, your complexion would be considered muted, or tonal.

Having now matriculated into one of the two prevailing male color fraternities, you might wonder how such a diversity of facial and hair colors can be so neatly divided into just two profiles. Although membership in the contrast club substantially outnumbers that of the muted, both complexion types contain one important subgroup. The higher-contrast contingent shares the spotlight with the medium-contrasts, while the muted's limelight is partly shadowed by the light-brights.

In an effort to simplify the subject, our discussion will be limited to the more graphic dark-light differential. Since relatively few men have much knowledge or experience in this area, if the reader can come away with a rudimentary understanding of the larger contrast/muted picture, he will be well ahead of the pack.

Look at Tyrone Power's invigorated facial tones as they interact with his black-and-white ping-pong regalia. When a man's skin and hair tones are in such powerful counterpoint to each other, surrounding them with contrasting colors of equal strength serves to enliven the face's natural vitality. Conversely, observe the dampened drama of Mr. Power's visage when visited by the monotone shadings of his tonal khaki turnout.

Alternatively, Woody Allen's muted countenance of sandy hair and fair-toned skin requires the nurturing effect of a softer, more monotoned color format, as provided by his beige polo shirt. Encasing a low-intensity complexion within a higher-contrast setting dilutes the face's natural pigmentation in addition to distracting the viewer's eye. As low-contrast complexions are easily overwhelmed by aggressive color coordination, these skin tones demand more attention and a

Woody Allen uses black eyeglasses to call attention to his low-intensity complexion.

lighter touch. And because the man with a complexion of average contrast can tolerate a fuller range of color coordination than his muted counterpart, he also enjoys more latitude and margin of error with colors.

The photograph below illustrates the importance of such color strategies. Here are two models with different complexions but attired in the same outfit. With the fairer-haired man, because of his tonal complexion, the necktie's stark black and white stripes jump out, jarring the eye and leading it away from his face. Conversely, with the darker-haired model, the necktie's high-contrast format actually invites the eye to look at his face because of its compatibility with his black hair and light skin.

Learning color management can produce immediate dividends. Take the example of a light-complexioned man in pursuit of the classic navy blazer. Armed with the knowledge that the blacker the blazer, the more it will contrast with and thus weaken his lighter complexion, he will concern himself only with brighter, richer-hued blues. By circumscribing his range of choices, he will not only save time but be rewarded with a superior purchase.

Same outfit, different complexions:
On the left, your eye goes to the tie;
on the right, your eye goes to the face.

The second color technique focuses on the enhancement of the face through repetition of one or more of its tones in the surrounding apparel. This principle can frequently be found informing the presentation of an art piece or the choice of eyeglasses. A picture matting or frame will often be selected just to highlight one of the painting's key colors. Similarly, a blond man tends to opt for gold-toned spectacles, while the salt-and-pepper brow favors the more silver-toned rims.

The early menswear magazines thought it was important that a man know the whys and wherefores of proper complexion and clothing coordination. Take this gent with brown hair and a slight ruddiness to his face *(below left)*. Following the second technique's imperatives, the obvious choice of suit shade would be that which repeated his hair color, thereby drawing the observer's attention to what was bracketed in between—in other words, his face. The fashion editor employed the same logic relative to the necktie—it's no coincidence that the tie's reddish cast just happens to pick up its wearer's ruddy facial pigmentation.

By sporting a scarf around his neck in the same pale hue as his ashen skin and hair tone, this next gent vouchsafes that his visage won't vanish from view *(below right)*. And to prove that

Echoing the hair's color under the face does wonders for one's complexion.

the tradition of augmenting one's facial coloring transcends even social station, here's the future king of England *(opposite)*, colonizing his auburn-tinted face in a sea of rubescent trappings.

Eye color follows skin and hair as the next most important facial indicator, especially when a man happens to look out behind the baby blues of a Paul Newman or a Frank Sinatra. Nothing brings an azure-eyed countenance into more engaging focus than a blue-toned shirt or like-hued necktie cavorting just below the chin.

The last facial feature to consider is any special pigment like rosy cheeks or suntanned skin. In trying to enhance the face's glow and primacy, the idea is to play up such colorations by keying them to apparel in close proximity, such as a scarf, necktie, or sport shirt. Because the bronzed skin's darker hue increases its level of contrast, clothing colors should be stepped up incrementally in strength. This is one reason why warm-weather climes tend to bring out the peacock in a man.

Captured in the autumn of his life, here's our man from Omaha, Fred Astaire, still choreographing himself into sartorial perfection. Recognizing that age lightens one's hair and skin tone, Fred enacts the first color strategy by adopting a muted toupee with tonal clothes to type. His pale blue Brooks button-down and soft-hued tweed jacket ensure that his features remain center stage. Plumbing the second technique with typical Astaire pomp, he highlights his cheeks' slight pinkishness with a lilac scarf and pocket square.

Let's look at some typical male complexions to see how these two color techniques can be applied to improve them. Think of the face as the picture and the clothes as their frame. While the frame should be attractive in its own right, its primary function is to help focus the viewer's eye on that which it contains. With a neutral-toned subject, the frame needs to recede into the background without losing its ability to define the content's borders. With a more graphic subject, the frame must be strong enough to delineate its perimeters without distracting from it.

OPPOSITE & RIGHT:
*Proper complexion and
clothing coordination—
Fred Astaire and
the Prince of Wales
coordinate colors with their
hair and skin tones
to enhance their appearance.*

TREVOR: MEDIUM CONTRAST

As a medium-contrast complexion, Trevor enjoys the most latitude of any type relative to his selection of clothing colors. Although still darkly stylish, Trevor's black hair and swarthy skin appear almost in shadow when framed by the monotoned gray ensemble (*above left*). The lack of opposition between the gray suit and gray dress shirt underplays the higher level of counterpoint found in Trevor's face above.

Now observe what happens when the gray shirt is replaced by white. The relief yielded by its lightness against the suit's darker background illuminates Trevor's face and skin. The tonally accessorized suit makes his tanned skin look lackluster; the high-contrast one makes it glisten. Because of his hair and skin's substantial distinction, Trevor is free to experiment with almost any medium-to-strong color coordination, confident in the knowledge that it can only strengthen his own complexion.

FUMIHIKO: HIGH CONTRAST

Compared to the rainbow of European complexions, the classic Far Eastern coloring is generally confined to one high-contrast format—light skin and dark hair. Here's a handsome representative. Although he is well turned out by most sartorial standards, Fumihiko's monochromatic coordination can never fully underscore the boldness of his high-contrast complexion. Like the dampening effect of Tyrone Power's khaki outfit shown earlier, its sobriety actually diminishes the drama unfolding *(below left)*.

However, set such dynamic good looks amid the garnishment of a blue-bodied dress shirt with contrasting white collar, dark navy suit, and a dashing burgundy silk necktie and, presto, resplendence results. All it took was a simple change of facial scenery to transform Fumihiko from pedestrian to prince.

JOHN: MUTED COMPLEXION

Although less graphic in content, the muted or toned visage demands more vigilance and skill to enliven. Due to its lower tolerance for too noisy or overly quiet color mixes, the muted facial type invites anonymity if not handled with appropriate care.

Just as watercolors need a lighter frame to complement what they enclose, so does John's low-key frontage. Without a contrasting dark hair shade to counterbalance the opposition underneath, John's muted complexion is bullied into submission by the starkness of his black-and-white outfit (*below left*).

Alternatively, when the less contrasting warmer shadings of his two-tone sport jacket and knit shirt enter the picture, suddenly, John's doughy skin shade picks up luster while the tint of his hair color gains prominence. Once again, whenever the face can be bracketed below in the same color as the crop above, it's bound to end up the clear beneficiary.

EDWIN: LIGHT-BRIGHT

If some of your clothes—even if they are exquisitely crafted or luxurious to the touch—make your face look more dulled and aged than others, it is certainly because their colors are probably incompatible with your own. Edwin is a perfect case in point.

As mentioned earlier, low-contrast complexions are highly susceptible to further washing out by careless color-coordinations. Edwin needs to pay special attention to those colors capable of siphoning off additional pigmentation from his fair skin and blond-turning-white hair. In the left picture, Edwin wears a midnight navy suit with a pale blue dress shirt. The suit's near-black shade of navy coupled with the ice blue dress shirt work to drain color from his face.

In the picture to the right, Edwin's dark navy suit has been changed to a brighter, warmer shade of navy while the cool blue of his dress shirt is now a deeper shade of blue. Although the difference is subtle, with richer tones now throwing more warmth around his face, Edwin's blue eyes suddenly spring to life, and his ashen skin appears flush and invigorated. With his tie pulling his hair color into the mix and his blue-accented pocket square reinforcing his eye shade, the overall effect is measurably advanced.

ALEX: LIGHT, BRIGHT, AND BLOND

Another classic male complexion is fair skin crowned with golden blond hair. Once again, the surest way to ensure your visage its rightful due is to buck it up with the relevant pageantry, as exemplified by these two fashion plates *(right)*, whose sport jacket and suit ensembles clearly publicize their gilded crowns.

Likewise, Alex, who has built his dressing style around his distinctive coloring, makes sure at least one item in each ensemble reflects his gold-toned complexion. In his first outfit *(below left)*, Alex looks classy, yet not enlightened, since his white shirt and bold striped tie do little to enhance his specially-hued countenance. In his next, by pressing into service an array of colors more congenial to his own, he elevates his face to a higher level of stylish sophistication. As long as Alex continues to wreathe himself with those warm golds, rusts, and browns found in his hair, his face will remain center stage.

TOM: MEDIUM CONTRAST

When you are as debonair as Tom here, there is an abundance of riches to work with, making it a challenge to render him in sub-par raiment. His plaid suit's light-and-dark pattern synchronizes well with Tom's own medium-contrast features. His countenance would suggest starting with a blue dress shirt to play up his bespectacled orbs of cobalt blue, and reddish or burgundy neckwear to work the same magic on his slightly ruddy skin tone.

Although Tom's no slouch when swathed in this first combination of somber gray shirt and maroon necktie *(above left)*, that look pales by comparison when juxtaposed to the next one. Things can't help but perk up when a strong blue shade of shirt and a very pink tie are lobbed into the proceedings. Once again, echoing skin tone and eye shade in clothing helps lift the face from smart to smarter.

AFRICAN AMERICAN:
MEDIUM TO HIGH CONTRAST

Trying to apply the contrast-muted paradigm to the African-American complexion requires some explanation. The fact that the average African-American face, whether black or light brown, exhibits little contrast between its hair and skin tone would seemingly qualify it as a muted facial type. However, when a dark face, regardless of shade, is surrounded by a white shirt, considerable contrast results. Therefore, for the African-American man to get the most out of his clothing combinations, he should approach the enterprise as a medium- to high-contrast complexion, the degree of which is dictated by his individual face's relative depth of color.

Ralph Lauren didn't put the black model Tyson Beckford (*opposite*) in this highest of high-contrast mantles because of his bland countenance. Beckford's extremely dark skin produces tremendous contrast with any clothing color. Therefore, the brighter and more dramatic the shade of his clothing, the better he looks and the more radiant his skin tone.

Stepping down one rung on the contrast ladder, this next man's medium-brown facial tones do not produce the same stark effect as Beckford's. Consequently, for this medium-contrast complexion, choosing clothes with a definite, but not deafening, intensity would be appropriate. Integrating his striking blue eyes into his ensemble is certainly a good way to start.

This third African-American man's skin shade is yet another gradation down in contrast, making his well-chosen sport jacket and matching T-shirt harmonize gracefully with his coloring. If one were holding up each of the three models' skin tones against a white shirt, the amount of contrast yielded would provide a dependable yardstick for determining the ideal amount of contrast that should be likewise used in the clothes.

Proportion ultimately determines any garment's potential longevity. The quickest way to transform one's provisional grasp of fashion into something more permanently stylish is by learning which clothing proportions best suit you and why.

The finest handmade navy cashmere blazer cannot be rescued from premature obsolescence if bought when the fashion gods decreed that its length should finish below your fingertips. Likewise, an inexpensive dress shirt can provide many more years of wear than an expensive one once you realize the latter's short collar points make your large face loom even larger. An old tailor's dictum goes, "Compromise on quality if you must, never proportion."

3

PROPORTION:
THE FOUNDATION

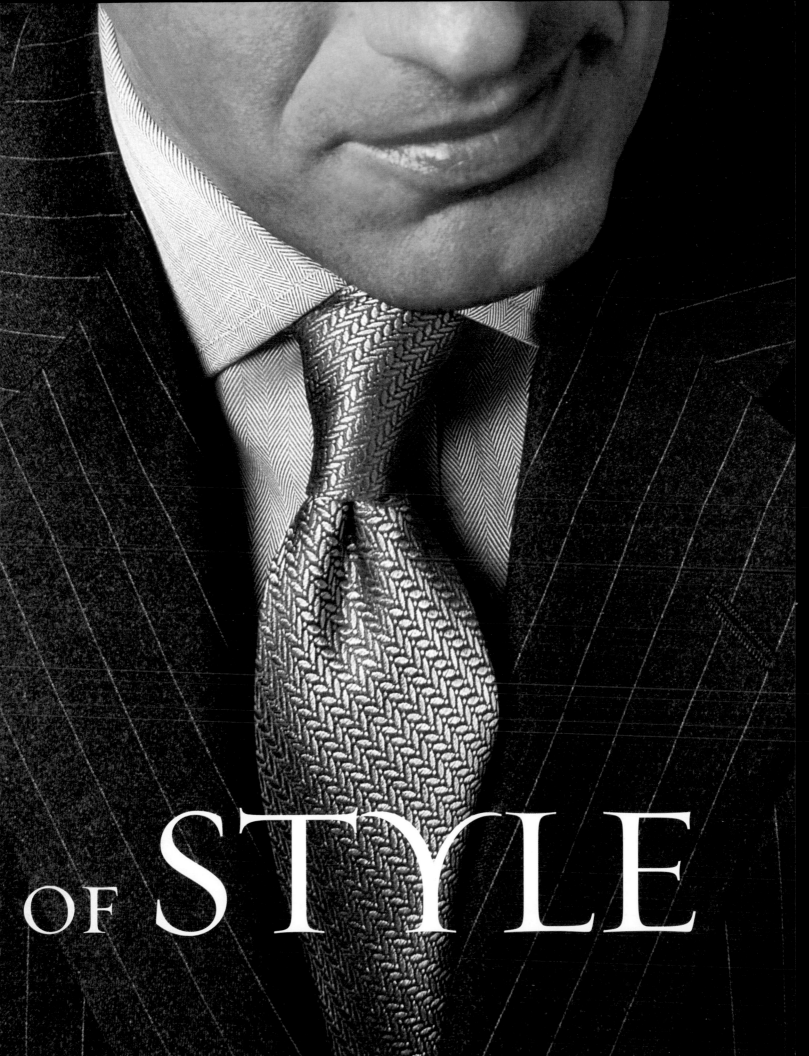

OF STYLE

Inappropriately scaled clothing is the root cause for the contemporary man's current lack of sartorial distinction. Obsolescence in menswear is built upon the manipulation of the classic proportions, sometimes in ways that do not flatter, as flared bottoms, overly shouldered jackets, and square-toed shoes attest.

It is said that the quality of a chef can be judged by his consommé. Likewise, a man's dressing skill rests on his ability to wear the simplest clothes to individual perfection. This is essentially a lesson in proportion. The first step in evolving a distinctive yet long-term dressing style is for each man to master the standard scheme of tailored suit, white dress shirt, solid necktie, white pocket square, with dark socks and shoes. This is not to suggest that he adopt such formulaic attire, although it can come in handy for certain occasions.

While this classic outfit does not constitute a study of all possible dressing proportions, its curriculum is fundamental to moving up to the next level of sartorial sophistication. The relevance of this specific sartorial paradigm is that within it resides a series of mini-portraitures, which, when knowledgeably rendered, form a choreography of ideal dressing proportions unique to each man. Once familiar with how best to exploit each for maximum personal advantage, one can use them as the blueprint for future fashion explorations. As stated earlier, genuine innovation has always taken place with an awareness, rather than an ignorance, of restraints.

Breaking down this ensemble into a corporeal map, you discover that in order to traverse it smartly, five major intersections must be negotiated—the neck, shoulder, waist, wrist, and ankle. Each contains a network of lines and curves that when correctly connected to one another enhances the overall aesthetic. Applying the whys of its collar decor to your face, or jacket length to your body, improves your faculty for less ritualistic raiment, such as tailored sportswear or casual attire.

Fortunately, the face's shape, the neck's height, the shoulder's width, the arm's length, the torso's structure, and the foot's size remain fairly constant over time, even allowing for some weight fluctuation. Unlike fashion, which is obliged to change seasonally, learning how to dress well does not have to be a case of stalking a constantly moving target. Confining one's fashion focus to those physical characteristics found between hat and hose will facilitate one's mastery of scale and proportion. Once these rules of classic form relating to his own unique physiognomy are understood, a man has every reason to feel confident about getting his arms around this stuff. Let's examine in more depth the architectural logic and fashion rationale at work here.

THE SUIT JACKET

While fabrics and patterns usually attract the eye first, the suit's proportions anchor it in time. A suit extreme in silhouette is more likely to go out of style before it falls apart. In assessing a suit jacket's potential life span, five elements of design require particular attention; these are the garment's "bones." Should the coat's architecture conflict with that of the wearer or deviate too far from the archetype, the coat's staying power will be significantly weakened.

THE JACKET SHOULDER   As its widest dimension, the shoulder sets the mood for the rest of the jacket. Since the jacket's shoulders frame the head, if they are too narrow, the head will appear larger than actual size; conversely, if cut too wide, the head will appear disproportionately small. Notice the difference in the shoulder expression between Doug Jr.'s suit jacket and that of Master Gary (*following page*). Doug's shoulders are built up to offset his wider head, while Coop's are narrow and more sloped to harmonize with his thinner face and longer frame.

THE CORRECT SHOULDER-
WIDTH PROPORTION.

SHOULDERS CUT TOO WIDE
DIMINISH THE HEAD.

SHOULDERS CUT TOO NARROW
MAKE THE HEAD APPEAR
LARGER THAN IT IS.

ABOVE LEFT:
Douglas Fairbanks Jr.'s shoulders are built up to offset his wider head.

ABOVE RIGHT:
*Gary Cooper's shoulders are narrow and sloped to balance with his
thin face and narrow frame.*

OPPOSITE:
Dean Acheson in a natural-shoulder suit silhouette.

The natural-shoulder suit silhouette adopted by the Ivy Leaguers in the 1920s came to be identified with America's upper class and its principal purveyor, Brooks Brothers. Here is the late secretary of state Dean Acheson in typical New England understatement, his Brooks Brothers natural shoulder and fully rolled button-down whispering their patrician provenance. Compare his jacket's rounder sleeveheads with those lightly puffed and contoured confections smarting up Gary Cooper's shoulders.

Unless a man is extremely slope-shouldered or so self-consciously short that he wants his shoulder line raised to produce an illusion of height, sharply angled or conspicuously built-up jacket shoulders should be avoided. They look artificial and arriviste in taste, signaling that their wearer is attempting to appear more important than he feels.

JACKET LENGTH The principal criterion governing a jacket's length is that it be long enough to cover the curvature of the buttocks while giving the leg as long a line as possible. Whereas the ideal measurement of a man's jacket can vary by up to ½ inch without compromising its longevity, any more variation can play havoc with the hip pockets by moving them out of proper balance with the whole. It is quite normal for a jacket to be slightly longer in front than back in order to hang properly.

Due to the longer swathings of the 1980s, the so-called Armani era, the majority of men wear their jacket and jacket sleeves far too long, foreshortening both their legs and arms. This is especially evident in the Far East, where the average person's torso is longer in relation to his legs, in comparison to the average person's build in the West. Such a man needs to pay particular attention to his jacket's length to help him reproportion his longer torso with his

RIGHT:
*The long jacket
diminishes the
man's leg line.*

JACKET LENGTH
IN RELATION TO
THE TORSO:
DIVIDE IN HALF THE
DISTANCE FROM THE
COLLAR'S SEAM
TO THE FLOOR.

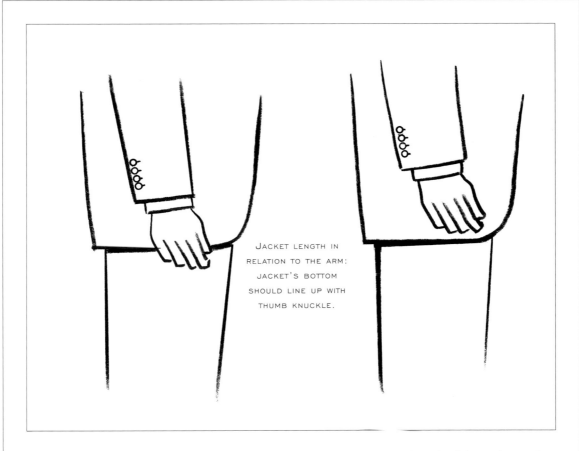

JACKET LENGTH IN
RELATION TO THE ARM:
JACKET'S BOTTOM
SHOULD LINE UP WITH
THUMB KNUCKLE.

shorter leg line. In the illustration on the previous page, examine the length of the jacket and its diminishing effect on the man's leg line.

Two methods for determining the correct jacket length originated with America's development of ready-made men's clothing, which needed general guidelines upon which to establish its standards of fit. The first employs the arm as a guide; when your hand is dropped at your side, the bottom of the jacket is supposed to line up with the outstretched thumb (*above left*). Though generally reliable, this formula has one drawback: arm length varies from person to person.

The second approach (*previous page*) measures the distance from the jacket's back collar (at the point where it joins the coat's body) to the floor, which is then divided in half. This is the procedure taught in most tailoring schools. Either of these two approaches can be influenced by dimensions unique to the wearer; a top tailor will use neither, trusting his practiced eye to take in the whole picture before deciding on the jacket's ideal length.

THE WAIST BUTTON   The waist button is to a suit jacket what the fulcrum is to a see-saw. If incorrectly positioned, a delicate balance is lost, calling the garment's pedigree into immediate question. The button functions as an axis: raise it too much, and the torso becomes abbreviated; lower it too much, and the torso is elongated at the expense of a longer leg line.

When the waist button of a coat is fastened, it should divide the body so that the torso and legs appear at maximum length. Observe the navy suit's elegant silhouette by following the

The placement of the coat's waist button should divide the body so that the torso and legs appear at maximum length.

line from its trouser bottom up to the jacket's waistline. The trousers' fullness smoothes the transition between the bottom and top halves of the suit, stretching out the overall figure, and the coat's waist button placement enhances the illusion of a long leg line while helping to articulate its inhabitant's chest and shoulders.

The correct placement of this critical detail occurs ½ inch below the natural waist. To find your natural waist, place your hands around the smallest part of your torso and then press down at the sides into the hollow above the hip-bone. Because this all-important button functions as the coat's center point, a top Savile Row–trained tailor will grab the waist button in the final fitting and pull it from side to side to make sure the coat has enough room to move gracefully on the body.

In an effort to defang the overly stiff tailored suit jacket, along with cutting its guts out, Giorgio Armani lowered its waistline and extended its length. Although he created a more fluid-looking jacket with a totally different feel, he doomed his early low-waisted jackets, along with their numerous wannabes, to lives of quiet obsolescence in their owners' closets. (Of course, thanks to Giorgio, all tailored clothing is much more comfortable nowadays. His positive innovations, on balance, transcended any fashionable excesses.)

THE GORGE AND LAPEL WIDTH

The gorge is that point where collar and lapel meet to form either a steplike "notch" or a pointed "peak" effect. The positioning of the gorge on the jacket's chest should be a function of one's build, not fashion. Drop it too low, and the truncated lapel's line makes the short man appear shorter and the heavy man look heavier. If he is short, a man's lapel notches should sit higher up

Gary Cooper's lower-sitting lapels play down his height.

on his chest, the longer lapel line emphasizing verticality. As Coop's lower-sitting peaked lapels illustrate, the taller man's lapel notches can rest a bit lower in the chest area, condensing the upper body's length while extending its breadth. Twenty years ago, this element of the coat's design rarely came into question. However, once again, while injecting more swagger into the conventional man-tailored jacket, Armani and others lowered its lapel gorges along with its waistline, loosening up both its classic demeanor and its hold on stylish longevity.

In order for a buttoned suit jacket's "V" opening to smoothly escort the viewer's eye upward toward the face, the jacket's lapels and the necktie's width should harmonize. Since the breadth of the jacket's shoulder guides its lapel width, a broad-shouldered man will naturally require a fuller lapel for proper balance. Like the single-breasted notches on Gary Cooper's three-button (see page 38) or on Dean Acheson's two-button coat (see page 39), the single-breasted lapel should cover between two-fifths to three-fifths of the distance between the jacket's chest and shoulder line, which usually results in the average notch lapel measuring from $3\frac{3}{8}$ inches to $4\frac{1}{4}$ inches in width.

While peaked lapels need more breadth to accommodate their upsweep design, they should not be so broad as to become conspicuous, such as those gracing Doug Jr.'s chest (see page 38). In the invariably dapper Mr. Fairbanks's case, his dramatic shaped lapels fall more into the arena of period style than of classic taste.

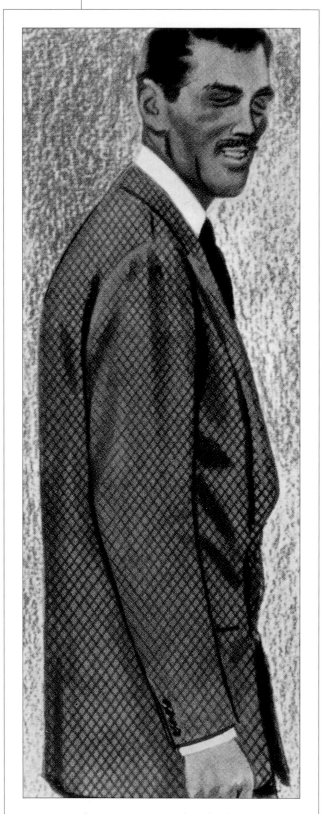

The proper tapering on the jacket sleeve.

THE JACKET SLEEVE Properly cut jacket sleeves lend a trim, well-formed grace to the arm. Full at the top, or sleevehead, and tapering down to the wrist bone, the sleeve's converging lines should conform to the broad shoulder and narrowing waist of the jacket. Sleeves that flap around the wrist not only lack smartness, but give the illusion of heft.

The band of linen between jacket sleeve and hand is yet another stylistic gesture associated with the well-turned-out man. It used to be said that a jacket sleeve without a bit of visible shirt cuff below made the hand appear as if part of it were missing.

THE SUIT TROUSER

Suit trousers should extend the line of the jacket. Fuller-chested jackets require fuller-cut trousers, just as more fitted jackets mandate slimmer-fitting trousers. The proportions of today's average suit have recovered from the hip-hugging jeans mentality of the sixties and the tight, low-waisted seventies fashions of the Pierre Cardin era. Today, most suit trousers are pleated for comfort with a longer rise, allowing them to reside at the wearer's actual waist, and fuller at the knee than bottom, following the natural line of the body.

Like the navy blue suit trousers seen earlier and the gray flannels of this traveler *(opposite right)*, suit trousers should be worn on the waist, not on the hip. Not only does the waist then appear smaller, but by raising the trousers' fullness, it can better fill up the jacket's bottom opening, thereby lengthening the overall figure.

*Suit trousers should extend
the line of the jacket thereby
lengthening the overall figure.*

THE DRESS SHIRT

Just as the suit frames the collar, making it the focal point of the shirt, the shirt collar frames the face, making it the cynosure of the ensemble. The choice of a dress shirt should be guided first and foremost by the appropriateness of its collar shape to that of the wearer's face. Think of the face as a picture and the collar as its frame. A small picture requires a like-scaled frame, just as a smaller man with delicate features requires a collar of restrained dimensions. Conversely, when the content is more expansive, the frame must correspondingly enlarge.

THE NECKTIE

The necktie's correct width has always been determined by the jacket's lapel. A man with narrow shoulders has less chest to drape a lapel across; therefore, the lapel's narrower dimension dictates that tie width follow suit. Conversely, a broad-shouldered man requires the services of a more generous lapel and thus a larger-scaled necktie. As the average single-breasted notch lapel ranges in width from 3⅜ inches to 4¼ inches, an equivalent range of bottom widths will immunize most neckties from the vagaries of high fashion.

The secret of tie aesthetics lies in compressing the knot so that it can dovetail high up into the inverted "V" of the collar's converging sides. To enhance its staying power, a dimple or inverted pleat should emerge from under the middle of the knot. If the tying procedure is not executed with an eye toward producing a taut knot, the knot will not have the necessary spring to arch out from the collar. Instead of looking crisp and distinguished, it will hang like a dead fish, undermining the composition's dignity. With the preferred four-in-hand smartly wedged high into the collar and its dimple lined up directly under the upside-down "V" point of the collar, a plumb line is formed, subliminally conveying authority on the wearer's part, as one who is in command of his own style.

Necktie width should relate to lapel width.

THE POCKET HANDKERCHIEF

One would be hard-pressed to find a picture of the Duke of Windsor, Fred Astaire, or any well-dressed Adam from the thirties in which some form of pocket square was not in evidence. The last American politician to be considered stylish, President John F. Kennedy, never left the White House in a suit jacket sans pocket linen. Although most men are intimidated by such vestigial raiment, no man can consider himself an *elegante* without knowing how to rig out the simple white pocket square.

But in terms of proportion, one way to ensure a natural effect is to angle the hank outward toward the shoulder, with its points irregularly arranged. When worn well, this eye cue of sartorial refinement can add more than just polish; by echoing the slant of the jacket's lapel, it reinforces the breadth of the wearer's chest and upper body. Jean Cocteau's casually furled pocket hank and unfurled jacket cuffs were trademarks of his unique dégagé dressing style.

THE TAILORED ANKLE

From hat crease to trouser cuff, the art of male habiliment can be divided into a series of mini-portraitures, the most southern being the rendezvous of trouser, hose, and shoe. To effect a permanently smart aesthetic below one's knee, certain rules of proportion must be respected.

Once again, it is the body rather than fashion that should take the lead—the general rule of thumb being that the trouser bottom should cover about two-thirds of the shoe. Narrow trouser bottoms make large feet loom even larger, while wide trouser bottoms make a small foot appear even smaller.

This symmetry in scale between trouser bottom and shoe remains an immutable linchpin of permanent fashion. Just like the slipper-type evening shoe worn under cuffless formal dress trousers, the round- or slightly-square-toed oxford, or blucher lace-up with a welt-constructed sole, ranks as *the* ideally proportioned shoe for suit-driven attire. The shoe's leaner line is enhanced by its beveled waist, the center portion of the sole that joins the heel to the toe, a feature of all dress shoes as opposed to the square waist used for stouter outdoors types, like the Norwegian model. The sinuousness of the shoe's form suggests its dressier intentions, while its sturdier (nonglued) welted soles offer the correct balance under the weightier-appearing cufffed trouser bottoms. For more on shoes, please see chapter 10, "Foot Decorum."

Trouser bottoms should harmonize with shoe scale.

PROPORTION AND BODY TYPE

Whether short or tall, portly or slim, most men aspire to look like some idealized version of themselves. Although the model male fashion figure has changed over time, for the past eighty or so years the principal goal has been to affect a tall, broad-shouldered, slim-waisted appearance. Therefore, that archetypal physique will serve as a reference point for the principles that follow.

The rules for downplaying girth or maximizing height can be helpful, but they should always be viewed as a guide rather than as dogma. There are many well-turned-out men who consistently dress against type. I can recall one portly patron of New York's famous "21" Club sitting down to lunch in a bulky three-piece Shetland wool suit tailored out of the most enormous estate plaid. While its scale violated every canon of anatomical logic, the man looked positively regal because of its impeccable cut and customized fit.

Back in the thirties, no group of swells was alleged to have exuded more collective swank than the Brazilian diplomatic corps. Contrary to conventional wisdom that swore short men off double-breasted jackets, these 5 feet, 7 inch plenipotentiaries not only preferred their lounge suits double-breasted but also finished them off with another sartorial no-no: leg-shortening cuffs. America's own guru of gestural elegance, hoofer Fred Astaire, always sported cuffed trousers, and he stood barely 5 feet 9 inches.

Dressing for your body type is a subject peppered with misguided prescriptions and arcane rules. For example, heavy men are advised to avoid double-breasted jackets, supposedly because they add bulk. However, in reality, if the jacket's peaked lapels roll below the waist, their long diagonal slant will do more for a man's avoirdupois than any line produced by the single-breasted model. Similarly, striped suits, which tend to elongate the figure, should not be automatically

The long-rolled, double-breasted lapel can downplay girth and maximize height.

NORTH AND SOUTH LINES
HELP THE SHORT, STOUT MAN
APPEAR TALLER AND THINNER.

eliminated from contention just because a man is tall. The important thing is for the scale and strength of the stripes to harmonize with the particular body type: narrow-to medium-spaced stripes for the thin physique; slightly broader and less pronounced lines for the fuller figure.

SCALING THE HEIGHTS: TIPS FOR SHORT, HEAVY MEN

Without question, correctly cut clothes can definitely aid the short, stout man in appearing taller and thinner. When an ensemble's north and south lines begin to replace those previously moving east and west, they stretch out and narrow the corpulent physique. To elongate the figure, the eye needs to be distracted from the waistline and led north to the shoulders and south below the knees.

Whether tall or short, the heavier man, much like the thin man, should always dress "large." Jackets should be cut with straight-hanging or slightly shaped body lines so they appear to hang loose from the shoulder downward. Close-fitting clothes reveal more than they conceal. There is nothing like the look of a stuffed sausage to call attention to a man's heft.

In general, short men are short, physiologically speaking, because their legs are proportionally short in relation to their torso. Therefore, for a jacket to endow such a physique with the illusion of greater height, it must create the impression that the leg line is actually longer than it really is. To accomplish this, the jacket's length needs to be kept on the short side, which is tricky, because the coat's length must remain as short as possible and yet cover the seat of his pants. If too short, the jacket will saw him in half; if too long, it will abbreviate the appearance of his legs.

Along with a shorter coat, the torso can be optically elevated by raising its shoulder line. The slightly higher shoulder gives the added illusion of elevating the torso while elongating the leg line. This is not to recommend squaring the shoulder, since you want to avoid the appearance of two right angles bracketing the head. Ninety-degree angles punctuating the head of any height-challenged man only emphasize that which he wants to diminish—his physique's lack of statuesque distance from the ground.

The single-breasted, two-button jacket with a medium "V" that opens down to the waist is more flattering to the short figure than the higher, closed fronts of the three-button coat. Squat figures should avoid jackets with stubby or short-rolled lapels, because they accentuate breadth. This includes the low-gorge designs of recent fashion. Lapel notches for the short-legged should rest high on the upper chest, for a longer lapel line. Peaked lapels with their upswept, pointed ends accentuate verticality more than the notched variety. Jacket sleeves should finish to show a half inch of shirt cuff: this helps balance off the sleeve and shorter jacket length. The coat's sleeves should taper down to the wrist bone, so there is no excess material jangling about the hand, creating unnecessary bulk.

Slanting lines minimize rotundity. Take the double-breasted jacket: whatever extra thickness the double-breasted's overlapping layer of cloth may add across the midsection, the slimming effect of its asymmetrical lapels more than compensates for it. The DB's diagonally running lapels lead the eye away from the center of the torso, and their upcurving pointed ends elongate and narrow the frame. Additionally, the classic six-on-two double breasted creates an additional "V" effect down the front of the jacket, which helps sculpt the torso and slim the waist.

THE WELL-CUT DOUBLE-BREASTED COAT'S SLANTING LINES HELP SLIM ALL BODY TYPES.

When it comes to jacket detailing, less is more. Extra flaps, like the change pocket, tend to bulk up and shorten lines. Besom-style (unflapped) hip pockets create less thickness and clutter than the flapped variety, although the hacking (slanted) flap pocket can chisel away breadth from the hip. Flap pockets are preferable to the patch design, whose extra layer of fabric adds heft.

Like its front, the back of this body type's ideal coat should promote a straighter line by hanging from the shoulders with a minimum of contour at the waist. Viewed from the side, the nonvented back can lend the corpulent hip a trimmer line; however, from the back, its one-piece expanse does little to break up the heavy rear end, particularly if the jacket fits snugly. When tailored to lie flat, side vents escort the viewer's eye up the coat's sides, suggesting a longer leg line and overall impression of height.

As for the trouser, because the short man aspires to an illusion of height, he must wear the suit trouser on his natural waist, not below it. Pushing the trouser waist down below the belly is this body type's most common and counterproductive tendency. Shortening the trousers' front line and forcing the pleats to open destroy the suit's potential vertical fluidity.

The man with a prominent middle needs full trousers that hang straight from the waist. By sitting higher on the waist rather than lower on the hips, the trousers' elevated fullness also works to smooth the transition between jacket bottom and trouser. What is to be avoided is the impression of two legs pouring out of the jacket's oversize bottom cavity like two straws in a jar, creating a visual break that divides the figure in half. Following the same logic, men with shorter legs should wear self-supporting or suspended trousers since a belt's horizontal line interrupts the suit's vertical flow.

Pleated trousers offer the man with a prominent middle more fullness in front so the trouser can hang straight from the waist. If designed well, pleats also divide up the stomach expanse. The reverse-pleat style (facing the pocket) may be more flattering for this figure, because they tend to lie flatter than the forward-pleated model (facing the fly). Trouser legs should taper modestly from thigh to bottom and sit on top of the shoe with a slight break.

Although conventional guidance advises against cuffs due to their horizontal effect, if the trousers are pleated, the cuff's weight knifes the front leg crease while better anchoring the pant's bottom to the shoes. The cuff's mass also helps forge a more balanced transition between the trousers' smaller bottom and larger shoe, particularly important for the heavyset man, who needs larger footwear to counterpoint the volume above. The width of the shorter man's cuffs should measure 1⅝ inches. If uncuffed bottoms are preferred, they should break slightly on the shoe front while angling downward to the heel to prevent them flapping about.

In the matter of materials, to discourage the impression of bulk, solids and vertical patterning should predominate. Colors should remain in the medium- to dark register, because lighter colors tend make a stout physique appear larger. The mission is to stretch out and promote long, easy lines, and the less contrast between the two halves of the body, the lengthier the

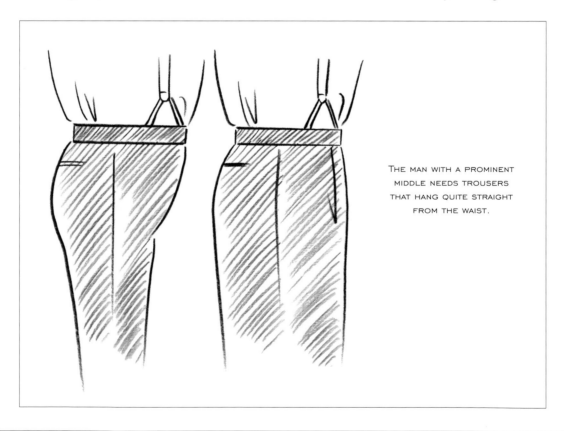

THE MAN WITH A PROMINENT
MIDDLE NEEDS TROUSERS
THAT HANG QUITE STRAIGHT
FROM THE WAIST.

appearance. One color from top to bottom, the suit's ultimate color lesson, should generally be the coordinating benchmark for this body type. Smooth fabrics such as fine worsteds minimize thickness, as do up-and-down patterns such as fine pinstripes, herringbones, and windowpanes longer in the warp than woof.

TIPS FOR THE SHORT, SLIM MAN Like the heavyset frame, the thin physique should always dress "large." Closely fitted clothes serve to accentuate the narrow frame. The major difference between the short, stout body and the short, thin one is that the latter's leaner scaffold can entertain more definition to the torso, especially around the waist. In order to construct this slightly hourglass shaping, the short, slender physique needs more breadth across his shoulders and chest and fullness in the upper trouser.

The single-breasted, three-button jacket would be welcome here, as when worn unbuttoned, each side forms a panel down the front that creates an illusion of verticality. The double-breasted model with lapels rolled below the waist would also serve to elongate this body type. Flaps or patch pockets add weight to the jacket's proportionally smaller hip, effecting a better overall balance between the top and bottom halves of the jacket. The height-challenged man, whether wide or narrow, should avoid ensembles in which there is a pronounced contrast between upper and lower halves. However, the thin man can wear lighter colors to better advantage than his corpulent confrere. Fabrics with strong vertical lines, such as some plaids and windowpanes, as well as more textured flannels and tweeds, are very sympathetic to this body type.

TIPS FOR THE TALL The higher the tree, the broader its branches; ergo, the six-footer and above needs full-proportioned clothing for both naturalness and style. As this guy has plenty of vertical lines, he needs to produce more horizontal ones. His suit jacket should affect an easy-fitting demeanor, particularly around the torso and waist, with ample breadth across the shoulders and sufficient length for symmetry and balance. The rule of thumb on jacket length: short jackets on short men, long ones on tall men.

Since this body type's shoulders already tower high above the floor, his jacket's shoulders should slope gently downward. The only reason for any extra padding or thickness would be to build them out a little. Although slightly augmented in scale, the tall man's jacket shoulders should pitch forward ever so slightly, contributing to the suppleness and softness encircling his upper strata.

As for jacket model, this man can wear them all. Double-breasteds are helpful to the cause, because the horizontal thrust of their lapels can build out a man, especially if fastened on the natural waistline, not below it. Another option would be the single-breasted, three-button jacket with generous width notch lapels that sit a fraction low on the chest, such as those of Mr. Cooper's illustrated earlier (see page 38).

Details like the patch and flap pocket, an extra ticket pocket, or turn-back sleeve cuffs inject a sense of stylish clutter that impedes the eye from making long, vertical sweeps. Here's one case where a belt's horizontal personality could come in handy, interrupting the occupant's vertical roulade.

*Details like a ticket pocket, pocket flaps,
and sleeve cuffs help break down verticality.*

Trousers should be long in the rise and tailored with deep, forward-facing pleats to bring a comfortable fullness to the front. Naturally, trousers positioned any lower than on the natural waistline would spell sartorial disaster for the long of leg. Generously cut thighs need to taper gently down to 1¾-inch cuffs, which are to rest on the shoe with a generous break. And should this high-rise gent be able to afford the custom route, his prominence would profit handsomely from the double-breasted, shawl-collar waistcoat's straight-fronted design (see page 91).

Small-patterned clothes only serve to exaggerate a tall man's length. To achieve a more natural proportion, long-limbed lads need larger-scaled patterns, preferably those having some weight and texture to them, like flannels, cheviots, and surface-interest woolens. If stripes are favored, they'll need some width for symmetry and softness for refinement. The horizontal formation of checks, overplaids, and boxlike designs has always been of benefit in the beam department. High-profile Gary Cooper enlists the patterned sport coat and contrast trouser to chip away at his elongated plumb line.

TIPS FOR THE ATHLETIC BUILD An athletic physique is defined by the clothing industry as a man whose chest measures eight inches or more than his waist. With such an exaggerated V-shaped torso, the goal would be to forge a more architecturally harmonious relationship between the highly upholstered upper half of the body and the disproportionately smaller lower half, without sacrificing the overall athletic image.

Beginning at the top, expansive shoulders and chest mean that the jacket's shoulders must be as soft and natural-looking as possible. The jacket's length is critical and should, if anything, err slightly on the long side. While its dimensions need to balance the shoulder's bulk, its extra length must not shorten the leg's line.

The single-breasted, two-button model with generous lapels positioned on the upper chest will help play down the shoulders' breadth. So as not to play up the already top-heavy look, one

Tall men like Gary Cooper can wear larger patterns.

should avoid any unnecessary waist suppression in the jacket. Just as the jacket should be gently shaped through the waistline, the sleeve should likewise taper gently downward to the wrist. Jacket detailing should be kept at a minimum to accentuate the vertical line, although flap or patch pockets can add weight to the hip for a better balance with the shoulder.

The suit trouser for the athletic build should be cut as full around the hip and thigh as possible, fitting as high on the waist as comfortable. Its fullness works to fill up the jacket bottom's large cavity, and its high-waisted placement translates to a longer leg line. Trousers should taper down to a cuffed bottom that rests on the shoe with some break, pulling the eye all the way down to the floor. Fuller-scale footwear plus the cuff's mass aid in countering the upside-down pyramid effect of the upper body.

Trying to emphasize the up-and-down while playing down breadth, smooth-faced fabrics, such as worsted stripes, herringbones, and even window-panes longer in length than width, will do very nicely here. Assuming a broad face and thick neck, vertical-pointing dress shirt collars, such as tabs or straight points, are the ticket to ride here.

INTO THE FITTING ROOM

Here is an all-too-poignant example of why today's fashion-conscious male does not dress better. As this contemporary photograph graphically illustrates, even the most classic clothing can be compromised by poor fit. While this black-and-white shot projects an unmistakable aura of elegance, the poor fit of the model's jacket and shirt collar, not to mention his dress shirt and jacket's voluminous cuffs, is one more reminder of the need for self-sufficiency in all matters sartorial, particularly fit.

      Once inside the fitting room, surrounded by mirrors, tape measures, and the like, most men relinquish questions of styling and fit to the store's salesperson or tailor. Years ago, when men's fashions were less fickle and tailors were better trained in the protocol of proper dress, this was a reasonable act of faith. However, today's fitting tailor is often obligated to alter clothes in conformity with the wishes of the suit's designer or the store owner. While the independent-minded tailor with real expertise can be found, the preponderance of floor tailors are simply duty-bound cogs in the store's assembly line, anxious to get you out with as few alterations as possible—hardly people to defer to in matters concerning taste or correctness.

An example of a bad fit.

      Fortunately, the correct fitting of a man's suit is not the arcane science that it is often made out to be. It is something that can be learned. Since a man's suit is made to fit a standard form and no two people are built exactly alike, only one man in a hundred is likely to step into a ready-made suit and find that it needs no alterations. Once again, the more knowledgeable you can become about how your clothes should fit in relation to your unique architecture, the more likely you are to walk out with an elegantly tailored result.

      As for the preliminaries, when first putting on a ready-made suit to be fitted, make sure you have your wallet in your pocket and your keys or cell phone wherever you normally keep them. No sense in having a breast-pocket billfold produce a bulge when the suit can be altered to hide it. It is also a good idea to wear or bring along a representative dress shirt with the correct sleeve length and collar height to help in the fitting process. Dress shoes with the proper heel height can aid in establishing the correct trouser length and bottom width.

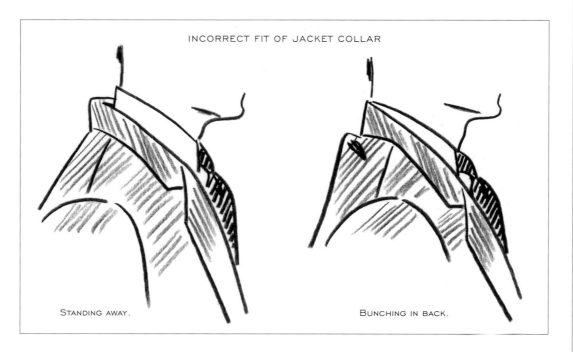

STANDING AWAY.

BUNCHING IN BACK.

Proper fitting can do much for an inexpensive suit, while a poor fit can scuttle the most expensively hand-tailored creation. If a three-thousand-dollar suit's collar bounces off your neck as you walk, the suit's value will be severely compromised. The jacket collar that creeps up or stands away from your neck is the fault of the tailor, unless you assumed a posture other than your normal one during the fitting. After slipping on the trousers and jacket, stand naturally in front of the mirror, and not as if you had just graduated West Point or are anticipating losing ten pounds.

Having already established that the jacket's "bones" harmonize with your own, you should begin the suit's fitting at the top. In addition to the shoulder's relationship to the head, its width needs to be generous enough to permit the jacket's fabric to fall from the shoulder in an unbroken line all the way down the sleeve. Also needed is enough fullness across the back and chest for the lapels to lie flat without gapping open.

This part of the fitting procedure can cause all kinds of problems, because there are those men, frequently accompanied by like-minded women, who feel that for a man's jacket to fit to perfection, it should be wrinkle-free, meaning it should look as if the fabric were painted on the body. For starters, there should be sufficient fullness over the shoulder blades for a slight break, or fold of fabric, to extend up the back from below the armholes. Unless the wearer doesn't mind donning a flawlessly fitting straitjacket, these folds ensure that there is enough room for movement and comfort.

Fifty percent of all tailored jackets need some kind of collar alteration to make them hug the wearer's neck. Watch that the collar does not stand away or have horizontal ridges below the base of the neck, a sign that the collar must be lowered by cutting away the excess fabric under the collar (above). If there are tension lines pulling across the shoulder blades, the back is too tight and must be let out a little.

FULLNESS OVER THE BLADES
ALLOWS THE JACKET TO DRAPE
COMFORTABILITY AND RELEASES
THE ARMS TO MOVE FREELY.

The jacket collar at the back should always be at such a height that at least half an inch of shirt collar shows above it. This way the jacket not only looks best but hangs correctly. Were it any higher, the collar would chafe against the neck; were it lower, the jacket would look as if it was sliding off your back. Since many fabrics fit and drape differently, this is a common alteration that can be competently performed by most store tailors.

Once the jacket's shoulders, chest, and neck are deemed satisfactory, continue the inspection downward. The waist should be slightly suppressed, responding to the natural curves of the body underneath. You can tell if the fit is too tight by looking for X-shaped lines forming on either side of the fastened waist button. If too pronounced, the waist should be let out. When buttoned, it should have enough room for you to sit down comfortably, although no style points are lost for unbuttoning a jacket when seated. The tailor can usually adjust the waist to your liking, but be careful not to have it taken in to the point where horizontal creases appear in the small of the back,

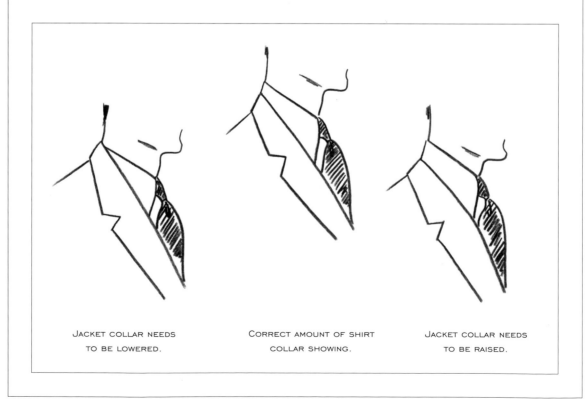

JACKET COLLAR NEEDS
TO BE LOWERED.

CORRECT AMOUNT OF SHIRT
COLLAR SHOWING.

JACKET COLLAR NEEDS
TO BE RAISED.

"X" MEANS
THE JACKET IS
TOO TIGHT.

CORRECT
CLOSURE.

tugging on the jacket's hip and pulling the rear vent(s) open. Back vents should hang in a straight line perpendicular to the floor.

The jacket sleeves should also hang straight, with no horizontal wrinkles or breaks forming on the upper arm. If a man carries his arms either too much to the front or back of the coat, the sleeves will not lie smoothly, and they should be removed and rotated accordingly. A good tailor will recommend such an alteration (and charge you for it). The jacket's sleeve should taper to the wrist bone, with a bottom opening measuring around six inches in diameter, or no larger than to frame the shirt's cuff.

Most men wear their jacket sleeves too long, either because of recent fashions or their tailor's lack of sophistication. As for the correct length, a man's arms ought to be his guide. The jacket sleeve should extend to where the wrist breaks with the hand. If the arms are on the short side, ½ inch of shirt cuff can peep out below the coat sleeves; if longer, like Gary Cooper's, ¾ inch to 1 inch will give the arm a better proportion. The band of linen between sleeve and hand is one of the details that define the sophisticated dresser.

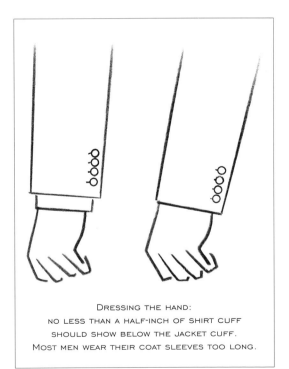

DRESSING THE HAND:
NO LESS THAN A HALF-INCH OF SHIRT CUFF
SHOULD SHOW BELOW THE JACKET CUFF.
MOST MEN WEAR THEIR COAT SLEEVES TOO LONG.

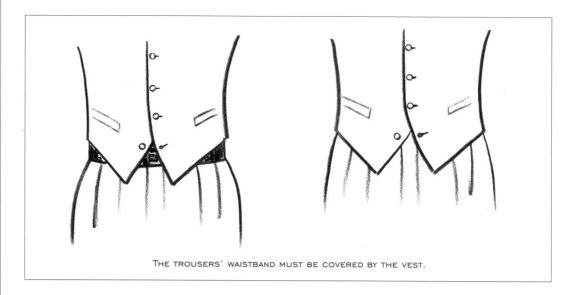

THE TROUSERS' WAISTBAND MUST BE COVERED BY THE VEST.

WAISTCOAT   The fitting of any tailored waistcoat should be done with its back strap fastened. The adjustable rear belt gives shape to the vest's waistline and discourages the vest from riding up the torso during the course of wear. The waistcoat's chest should be full enough to allow its wearer to sit comfortably with no hint of looseness at the waist. Only a small segment of waistcoat, revealing no more than the top button, should be visible above the jacket (see page 32).

Tha vest must be long enough to cover the trousers' waistband, stopping in front before its points extend below the hipbone. A delicate balance must be forged between the trousers' waist and the depth of the vest's "V" points: the whole edifice would crumble should it expose a patch of shirt or belt buckle.

Suspenders are the recommended antidote for the gap that typically develops between suit trouser and vest. They raise the trousers' waistband so it remains covered by the vest, while bringing the trousers' pleats and vest's points into better harmony with each other. Vests and belts should choose different dance partners. A strip of leather encircling the stomach adds more bulk to an already layered waistline, and belted trousers also tend to slide down the hip, frequently revealing the undesirable presence of a belt buckle.

Top-quality waistcoats have slits on either side, the back vents extending below the front so as to keep the trousers' rear waistband from showing when its wearer bends forward. High-class tailor-made waistcoats have slightly curved fronts, echoing the rounded shape of the single-breasted coat's fronts (see page 157). The vest's button stance is designed so that its bottom button is left undone, a custom dating back to the eighteenth century, when Edward VII, a corpulent sovereign, forgot to button his after an unusually vigorous repast, with the oversight ultimately taken and handed down as a style indicator.

TROUSERS   When fitting trousers, the cardinal rule is to wear them as high on the waist as comfortable. Hip-positioned pants will make the crotch hang too low and look sloppy. Moreover, the curvature of the hip tends to spread pants pockets and pleats. Like the jacket's armhole, the trousers' fork should fit as high as hospitable if it is to facilitate movement comfortably.

With pleated trousers, the hip and thigh must be cut full enough so that the pleats lie flat and do not pull open when standing. The function of the pleat is to respond to the natural widening of the hip and seat when sitting down. If you are not prepared to wear trousers with a more generous front, stick with the plain-front trouser. When one is standing, the trousers' front leg crease should bisect the kneecap and finish in the middle of the shoe. Trouser creases should err toward the inside of the knee; those falling to the outside create the illusion of breadth, something most men prefer to avoid.

If it is to be worn on occasion with suspenders, make sure the trouser is fitted with them, since suspendered trousers can change the fit of the waist, back rise, and inseam. Try them on in the standing, sitting, and legs-crossed positions. Trousers intended to be worn exclusively with suspenders should allow more room in the waist so that they can "suspend" from the shoulders.

Today there are several schools of thought on the length of a trouser. In the States, they are often worn to rest with a slight break, or "shiver," on top of the shoe. In this case, they should be long enough to cover the hose when a man is in stride, with a width that conceals the shoelaces. Plain-bottom trousers should slant downward from front to back so as to not fly away at the heel when the man is walking. If cuffed, their width should be neither so narrow nor so wide that it calls attention to itself. For time-honored balance, the proper width of trouser cuffs should be 1 ⅝ inches for a man under 5 feet, 10 inches, and 1¾ inches if taller.

Another approach is that of the Europeans or, more specifically, the Milanese, who wear their trousers narrow cut and a little on the short side, even showing some sock. In this case, the pants sit just lightly on the shoe. Signor Luciano Barbera, head of an Italian menswear company that bears his name, calls it the "mid-Atlantic solution," since it is halfway between Europe and America. Although he doesn't want to see your socks, he does want to see your shoes.

TROUSERS SHOULD BE WORN ON THE WAIST, NOT BELOW.

THE TROUSER CREASE SHOULD INTERSECT THE MIDDLE OF THE KNEE AND BISECT THE MIDDLE OF THE SHOE.

CUFFED BOTTOMS SHOULD REST WITH A SLIGHT BREAK ON TOP OF THE SHOE.

THE MID-ATLANTIC SOLUTION.

CUFFLESS BOTTOMS SHOULD SLANT TOWARD THE HEEL.

The good news is that in order to dress well one does not have to brandish a tapestry of pattern; the bad news is that if one wants to develop a unique and enduring dressing style, familiarity with the prerogatives of pattern is a must. Dressing would be monotonous without the graphic interest of a variety of designs. This is not to suggest that multipatterned ensembles are inherently more stylish than plainer ones. (Take another look at the monotoned elegance of Messrs. Agnelli and Fairbanks on pages 6 and 7.) From time to time, however, the sophisticated dresser will find himself switching gears. Some days he will swear off anything

4

THE PREROGATIVES OF

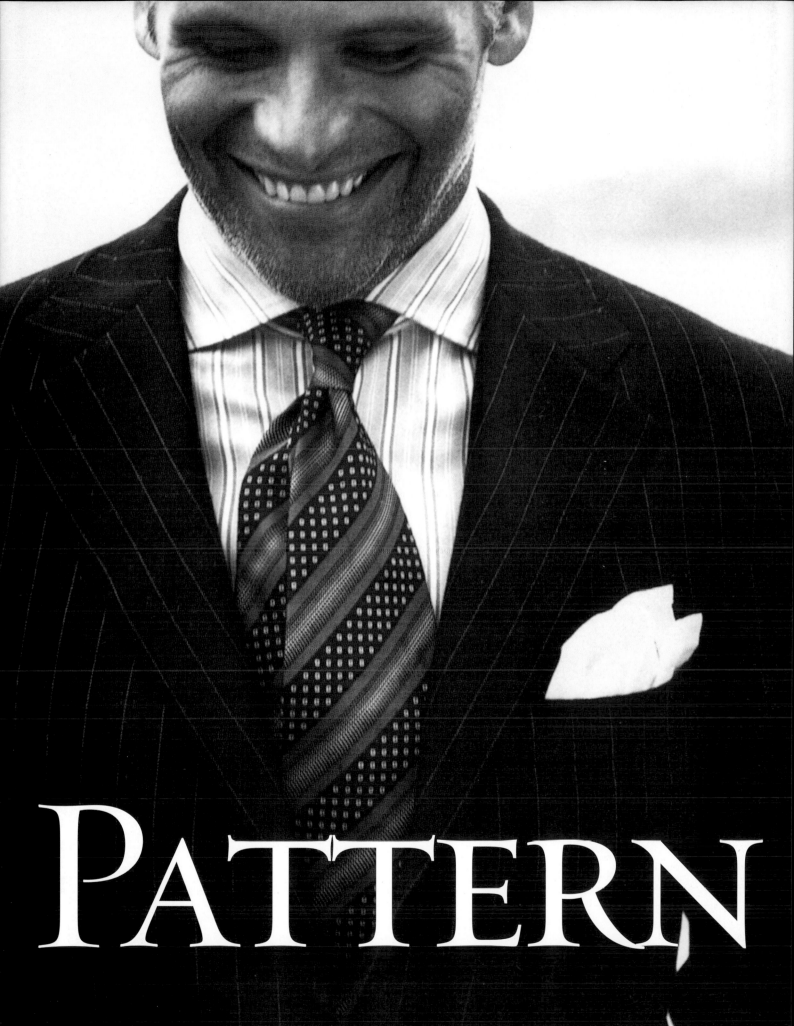

PATTERN

but the sparest outfit, while on others he will not be able to get enough decoration. Regardless of the approach, the ability to switch from one mode to another is an essential skill in any man's dressing arsenal. On the practical front, a dexterity for harmonizing patterned clothes can lend versatility to a wardrobe of modest means as well as increase the number of combinations when traveling with limited luggage.

The history of patterned fashions and their rise to sartorial sophistication has its origins in the early 1920s, when men began to experiment with a variety of less formal garments as a result of spending so much time in the function-driven gear of World War I. Patterned attire also represented a departure from the stiff, stolid Victorian dress of the prewar years. The new lounge coat's easy, flowing lines inspired men to loosen up and smell the roses.

While the dashing Prince of Wales established many of the styles that came to be identified with the era's "man about town," perhaps his most defining contribution to popular taste was his insatiable appetite for pattern mixing. Throughout his life, the Prince was routinely photographed in any number of audacious consortiums of checks, stripes, and plaids. And he wore them all with an aplomb devoid of arrogance, formal and fastidious without a hint of stuffiness. While his interest and affinity for clothes was no doubt exceptional in the annals of modern menswear, his particular fondness for patterned attire was as much a function of his Britishness as his royal birth.

The English aristocracy spent considerable time on their country estates, and their dress aptly reflected their outdoor lifestyle, with large-patterned, splashy-hued estate suits as the favored regalia. The Scottish influence of Balmoral Castle and other royal hunting lodges paved the way for the introduction of individual district checks and clan tartans into estate living. Hosts and guests were regularly kitted out in local Highland fare of tartans, tweeds, plaids, and argyles. As the philosopher and confessed Anglophile André Maurois once observed, "There is something affected and deliberate about the casualness of shaggy fabrics in which a continent dresses, while the English know how to be truly casual and therefore truly elegant."

As for the nobleman's seat itself, melanges of color and pattern were strewn about to warm up the typically cold, cavernous manor house into a place of lived-in warmth and casualness. The typical English country room was an eclectic amalgam of ancestral heirlooms, antique tapestries, and chintz-covered furniture, punctuated by oversized shocks of fresh flowers. Thus the English country squire found himself surrounded by a plethora of visual stimuli.

However, unlike other young men of regal birth, the future king of England devoted a considerable part of his ado-

ABOVE:
The young Prince of Wales in royal attire.

OPPOSITE:
The Prince of Wales had an insatiable appetite for pattern mixing—here are four.

lescence to the fitting and donning of vividly colored and elaborately decorated clothes that bore some royal, military, or family significance. Such a diverse and extensive wardrobe required the full-time services of four men just to organize and transport it when the Prince of Wales traveled.

Given the strict dress requirements of his youth, with its disciplined and nearly fetishistic attention to detail, it's no wonder that as soon as he was old enough, the Prince threw off the shackles of his parents' Edwardian formality. In doing so, he created a worldwide awareness and demand for his liberated dress, which the French later termed "chic fatigué," denoting an easy, casual stylishness.

With affluent Ivy League collegiates taking their fashion cues from vacations spent attending the rowing races at Oxford and Cambridge, Anglomania was at a fever pitch. While they brought home interpretations of the clothes worn by the dashing Prince of Wales, men from around the globe turned to the British heir for clues on how to dress for sport and travel. Pretty soon, fashionable men everywhere began to realize that combining two or more patterns within an outfit imbued them with an aura of distinction and urbanity.

MIXING TWO PATTERNS OF
THE SAME DESIGN

Narrowing the working canvas to the interaction of the suit, dress shirt, and necktie greatly simplifies the pattern-coordinating tutorial. The first step toward pattern-mixing prowess is learning how to mate two like-patterned garments, such as a striped tie with a striped dress shirt, or a checked necktie with a plaid suit. When combining two patterns of the same design, the size of each should be as different from the other as possible, otherwise the similarity will produce an optical illusion of movement or vibration.

Cary Grant ensures the visual compatibility of his two stripes by varying their spacing, allowing the viewer to easily distinguish one from the other. The solid necktie's subtle dialogue

*Cary Grant keeping his stripes
different scales.*

with each stripe also enhances the overall ease on the eye.

Ever the style setter and ever comfortable with his clothes, Fred Astaire was certainly no stranger to shuffling around different patterns. Here he chooses the perfect dance partner for his four-in-hand; his Brooks button-down's closer-set stripe arrangement has no difficulty following the lead of the repp tie's larger-spaced-stripe design.

Alternatively, here's a lesson in how *not* to mate two stripes. Although the overall ensemble is artfully arranged, the tie's bar-stripe design almost duplicates that of the suit's, forcing the eye to work overtime and strain for focus.

ABOVE:
*Fred Astaire achieves compatability
with two stripes of varying spacing.*

BELOW:
DON'T *mate two two stripes that are similar in size.*

MATING TWO CHECKS

Stylishly combining two checks requires a bit more savoir faire than combining two stripes. However, the risk can be held "in check" by once again imposing a healthy dose of contrast between the scale of each player. Following closely in Mr. Lauren's footsteps (*above left*), Mr. Agnelli (*above right*), another men's style innovator of established legend, takes no chances on his two checks clashing, keeping them about as different in size as a Fiat is from a Ford.

  If this assemblage to the right doesn't make you squint, please collect two hundred dollars and proceed to the nearest optometrist. When two similar-size checks are placed in close proximity, familiarity can breed confusion. Not only does their lack of congeniality undermine the ensemble's overall effect, but with the battlefield situated right below the face, life is unnecessarily difficult for the observer's eye.

DON'T *wear two checks that are similar in scale.*

MIXING TWO DIFFERENT PATTERNS

While the agency of scale was used to separate two like patterns, in the case of two unlike patterns, scale must also be employed to harmonize them—but with a converse rule applied. Two similar patterns necessitate varying sizes to avoid opposition; however, coordinating two different patterns, such as a striped suit and a check dress shirt, or a plaid jacket and a figured necktie, necessitates keeping them close in size.

The shirt-and-tie merger below illustrates this point. A dominant-patterned dress shirt requires a necktie with a design at least equal in scale; otherwise, the strength of the shirt's aesthetic will eclipse that of the necktie's. This open-spaced striped shirt *(below left)* demands a large-figured print necktie for proper pattern parity. The fact that the tie's color reflects that of the shirt further advances the combination's smartness.

This next svelte boulevardier *(below right)* emphasizes his distinct bold suit by mating it with an equally spirited necktie. Notice how the spacing of his necktie's stripes melds with the size of the suit's plaid. When in doubt about coordinating a second prominent pattern with a first, choose a larger rather than a smaller design. As previously demonstrated, the arrangement of the two patterns is further abetted by the necktie's repetition of the garnet-colored overcheck in the suit's plaid.

Like all guidelines, there are always exceptions. The biggest challenge in combining two patterns harmoniously occurs when one design happens to be particularly small. Placing two small patterns near each other, whether similar or not, will wreak havoc on the eye of the beholder. You rarely see a man on television wearing two small patterns, because their vibrating effect distorts the camera's focus.

To safeguard optical clarity when coordinating one small pattern with a second, one design must be significantly larger. Consider this next coordination of two small patterns *(above right)*, and you will immediately realize that its miniature scale forces the eyes to work overtime to avoid a blur. Alternatively, the mini-houndstooth composition manages to forge a visual harmony, because the necktie's foulard motifs are spaced far enough apart to distinguish themselves from the suit's diminutive check pattern *(opposite right)*.

Keep the scales equal to harmonize two different patterns.

TOP:
Two small patterns
create discord.

BOTTOM:
A *small pattern*
needs to be relieved
by a larger one.

MIXING THREE PATTERNS

Conventional taste has guided us safely to this vantage point, but scaling the next peak of patterning will require a bit more sartorial rope—from this point onward, reward and risk go hand in hand. The safest route to the happy rendezvous of three patterns within one ensemble is where each design differs from the others.

Following the same trail that helped us unite unlike patterns, we again rely on the medium of scale to safeguard our footing. Observe Tyrone Power's strategy (*opposite*). By maintaining a consistent amount of contrast and scale within his ensemble's components, he makes the overall enterprise appear relatively effortless. Similarly, in the illustration to the right, the dimension of the suit's herringbone pattern, the size of the dress shirt's check, and the width of the necktie's stripe all accord in proportion and weight with one another. Even the border of the pocket handkerchief reflects the bolder stature of this multipatterned town outfit.

OPPOSITE:
Tyrone Power wearing three different patterns.

RIGHT:
Using the same scale to hold together multiple patterns.

MIXING THREE PATTERNS WHEN TWO ARE THE SAME

We encounter an even more demanding slope when two of the three players share the same design, such as two stripes and a check, or two checks and a stripe. In this case, safe passage can be assured only by separating the two like designs in size while selecting an unlike pattern that is visually compatible with both. In this example, the two stripes are kept at arm's length by virtue of their differing scales, while the necktie consorts handsomely with either stripe.

Ditto for the check-on-check classic below. The dress shirt's smaller check is appealingly framed within the suit's bolder check. When sporting a triumvirate of patterns in which two share the same design, the odd one out (in this case, the necktie) must take its cue from the more prominent of the two partners.

Notice the usefulness of a larger-patterned necktie in harmonizing many of these multipatterned compositions. Of all neckties, the open-ground, large-spaced motif affords the greatest possibilities for textural harmony. Multiple-patterned ensembles often require at least one larger-scaled design for proper balance, and these bolder-all-over neckties are indispensable for accomplishing just such an aesthetic accord.

TOP:
Correct balance—large stripe, small stripe, large paisley.

LEFT:
Correct balance—large check, small check, large stripe.

MIXING THREE PATTERNS OF THE SAME DESIGN

The air continues to thin at this altitude as we leave solid ground and rule of thumb, guided now only by intuition and experience. Brandishing three plaids or three stripes falls very much within the parameters of traditional elegance; however, such an enterprise is fraught with the risk of contrivance and self-consciousness. Whether such a convergence strikes the observer as the summit of style or the edge of arrogance depends on the wearer's skill.

Once again, scale becomes the blueprint for success. Following the technique for dealing with two like patterns, scale must now work overtime to impose a similar discipline on three. Sometimes these creations go easier when graduating in size from small out to large, begin at the base with the smallest step and proceed on up.

Take a look at Basil Rathbone's graduated arrangement of checks (top). Starting with his shirt's small tattersall, he builds up to the jacket's larger houndstooth check, and then extends things outward to the jacket's larger plaid pocket square. Likewise, Prince Charles (center) jumbles around three plaids with a display of aristocratic aplomb.

The same basic geometry applies to successfully choreographing three stripes (bottom). Once again, such a linear scenario falls very much within the mainstream of sophisticated taste, and, like the plaid trio, its fortune rests squarely on the skill of the wearer. In melding three stripes, start with the smallest at the base and then branch up and out in scale. By building upon each stripe's graduation in size, the arrangement is infused with dimension and proportion, minimizing the potential for contrivance inherent in such repetition.

TOP:
Graduating checks from shirt outward.

CENTER:
Prince Charles in three checks.

BOTTOM:
Graduating stripes from shirt outward.

MIXING FOUR PATTERNS

Having now arrived at the summit of pattern pastiche, we have reached the point where inspiration trumps imitation. Collectively, these next toffs probably violate every rule of pattern mixing in the book, lobbing a few of their own in for good measure. This super-secret worldwide Order of Dandies (a Tom Wolfe appellation) dress almost exclusively for themselves, undaunted by an outcome that might contravene convention or raise eyebrows. They relish the challenge of a fine match. Is this art or simply vanity?

Fred Astaire *(center right)* once compared dressing well to putting on a show—he had to rehearse in order to get it right. Here are just a few of the fellows who have practiced long and hard, and have everything to show for it.

Luciano Barbera *(opposite page)* is one of those few contemporary men whose personal taste and code of conduct set the standard by which many in the business of menswear measure genuine elegance. Let's study one of the "maestro of mix's" own confections. Although he is swathed in four differently patterned garments—windowpane jacket, striped oxford shirt, checked tie, and foulard pocket handkerchief—none of them calls attention to itself. Granted, in such hands, such details of dress become elements of design. Barbera understands that in order to don four different patterns without appearing overly decored, the clothes must be worn with a slight disorder and looseness. Dressing at this rarefied altitude pivots on something of a paradox: the more imagination and taste one puts into his appearance, the more subtle the results should be.

Although not quite at the same level as these other three paragons of men's style, young Tyrone Power *(top)* may have been the handsomest man to know how to wear clothes well. Here he is, mantled in motif—four of them, allied by their mutuality of scale and degree of contrast. While he exudes "nothing but naturalness," the mélange hangs together superbly.

Whereas the Duke of Windsor would knock about in combinations of garments that no other mortal could conceive of, Fred Astaire's *(opposite center)* innate sense of style endowed everything he wore with a grace and charm. Few men could sport such a consortium of apparel and not appear foolish. Shall we go out on a limb and speculate that a fifth pattern is probably gracing his ankles?

This exposition couldn't end without going to the well one last time with a favorite D-of-W snap *(opposite bottom)*. Even though we all know that he had little else to amuse himself with besides his clothes, here's yet another inimitable concoction in the Duke's seemingly inexhaustible supply of sui generis, patterned perspicacity. This guy was a one-man fashion institute.

OPPOSITE TOP:
*Tyrone Power
in four patterns.*

OPPOSITE CENTER:
*Fred Astaire donning four
patterns (maybe five—
if his socks were visible).*

OPPOSITE BOTTOM:
*The Duke lived
on planet "pattern."*

RIGHT:
*Luciano Barbera
looking as if he were
wearing nothing unusual.*

If a man runs for president, interviews for a high-level job, or needs a good table at a smart restaurant, chances are he'll be wearing a suit. The tailored jacket with matching trousers remains the uniform of official power, suggesting civility, diplomacy, and physical self-control. Suits have a way of looking superior.

While the context and connotations of men's suits have changed, their basic form hasn't. For more than one hundred years, through periods of extreme social upheaval, the dress suit's insistent longevity testifies to the dynamism of its unique composition. No one has yet to devise any surrogate

"I'll throw in a few extra pinstripes."

5

THE SUIT

garment or ensemble that affords such a complete yet variable envelope for the male body. Although the fashion community seems congenitally disposed to seasonally remodel it in the name of "modernism," all this invention has managed to proceed without radically undermining the suit's eminence among hierarchical male vestments.

The Peacock Revolution accelerated the movement away from tailor-dictated taste to designer-inspired fashionability as the basis of men's style. The popularity of the Pierre Cardin hourglass suit in the seventies, followed by Hugo Boss's airplane-shouldered power suits and Giorgio Armani's low-gorge swathings in the eighties, transformed the business suit from the standard-bearer of conformity and membership into a vessel of currency and fashionable energy.

By the mid-eighties, having established itself as the contemporary clothier's high-profile calling card, the designer saw suit sales begin to eclipse both national brands as well as the top retailers' own private-label offerings. Whereas previously men tended to pay allegiance to one suit shape and dressing style, by the end of the go-go eighties, fashion's newest exponents began to experiment with clothing silhouettes the way women did with makeup, thinking nothing of buying three new suits a season, from three different designers, in three different cuts.

For most of the last century, the corporate uniform virtually guaranteed the suit an ever-widening audience. However, the latest workplace freedoms have encouraged more comfortable and collegial garb. With business attire no longer fettered by strict social codes, casual dress now shares the office with the tailored uniform.

Despite the suit's current bad press and steady decline in unit sales, more fifteen-hundred-dollar-and-up suits were sold in the last five years of the twentieth century than during the previous thirty. The sophisticated dresser understands that while no longer mandatory corporate fare, the suit is here to stay. With the classic dress suit now pressed into service more for ceremony than ordinary day wear, men want their tailored attire to be no less a talisman of success than their cars, wines, and watches, and when a man needs real sartorial firepower, he looks for the best armaments money can tailor.

Another contributor to this collateral trading-up is the maturation of the contemporary male's taste level. The style-conscious man has graduated from the high-fashion suit's two-year cycle of disposability toward one with a longer life expectancy, and thus, value. Old-world verities such as handwork and artisan craftmanship are making their way back into modern fashion parlance.

And bespoke tailoring is by no means dead, still setting the standard for today's top tier of ready-mades, so that clothing merchants assure you that, except on close inspection, their hanging product is indistinguishable from custom-made examples.

Instead of shedding value, the tailored suit has actually returned with interest. Even the Gucci-Prada colony portrays its postmodern two-pieces as tonics rather than tyrannies, the lone garment capable of transporting their urban knights from day to night, uptown to downtown. Despite the new haute corporate regime of casual dressing, when success is in the air, no ensemble can deliver such a message more poignantly than the well-tailored dress suit.

THE SILHOUETTE

Forty years ago, one could break down the dominant suit silhouettes into three or four "schools" of custom tailoring. In England, they call it "bespoke." In Italy, the word is *sartoria*, In France, it's known as *tailleur*. Each generic suit shape could be identified by its national custom-tailoring tradition, which filtered down into a variety of ready-to-wear suit styles, several of which emerged over the long term to be almost immune to the vagaries of fashion. .

The first archetype silhouette was the so-called English look, which took its lead from royalty, who in turn were invariably clothed by one or more of Britain's legendary of Savile Row tailors. The British style modeled itself along the lines of the military uniform as exemplified by the long-fitting, hourglass-shaped hacking jacket. Adhering closely to the body, with subtle emphasis on the chest and a soft shoulder, the silhouette's marked waist, slightly flared skirt, and deep side vents, trimmed sleeves and trouser line gave a man a firm, almost regal bearing, especially if he happened to be aristocratically slender.

A second generic suit shape was popularized by Brooks Brothers in America, which became known as the "Ivy League look" in the 1950s. Characterized by a three-button, single-breasted jacket with natural shoulders, undarted fronts, flap pockets, center vent, and plain-front trousers, Brooks' "Number One Sack Suit" was the first mass-produced suit, its shape undifferentiated and unsexy, offering the wearer a soft-spoken, calculated anonymity. The American suit makers were the first to learn that the less there was in a garment, the better one felt in it.

The third basic tailored expression became the Continental or European look. Continental style revolved around Italian and, to a lesser extent, French fashion. Virtually the polar opposite of the shapeless American sack suit, the European cut relied on severity of line to project its style. Characterized by high squarish shoulders and a short overall length, the jacket demanded small, high armholes to give the chest the length that short jackets denied it. Cut close through the chest and hips, the coat was usually single-breasted, two-buttoned with high notched lapels and slimming flapless pockets, and a ventless back. Its trousers had a lower rise with figure-hugging legs. The European's wedgelike torso and lean-fitting trousers turned many a young male into a walking phallic symbol.

The last or fourth type of suit style was a blend of American and English, Brooks Brothers and Savile Row. Long the staple of fine dressers, from Fred Astaire to Gary Grant, this updated American suit combined the Row's trademark smartness with the understated comfort of the sack suit. Introduced to the Gotham gent in the middle sixties by Madison Avenue retailer Paul Stuart, this shaped, two-button suit was later offered to the general public through the fashions of designer Ralph Lauren.

Featuring higher armholes and a smaller chest with darted fronts for a more shaped waist, the updated American suit's longer rolled lapels opened the coat's front to reveal more of the man's furnishings while emphasizing his V-shaped torso. Whether Americanized by a center vent or anglicized with side vents, for several decades, this soft-shoulder hybrid was the keynote of traditional American fashion, breathing fresh air into the East Coast Ivy League look.

For years, the terms "English" or "American" seemed frozen in time, denoting a particular style of suit and manner of dress that cut across continental and cultural divides. To be described as "Italian" in one's sartorial proclivities was to suggest that a man preferred his clothes fitted and worn with a certain flair. Today such references have lost all practical meaning. The last thirty years of global fashion have transcended national boundaries and cross-pollinated indigenous tastes to such a degree that those standard suit silhouettes have been completely unhinged from their former territorial or tailoring moorings.

Today, *Le Style Anglais* is more popular abroad than in England, where only an aging landowner or steadfast client of a Savile Row tailor might still adhere to the old Bond Street bromides. One would be equally hard-pressed to find the authentic sack suit for sale in Manhattan. The former European fig, with its tight fit and wedge shoulder, has now evolved into a slope-shouldered, side-vented, softly sculptured three-button affair, more Anglo-American than Continental, more Metropolitan than Milanese.

Therefore, rather than getting sidetracked by fashion's latest runway of moving suit silhouettes, arriving at that suit shape relevant to permanent stylishness will be made much simpler if one basic silhouette can be employed as the starting point. In fact, such an assumption is not as big a leap of faith as one might think. Due to a unique confluence of events, for the first time since menswear's golden age, present-day suit makers agree on the suit jacket's most defining yet variable feature, its shoulder expression. By the dawning of the twenty-first century, Italy's leading fashion designers, England's Savile Row tailors, France's top retailers, and America's sartorial elite basically agree that the sine qua non of tailoring sophistication is a suit that brackets the wearer's head with gently sloped, natural-looking, but defined shoulders.

This is not to suggest that men's suits have become so homogeneous in cut or detailing as to be indistinguishable from one another. However, it is to affirm that the real differences in today's top-rung suit silhouettes have seldom been less remarkable or more subtle. And if you throw into the mix the fact that most better suits' shoulder lines now appear to share more similarity than ever before, then, whether a man favors a suit shape that is slightly boxy or fitted, fuller cut or tapered, the exercise becomes more an expression of personal taste rather than sartorial correctness.

Therefore, assuming that the suit's proportions accord with those of the wearer and this "international silhouette" can be used as a constant in our discussion, we are freed to focus on those models, details, and fabrics that translate into permanent fashion, at least for the foreseeable future.

CLASSIC SUIT MODELS

TOP:
Gary Cooper demonstrates the classic buttoning of a three-button suit with its center button closed.

BOTTOM:
Jean Cocteau shows the larger "V" opening of the two-button suit.

THE SINGLE-BREASTED SUIT The single-breasted two-piece is the mainstay of most men's suit wardrobes. Early single-breasted suits were usually three-button, mostly with notch lapels, and always vested. Following the lines of its two progenitors, the riding jacket and then later on, the morning coat, the single-breasted lounge coat made the transition from country to city when its curved fronts were cut away below the waist button. As the curve prevented the bottom button from fastening, the top button was worn undone to balance the trio, giving the lounge suit a distinctly dégagé air.

An alternative mode of wearing the three-button coat was to fasten its top two buttons, although the lapel had to be designed to roll high enough to permit the top button to be closed. Compared with the openness of Mr. Cooper's single-button fastening, this arrangement closes up the coat, somewhat formalizing the presentation. Its two upper buttons also form a vertical line in front, promoting a more up-and-down dynamic, thought to add length to a man's torso. Here is an elegant *Apparel Arts* stripling taking in all measure of three-button stylishness.

Warm weather found men removing their vests, and over time, the matching vest's high "V" front began dropping lower and lower. Not surprisingly, the three-button jacket's high-button stance was likewise lowered, ushering in the two-button suit model. Ultimately eclipsing the three-button in popularity, the two-button with its open front not only exposed the wearer's furnishings to better advantage, but its darts and defined waistline gave occupants a trimmer look. Who says that the conservative two-button business suit necessarily stifles self-expression? This classic dark worsted doesn't seem to have inhibited Jean Cocteau from imposing his stamp of individuality on it.

The three-button suit with its top two buttons closed.

THE SINGLE-BREASTED PEAK LAPEL SUIT In the 1920s, the peaked lapel
masterminded the metamorphosis of the male torso. Throughout the interwar period, whether
for single- or double-breasted suit jackets, overcoats, or blazers, pointed revers or lapel peaks
spearheaded the popularity of the V-shaped male chest. The acceptance of the single-breasted
dinner jacket with peaked lapels in the late twenties ultimately spilled over into daywear.

By rigging a single-breasted jacket with a double-breasted rever, this lapel treatment
virtually neutralized the double-breasted edge in formality. This option offered particular relief
in the summer months, since single-breasted styles eliminated the warmth of the DB's overlapping fronts. Rarely found on ready-to-wear racks, this mildly offbeat suit model remains pretty
much confined to the custom-tailored crowd. Bespoke and vested with walking stick in hand,
two of the Home Country's better-upholstered public servants, Sir Anthony Eden and Sir
Samuel Hoare, show their take on the smartly stocked city wardrobe.

LEFT:
*Sir Anthony Eden and
Sir Samuel Hoare in single-
breasted peak-lapel suits that
spearheaded the popularity
of the V-shaped male chest.*

OPPOSITE TOP:
*Adolphe Menjou in a natty,
classic double-breasted suit.*

OPPOSITE BOTTOM:
*The Duke of Kent in the
"Kent," a longer-line version.*

THE DOUBLE-BREASTED SUIT Prior to World War II, single-
and double-breasted suits sold in almost equal numbers. As the driving
force behind tailored menswear in the twenties and thirties, the double-
breasted suit's most popular rendering was the six-on-two button front,
with broad lapels marking a high waist and straight ventless tails hugging
cylindrical hips. Long, wide trousers supported this columnlike shape,
serving as the base of an athletic silhouette that came to define masculine
elegance throughout the period.

Actor Adolphe Menjou's wardrobe was supposed to have been a
virtual anthology of men's fashion. Reportedly, it included at least one
jacket from every famous European tailor up through 1956. Here's one of
his killer DB's, natty in every nuance, from its soft, contoured shoulders
and smoothly draped chest down to his full-cut trousers' symmetrical and
centered crease.

When America's elite adopted London's famous drape cut as their
own, new double-breasted versions emerged. One model in particular spirited itself to the top of the charts, the six- or four-button front with lapels
designed to roll down below the waist and fasten on the bottom button.
Known as the "Kent," it was named after the Prince of Wales's younger
brother, Prince George, the Duke of Kent, who was generally credited with
its introduction in the late twenties. Because its longer lapel line extended
through the waistline, less emphasis was placed on the waist, thus giving the
wearer an illusion of height. Not only did the Kent seduce the superbly proportioned, its stylish swagger curried particular favor with the short and stout.

As to its style ranking, the double-breasted suit is to the single-
breasted what the pleated pant is to the plain front, incrementally more
stylish. The DB's pointed, diagonal lapels spiff up any worsted wool with
a slightly dressier panache. Because the jacket's overlapping fronts look
tidier when squared up, one of their front buttons should be fastened to
exploit the model's inherent swank. Like the pinned dress shirt collar or
suspendered trouser, the DB suit requires a bit more aplomb to effect a
natural stylishness.

Men are creatures of habit. When servicemen returned from
World War II, they opted for the single-breasted suit, having become accustomed to its comfort and ease of wear during their military service. As a
result, the fifties witnessed the popular decline of the DB. With the exception of a few random periods of limited renaissance, the double-breasted's
principal proponents have been the custom tailors and their style-conscious clientele. Although its
appeal comes and goes, as long as men regard the dress suit as a symbol of male elegance and
authority, the double-breasted suit will always justify its inclusion in the top-echelon wardrobe.

SUIT JACKET DETAILING

ABOVE:
Side pockets line up with the bottom button on the coat's front. Notice the pocket's D-tack finishing.

BOTTOM:
Patch pockets are considered the most casual of the three classic suit pockets.

SUIT JACKET POCKETS Early suit pockets were jetted, or flapless. In 1921 the Prince of Wales started yet another trend by reverting to flaps for his suit coat's lower pockets. Although he was not the first to wear them, his adoption sanctioned their vogue for his legions of followers. Regardless of their style or size, the jacket's side pockets (or the top edge of the flap) generally line up with the bottom button on the coat's front.

Flapped pockets add a layer of fabric to the jacket, therefore making it less sleek and dressy. This is why top-pedigreed tuxedo jackets feature jetted rather than flapped pockets. Better-quality flap pockets are "double-besomed," a tailoring term for a narrow welted edge sewn above and below the pocket's slit opening. Not only is this the most expensive type of pocket flap construction, but also should the wearer decide to tuck his flaps inside the pockets, these two welts give the pocket a more finished appearance.

Alternatively, flap pockets are dressier than the sewn-on patched variety. As such, the open or flapped style of patch pocket can usually be found astride the sportier two-piece or light-colored solid suit. Since patch pockets add another layer to the jacket's surface, they are considered the most casual of the three classic suit pockets. Were a navy or dark pinstriped dress suit adorned with patch pockets, it would be frowned upon as a sartorial oxymoron. Here's a trio sported by the White House's only president to do time in the menswear business, haberdasher Harry Truman.

The extra change pocket situated above the lower hip pocket, whether flapped or jetted, has always been a detail signifying a suit's custom-tailored genesis. Movie stars such as Fred Astaire had many of their on-camera suits made with them, thus introducing the ticket pocket to the male viewing public. As a rule of thumb, the flapped cash pocket diminishes a suit's dressiness, while the besom style heightens it. Years ago, if a customer wanted a cash pocket added to a ready-made suit, most better men's stores were equipped to accommodate him.

SUIT FABRICS

FALL

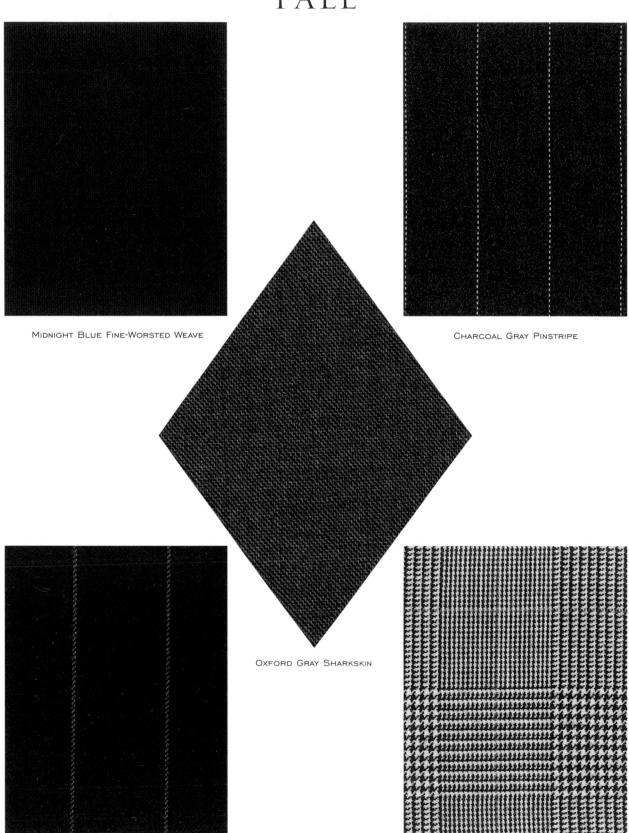

MIDNIGHT BLUE FINE-WORSTED WEAVE

CHARCOAL GRAY PINSTRIPE

OXFORD GRAY SHARKSKIN

NAVY WORSTED CHALK STRIPE

MEDIUM-WEIGHT BLACK-AND-WHITE
GLENURQUHART PLAID WITH BLUE OVERCHECK

Unless indicated, all suitings are constructed with fine merino wool yarns and two-ply fillings.

WINTER

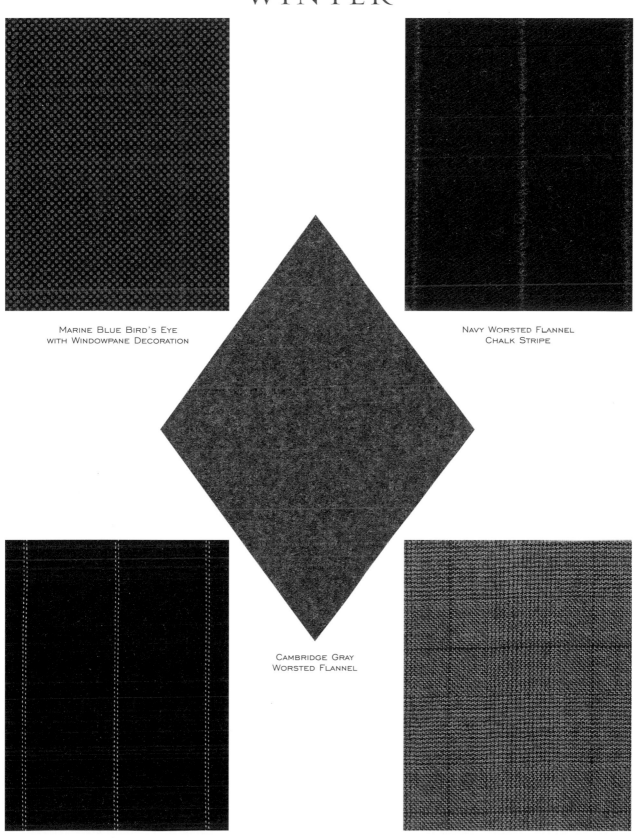

MARINE BLUE BIRD'S EYE
WITH WINDOWPANE DECORATION

NAVY WORSTED FLANNEL
CHALK STRIPE

CAMBRIDGE GRAY
WORSTED FLANNEL

CHARCOAL BROWN DOUBLE-BEAD STRIPE

TAUPE GLENURQUHART PLAID

SUMMER

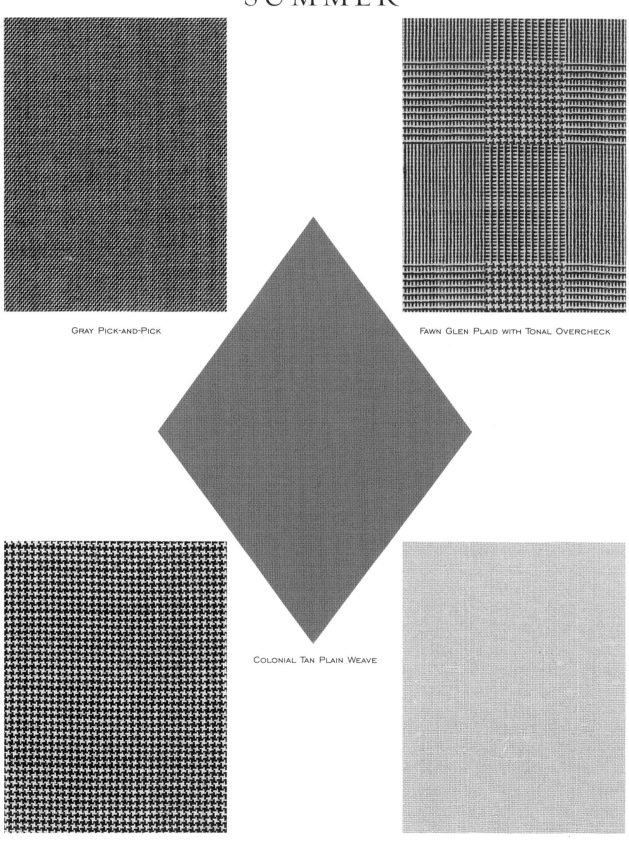

GRAY PICK-AND-PICK

FAWN GLEN PLAID WITH TONAL OVERCHECK

COLONIAL TAN PLAIN WEAVE

BLACK-AND-WHITE TROPICAL
SHEPHARD'S CHECK

CREAM DUPIONI SILK

SPRING

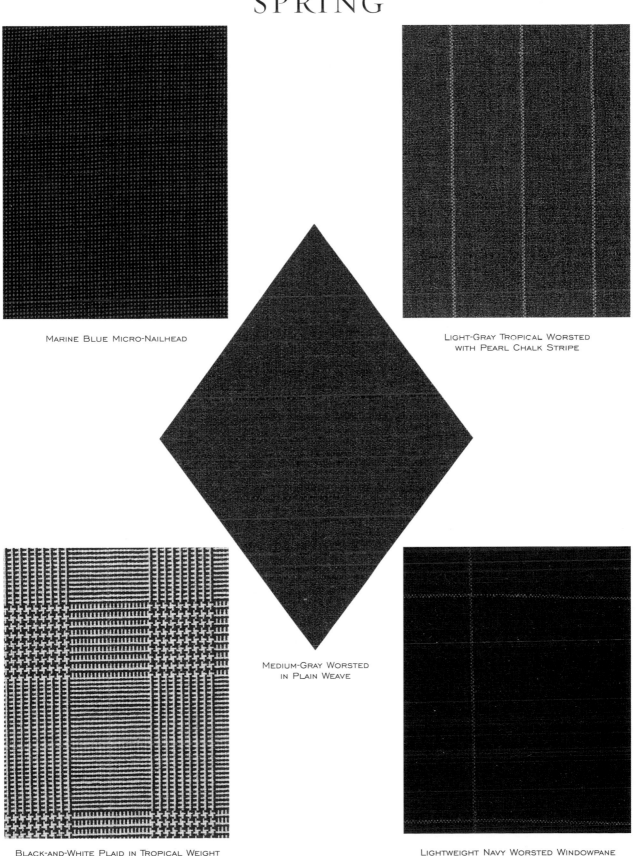

MARINE BLUE MICRO-NAILHEAD

LIGHT-GRAY TROPICAL WORSTED
WITH PEARL CHALK STRIPE

MEDIUM-GRAY WORSTED
IN PLAIN WEAVE

BLACK-AND-WHITE PLAID IN TROPICAL WEIGHT
WITH RED OVERCHECK

LIGHTWEIGHT NAVY WORSTED WINDOWPANE

RIGHT:
Cash pocket.

BELOW:
Angled hacking pocket.

The angled flap or "hacking" pocket, so called because of its ancestral connection to the English riding or "hacking" jacket, is another timeless suit-pocket option. Rarely found on non-British ready-mades, its presence tends to project a slightly Anglicized, if not bespoke, slant. A favorite detailing of the house of Huntsman, the famed Savile Row tailor known for their riding jacket–inspired cut, the flap's diagonal chisels breadth away from the hip while adding an illusion of height to the wearer. With its sporty roots, the slanting, hacking-style pocket works better with single-breasted clothes, although its angles harmonize handsomely with those of the peaked-lapel, single-breasted suit model. Occasionally accompanied by a like-pitched cash pocket, this arrangement is better left to rusticate the sporty country suit.

JACKET VENTS Vents have a military heritage. When men traveled on horseback, their coats were designed for comfort in the saddle. A single slit in the coat's back permitted its tails to fall naturally on either side of the horse, a very practical reason why even today the long single back vent still adorns most modern riding jackets. As the male suit jacket must be long enough to cover the buttocks, rear vents make the trouser pockets more accessible. There are three choices in jacket venting: ventless, single center vent, and the double-vented side vent.

The Ventless Back In the late seventies, the ventless suit was a rarity. Over the next ten years, the men's designer business catapulted the plain-back suit into mainstream fashion, establishing it as the most popular type of jacket, a status it retains today. Although its origins are frequently traced to the tight-fitting Italian suit of the sixties, nonvented suits are as time-honored as the British side vent. Between the wars, when English tailors ruled men's seams, the majority of bespoke lounge suits and, in particular, dinner jackets, were tailored without vents.

ABOVE:
The long single back vent adorns most
modern riding jackets.

LEFT:
The ventless back bunches up if forced to accommodate
a hand in search of a pocket.

The nonvented jacket hugs the hip, giving it a clean, trim contour and a dressier mien. While offering simplicity of line and form, it functions poorly. In order for the wearer to reach into a trouser pocket or to sit down, the ventless back must bunch up, frequently leaving a crease. Advocates choose to ignore such inconvenience, because of its supposed sexier allure.

The Center Vent The center-vented back, an American predilection, rose to prominence in the days when ready-to-wear clothes were first arriving on the scene. With the evolution of America's natural-shoulder fashions in the fifties, the center-vented jacket became a featured part of the Ivy League look. Initially designed for horseback, the single vent lacks any stylish form whatsoever when not in the saddle.

If a man's hand is in search of a jacket or trouser pocket, at the slightest tug the single vent pulls open like a garage door, revealing what it should be covering. This center slit

ABOVE:
*The single vent pulls open to expose a
man's derriére, once a hand is placed
in a trouser or jacket pocket.*

RIGHT:
*The side vent permits access to trouser pockets
while covering the buttocks.*

attracts undue attention to the man's exposed der-
rière, and, if cut high enough, the vent encourages a
fringe of disordered shirt to join the spectacle.

As the least expensive vent to manufacture
and, until recently, the most common style of rear
venting, the center-vented treatment usually confirms
the garment's ready-made provenance. The Italian
cognoscenti never succumbed to its middlebrow favor,
and most Savile Row tailors avoided it like the sartorial
sophomorism it is. Offering a bit more function than
the nonvented arrangement, the single slit's only saving
grace is that it can occasionally be employed to better
conceal a prominent hip than either the ready-made
ventless or side-vented jacket back.

The Side Vent Side vents
offer the wearer the highest union of function and
form, not to mention flexibility. Should a man try
a double-vented coat and
later decide that he doesn't
like the two vents, the back
can be easily converted
into a ventless by sewing
the side vents closed. As for
function, when the wearer
is sitting down, the side slit
allows its back flap to move

away, thereby minimizing creasing. And when one accesses a trouser
pocket, the double vent's back flap permits smooth entry while conceal-
ing the buttocks. Whether single- or double-breasted, the side-vented
coat can be worn buttoned and still provide ready entrance to the jacket
or trouser pockets without disturbing the line of the jacket's back.

In spite of its overwhelming upside, the double-vented scenario is the least popular of the three back treatments. Unfortunately, because side-vented coats demand better design and tailoring
to fit well, the public's negative opinion has been fed by the all-too-
common example of side-vented coats whose rear bottoms either
kicked out or stood away from the wearer's seat. Along with the pub-

The side vent minimizes creasing when a man chooses to sit down.

lic's lack of interest, side-vented clothes have never been enthusiastically embraced by the manufacturing or retail sector. The fact is that double vents are the most expensive type of jacket back to manufacture and also the most likely to involve additional alteration costs for the seller.

However, when its side slits fit properly, lying flat and perpendicular to the ground, the double-vented jacket offers a posterior guard of practicality and propriety. While this rear design dispenses its duties with simple élan, its benefits are not limited to a man's hindquarters. Side vents lead the observer's eye up either side of the coat's back, subliminally imbuing the wearer with an illusion of greater height. When the man is in stride, the subtle concert of motion between the rear vents above and the trousers' thighs below lend fluidity and grace to the male silhouette (an attribute that Fred Astaire exploited to the hilt for his on-camera dance routines).

The side vent's height constitutes another of those minute details that reflect a man's personal taste. In general, its length should not extend above the top of the jacket's hip pocket flap or below its bottom edge. If the pocket is jetted, the vent's length generally takes its cue from the pocket's height, although it can finish lower. Side vents cut above the height of a pocket flap tend to move about, calling undue attention to themselves by swinging open and shut like an unlatched gate.

DRESSING THE JACKET SLEEVE Buttons on jacket sleeves have passed through various vogues. Centuries ago, they were employed on jacket cuffs so the wearer could unfasten his sleeve to permit his ruffled cuffs to be pushed through without wrinkling them. These customs antedate Frederick the Great's order to have buttons put on the sleeves of his soldiers' uniforms to encourage them to use their shirt cuffs instead of jacket sleeves as handkerchiefs.

Jacket-button logic has historically operated as if it were a cabalistic language. No one knows for sure why four buttons on a suit jacket's sleeve convey superior sartorial breeding, but that's how London's master tailors have trimmed suit sleeves since time immemorial. And because they have mentored every civilized country in the fashioning of fine men's tailoring, England's Savile Row remains the "cultural arm" of the fashion papacy in such matters.

Regardless of their number or functionality, suit sleeve buttons should be set close together, their edges "kissing," with the bottom button finishing no more than ¾ inch above the sleeve's bottom. (Note Captain Eden's cuff buttons, in the illustration, opposite.)

THE SUIT WAISTCOAT

All tailored men's vests descend from the original postboy waistcoat of nineteenth-century England. Worn by the postboy, or postilion, who rode as a guide on one of the pairs of horses attached to a coach, the garment was intended mainly to provide warmth, so it was usually made of a woolen fabric, front and back, and cut high under the armholes.

The waistcoat is technically the most challenging garment to construct satisfactorily. As a high point of the tailor's craft, it is required to lie flat as a pancake on a surface as contoured as a potato as well as maintain a "touch fit" that is nowhere tight. The waistcoat has survived because it added gravitas to the single-breasted suit, held a tie in place, kept the shirt neat and tidy, and lent an efficient appearance to working in shirtsleeves. It was not only warm and decorative but utilitarian, since the wearer carried a heavy gold watch in one waistcoat pocket and his watch fob in another, with a gold chain extending across its front to connect the two.

Prior to the Second World War, most single-breasted as well as many double-breasted suits were worn with a vest. However, historical circumstances conspired against the waistcoat. Central heating and the arrival of warm-weather fashions in the late twenties encouraged the shedding of superfluous clothing. The double-breasted suit was the first to dispense with its customary waistcoat, and then wartime fabric rationing all but dealt the suit vest a deathblow. In the 1960s, three-piece suits began a slow recovery, but the inclusion of the vest increased the ensemble's retail price, diminishing its commercial viability. Today the vested suit is a remembrance of things past and accessible only to those able to afford one custom made.

The addition of the right "odd" waistcoat can transform even the most predictable two-piece, as shown here by Captain Eden's white linen single-breasted waistcoat with small notch collar. Following suit, the single-breasted, peaked-lapel model (*above right*) provides an ideal setting for more meticulous waist decor as worn by one of the dream machine's most debonair leading men, Randolph Scott.

THE SUIT TROUSER

The most fortuitous development in recent trouser fashion occurred in the eighties, when pleats and suspenders returned dress trousers to the flattering sanctuary of the man's natural waist. Whether plain-front or pleated, forward- or reverse-pleated, narrow- or full-legged, should a suit trousers' rise be so low that their waistband is obliged to rest between the wearer's natural waist and hip, the ideal balance between suit jacket and trousers will be doomed.

Although plain-front trousers have staged a comeback, today's suit trousers are pretty much a pleated affair, their shape dictated by the natural lines of the body, full across the hip and thigh, tapering down to narrower bottom. Pleated pants look dressier, and their pleated fronts provide greater comfort than plain-front trousers. Hips widen when the wearer is seated, and pleats facilitate this shift more easily and with less wear to the trouser. Objects placed in a front pants pocket are better concealed within the pleated trousers' front.

The classically designed pleated dress trouser has two pleats on either side of its fly—a deep one near the fly and a shallower one placed toward the pocket. This design fostered a working relationship between the two pleats, as the smaller one helps the larger one to remain closed. Having more than two pleats on a trousers' front interferes with this symbiotic function and is simply a gimmick of fashion.

COLORS AND FABRICS

As recently as ten years ago, men still spent the majority of their clothing budget on fall-weight suits. Nowadays, courtesy of high prices and fears of global warming, it is the midweight, eight-month two-piece that monopolizes most of their funds. Perhaps the single largest beneficiary of recent textile and manufacturing advances is the three-season suit, the workhorse of the male suit wardrobe.

Whether untouched by human hands or completely hand-tailored, today's $750-and-up suits are confections of unrivaled lightness, suppleness, and performance. Never before has a man's suit provided him with such comfort along with a sense of well-being. Advanced textile technology has enabled the top Italian and British mills to fabricate worsted wools that look and hang like cloths almost twice their weight. Yesterday's coarse wool yarns made tailored clothes feel heavy and boardy; conversely, today's high-count worsted yarns make dress suit jackets as light as cardigan sweaters. While vintage suits in old films appear impeccably suave, were you to slip one on today, it would probably feel more like an overcoat than a suit.

The orthodox view held that suits should be in neat patterns and quiet tones, ranging from midnight to slate blue, from dark charcoal to light gray. Blues and grays were considered the business basics because they facilitated the transition from work to after-work activity. In the fall, a rich-hued brown suit in cheviot or tweed could be added to the rotation.

While this limited color palette continues to direct the selection of most men's business suits, there are more options than ever before. Let's focus on those classic suitings that should form the backbone of the well-dressed man's tailored wardrobe.

THE CHARCOAL SUIT When it comes to starter suits, the dark gray two-piece gets the professional's nod. While navy is more formal, charcoal complements more men's complexions. In the case of the young man, navy's starkness frequently accentuates a pubescent face.

The dark gray dress suit empowers the knowing wearer with unrivaled flexibility. It can be accessorized with a white dress shirt and dark tie for uptown, black turtleneck or T-shirt for downtown. Such fashion fluidity makes the charcoal two-piece the blazer of male suits. As the well-heeled Milanese's most worshiped worsted, the perennially stylish charcoal affords the maturing master of the universe a neutral canvas on which to rough out the morning's vestiary possibilities, readily accommodating a larger variety of colored or patterned furnishings than any other single suit shade.

Ralph Lauren's bird's-eye gray dress suit.

THE NAVY SUIT At the turn of the century, if a man owed one suit, it was usually the old "trusty blue serge." Its navy jacket topped white flannels, making the first nationally accepted weekend leisure ensemble. Coming into its own as daytime wear for the man who needed a bridge between the informal and formal, the navy two-piece was the first lounge suit to be accorded the status of a modern business uniform. Recommended for town wear with a bowler hat, yet spruce enough to wear when taking a lady to an evening concert, the dark blue dress suit could transport its owner from day to night, weekday to weekend, even showing up at semiformal occasions when black tie was not required.

The quintessential power suit color, navy was the color called upon for the Michael Douglas character Gordon Gekko to deliver his infamous "greed is good" speech in the movie *Wall Street*, not to mention all serious-minded American presidential candidates, who seldom appear on national television wrapped in anything less patriotic than the color anthem of navy suit, white shirt, and red tie. More enriching than stark black, more ceremonial than charcoal, whether in twill or plain weave, 12 ounces or 8, a navy suit shows off the average man to best advantage.

THE STRIPED SUIT Of all men's suitings, none has ever matched the glamour and popularity of the striped suit. At one time or another in the thirties, the striped suit probably graced every pair of male shoulders, from the humble to the most famous, from the unemployed to the chairman of the board.

Although its stripes had to be positioned perfectly for maximum effect, this pattern's innate appeal derived from its vertical line. Elongating any physique, the striped worsted quickly established itself as the patriarch of all patterned dress suits.

The variety and scale of classy suiting stripes are endless. They can be in single, double, or triple tracks, against plain or fancy backgrounds. Lines can be faint or bold, from subtle shadows to hairlines to pins, up to pencils or chalks, in spacings ranging from narrow to wide. When the Prince of Wales launched the daytime vogue for shadowy chalk stripes, he elevated the stripe suit to new level of cosmopolitan consciousness.

The striped jacket and matching trouser formed their own partnership around the turn of the century when the lounge suit started to replace the black jacket and odd striped trouser for business dress. The montage of striped swells here illustrates the proposition that when executed knowledgeably, the two-color tailored ensemble can add up to more than just a simple two-color look.

ABOVE:
Ronald Coleman in early lounge coat formality.

RIGHT TOP:
James Mason in his stripes.

RIGHT BOTTOM:
The ever-stylish Ralph Lauren in striped repose.

THE PLAID SUIT While the Victorian era entertained tartans and the turn of the century hosted checks, it wasn't until the 1920s that plaid clothing revolutionized the rules of urban style, following the English trend in which "country" began to impinge upon "town" in matters of male dress. Although some checks like the houndstooth enjoyed a distinguished career, none would become as enduringly stylish as the glen plaid.

For the sartorial romantic, the glen plaid suit conjured up images of strolling in the fresh and radiant light of a spring morning. Its charm stemmed from the overall lightness achieved through a refined play of vertical and horizontal lines that intersected at regular intervals over a houndstooth check. Sometimes thin threads of bright color (red, blue, rust, pink) were woven through the checks.

Although the glen plaid could flatter almost any physique, for tailors, plaids posed numerous challenges and additional costs. Their horizontal and vertical lines had to match up exactly, requiring slightly more fabric than the solid or striped two-piece. However, the plaid's higher cost and complexity of production invested it with just the right allure to secure its position in masculine fashion mythology.

The man who raised the plaid suit: The Prince of Wales in his own "Prince of Wales."

THE WINDOWPANE The windowpane worsted has always featured low among the rank and file, while its standing with the well-starched set has never been higher. Rarely found hanging around average retail climes, the windowpane suit, when it did make one of its rare appearances on a selling floor, tended to overstay its welcome. As a result of its commercial disabilities, most men remain unfamiliar with the windowpane's insider charisma.

For the initiated, the pattern's individuality and popular neglect are two of its main attractions, the third being its salutary effect on the male figure. Longer in length than width, its upright rectangular formation subtly elongates, unlike the stripe, which works its magic in more conspicuous ways. Another plus is its facility for harmoniously combining with a second or third pattern. The windowpane's open-box setting encourages far more varied pattern mixes than the glen plaid's multilinear ground. However, the windowpane's clearly demarcated outline gives manufacturers even less margin for error in matching.

Whether in a charcoal flannel enlivened with a chalk-toned windowpane or a tropical worsted embellished with a colored overcheck, this erudite pattern is, like Caesar's wife, above suspicion.

THE GRAY FLANNEL Though the shrinking demand for winter-weight wools has diminished the appeal of this icon of male refinement, the classic gray flannel suit remains a paragon of cool-weather stylishness. Ever since the famous 1950s novel *The Man in the Gray Flannel Suit* immortalized this cloth as a symbol of corporate recititude, collegians, ad executives, and Madison Avenue clothiers have regarded it as a wardrobe staple.

Soft rather than stiff, with just a pinch of texture, the best gray flannel eschews any hint of sharpness or newness, exuding that slightly worn-in, old-money look associated with genteel taste. Owing to advanced textile technology, England's and Italy's top weavers now turn out lighter-weight worsted flannels with the authentic "English flannel" look.

Like the charcoal worsted, the medium-gray flannel is the perfect foil for accessories of all backgrounds. Whether a soft-spoken button-down or a starchy spread-collar, dress shirts and neckwear of every description are welcomed by gray flannel's sumptuous repose. Imbuing its wearer with a relaxed elegance, the well-cut gray flannel grows more flattering with wear (see page 43).

THE BROWN SUIT Perhaps no other male vestment has been more maligned over the past fifty years than the brown suit. First, there was the old British saw about never wearing brown in town. Churchill once impugned it as the mantle of a cad. The khaki-clad legions of the post–World War era eschewed brown because it reminded them of their military service, while their brides felt that the shade aged them. Finally, Charles Revson's highly publicized quip about brown making men look like "shit" pretty much resigned it to the wardrobe of the nonconformist.

Brown's reprieve from suiting oblivion came during the tenure of President Ronald Reagan, whose personal affinity for the disgraced color returned the brown dress suit to public currency. Fortunately for the modern swell reared on a steady diet of navy or charcoal, just as the twentieth century was about to close its books, fashion restored the brown suit to its former state of masculine grace. Following closely on the heels of the smarter set's partiality for walnut-toned lace-ups over black with their navy or charcoal suit, all sorts of brown worsteds suddenly started showing up on the backs of the better-shod.

In 1939 *Esquire* presented a "thoughtful study in charcoal brown," introducing an outfit it judged "almost perfect for maintaining a due degree of formality for definite town occasions." Back when menswear journalism focused on individual dressing strategies as opposed to generic fashion, a man's complexion, vis-à-vis his clothing's colors, used to receive extensive coverage. As a result, chocolate-, blond-, red-, or sandy-haired men were continually encouraged to consider brown as one of their staple wardrobe themes.

While there are those diehards who refuse to consider a brown suit, there is no man who cannot wear one to personal advantage. The dark brown suit offers many virtues, the first being its freedom from dependence on the predictable blue and gray. The second is that the dark brown suit is every bit as dressy as the navy; like charcoal, the richness of brown's darker hues harmonizes well with dress shirts of all shades, from gold to green to tan, with the recent mating of the dark brown worsted and medium-blue dress shirt attracting considerable acclaim. Whether in a winter or summer weight, plain or pinstriped, double- or single-breasted, the high-class brown suit will always be a power player in any male wardrobe aspiring to permanent stylishness.

The dark brown suit is every bit as much a power suit as navy or charcoal.

ABOVE:
Ray Milland swathed in silky gabardine.

BELOW:
*Sir Anthony Eden in mohair, when
a soupçon of sheen was viewed as a
touch of class rather than crass.*

GABARDINE For the ultimate in light-colored suit fare, nothing beats the colonial tan gabardine. Since its introduction in the thirties, the classic gab has consistently ranked right up there on the list of idealized dress suits. Costly to weave, expensive to tailor, and problematic to press, the top-quality gabardine is neither a winter nor summer suit, but an interseason option for those with deep-enough pockets to afford its delicate luxury and limited wearability.

While not as sumptuous as its wool confrere, the cotton gabardine two-piece offers a soothing alternative to the typically dry, firm-feeling tropical worsted. The fine Italian cotton gabardine suit will wrinkle, but its satiny freshness and cool suppleness offer the humidified epidermis a princely measure of comfort.

SUMMER STANDARDS For years, when the seasons changed from cold to warm, so did the texture of men's tailored clothes. Fabrics became more buoyant, drier to the touch, with increased porosity for better air circulation. Voiles, airtex weaves, and open-mesh dress shirts helped ventilate male torsos, while Palm Beach worsteds, cotton seersuckers, and nubby silks helped layer bodily zones for hot-climate comfort. Gauzy silk grenadine and spongy linen neckwear completed the surface-interest picture.

With the disappearance of the hand laundry and the commercialization of the dry-cleaning process, the majority of these higher-maintenance summer materials went the way of the two-toned spectator shoe. However, a few of the standbys are still available for those interested in unearthing them, although they are fast becoming extinct due to the public's lack of exposure to them. What has rendered them increasingly less commercial over the years are their surface properties, such as sheen or texture, which today are either misunderstood or neglected. The following are classic suitings whose particular fabrics were bred to provide the wearer with comfort and coolness, and still do.

Seersucker is America's most iconic summer suit. "Why should the very cheap remain the province of the very rich?" asked *Esquire* magazine in August 1936. This rumpled-looking cotton fabric first became a symbol of the rich and socially secure before the average man finally accepted it as something other than a poor man's suit. Although not an expensive fabric, the all-cotton seersucker will go right on ticking way after other luxury garments have tossed in the towel. Today, in medium blue, brown, or gray and white oxford stripe, single- or double-breasted, worn with a necktie or polo shirt, the seersucker suit offers a heat-beater stylishness transcending both low and high fashion. (See page 105.)

One of the few summer suits capable of holding its crisp good looks has always been the wool mohair suit. Today, when fine baby mohair is mixed with superfine merino wool, a crease-resistant fine blend results, leaving the old mohair suit stiff and old-fashioned by comparison. Unfortunately, because of the dulled luster of mohair's surface, its sensibility is frequently identified with its older enthusiasts, the white-on-white-shirted, bulbous Windsor-knotted boulevardier.

Since its debut on the Riviera in the late twenties, the pure silk dupioni suit has always been the last word in summer chic. From its well-bred beginnings, the silk suit with its natural glossy beauty and superior draping quality was a status symbol, an aristocratic garment made only by the prestigious custom tailors and top manufacturers. Today, only one mill in Italy weaves this unique fabric in its original quality and narrow width. The classic shades are cream, brown, blue, and elephant gray. Combining the best of natural fiber worlds, this shantunglike nubby silk material is drier yet more luxurious to the touch than cotton, resists wrinkling better than linen, and drapes with more fluidity than fine worsted wool.

Prince Charles, backdropped by the tropic paradise of Hawaii's Big Island, immaculately rigged out in silken Savile Row dupioni.

At the beginning of the twenties, the term "sport jacket," or "odd jacket," was still not in popular usage. The bulk of the male population wore for leisure the jackets, and often the vests, of their business suits with white flannel trousers and white shoes. Whereas the well-dressed man might have secretly hankered for something sartorially more exciting than a suit jacket, most men had simply not progressed to the point where they expected comfort from their clothes. In fact, it was not until 1923 that the style-conscious Ivy League undergraduate finally accepted the idea of a designated separate jacket for spectator sports.

6

ODD JACKETS, TROUSERS, &

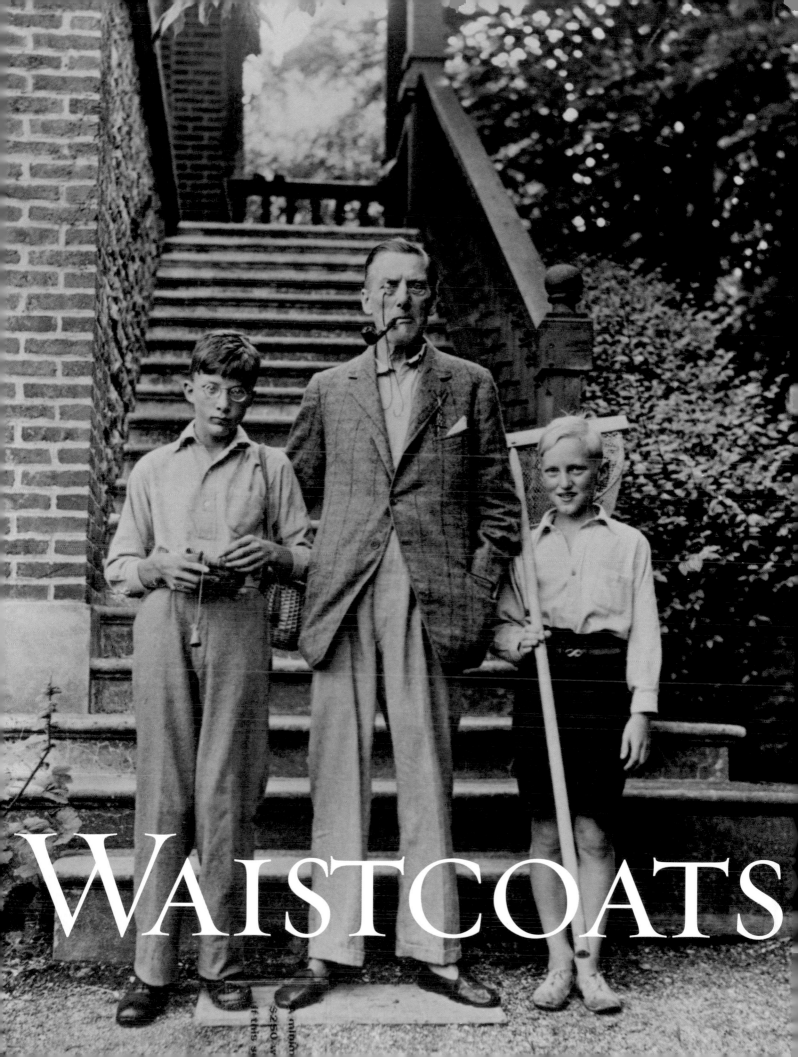

WAISTCOATS

In the period following World War I, discharged veterans thronged to department stores and haberdashers to make up for the deprivation suffered in the distant trenches of Europe. The era of flaming youth was unfolding, and never before was the American man more inclined to try something new and different. The postwar obsession with sports and outdoor activities encouraged fashion experimentation, with the main arena being sports clothes. The New York elegance of the period meant looking well turned out but comfortable. From this time forward, the virtue of comfort would be an evolving constant of men's fashion. In a few short years, the contemporary sport coat would become the hallmark expression of modern men's clothing.

Jackets for sport have a common progenitor in the Norfolk jacket of the mid-nineteenth century. Forty years later, it reappeared with its original detailing intact. The later Norfolk jacket of 1918 might be called the first American sport jacket, although it was borrowed from the Norfolk suit of Harris or Donegal tweed that manufacturers advertised as "a thoroughly serviceable suit for men who are young, either in age or spirit, and who want to be distinctly well dressed, even on their outings." When paired with white flannel trousers and a natty straw skimmer, this summer outfit passed muster at even the most snobbish vacation resorts.

Along with the dark blue serge suit jacket and white flannel slack "uniform" of fashionable resort wear, the affluent American was accumulating an impressive wardrobe of Norfolk suits and odd knickerbockers that he could mix and match. As the Great War had not undermined British supremacy in the realm of masculine stylishness, London was more than ever its capital. During the Anglomania of the 1920s, a variety of highland jacketings thrilled connoisseurs and neophytes alike. The rough, warm woolens of cheviot, saxony, and donegal brought a breath of fresh air to the sleek worsteds then popular. Scottish and Irish tweeds, countrified yet civilized, represented the apex of all fabrics associated with the British sportsman, with the well-worn-in tweed looked upon as the epitome of aristocratic aplomb.

Two silhouettes came to define the early sport coat: the English drape, with its broader shoulders, fuller chest, slightly shaped waist, and close-fitting hip, and the American Ivy League sack coat, an unpadded and undarted, straight-hanging jacket with pliable fronts, soft rolled lapels, and a three-button front. An elegant example of early American sport jackets is shown above—the Brooks Brothers Shetland sport coat, complete with its characteristic three-button, two-to-button front.

In those days, for a fashion to start off on the correct foot, it had to be seen worn by the right folk. American postwar prosperity created overnight millionaires, resulting in "new" money following "old" down to their favorite warm-weather watering holes. With a social season that demanded multiple changes of wardrobe and a concentration of society's leaders in attendance, Palm Beach became the fountainhead for American resort fashion. Representatives from national publications and sportswear manufacturers flocked to this elite turf to report on the latest leisure apparel of the upper brackets.

However, it wasn't until 1923 that fashionable denizens began to witness some of their regulars donning jackets that could claim to be separate "odd jackets." Profiled (*below*) in prevailing plage fashions is one of its northern habitués, New York socialite Milton Holden.

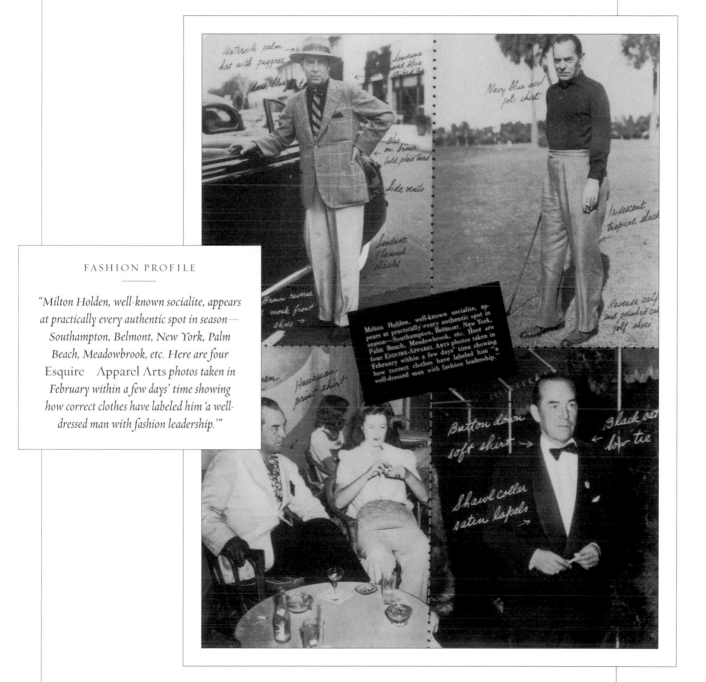

FASHION PROFILE

"Milton Holden, well-known socialite, appears at practically every authentic spot in season—Southampton, Belmont, New York, Palm Beach, Meadowbrook, etc. Here are four Esquire–Apparel Arts *photos taken in February within a few days' time showing how correct clothes have labeled him 'a well-dressed man with fashion leadership.'"*

ABOVE:
René Lacoste sporting the first designer logo.

OPPOSITE:
*Accompanied by his wife and a friend (in a suit coat),
best-dressed Anthony Drexel Biddle in a sport coat
was one of the era's legendary barometers of men's fashion.*

By the latter part of the twenties, the sporting jacket, trimmed of its countrified detailing and worn with separate trousers in contrasting fabrics such as flannel or gabardine, became the ideal expression of casual elegance for competitors and spectators alike. Ironically, it was this garment, as adopted by the upper crust for the sport of tennis, that begat the designer logo. Dubbed *Le Crocodile* by the sports press for his tenacity on the court, French tennis champion René Lacoste had his symbol embroidered on his blazer jacket several years prior to its debut on his legendary white piqué sport shirt.

If there was ever any doubt about the aptitude of America's leaders of male style to hold their own at the proverbial card table of international fashion, here's a guy who could do it in spades: Anthony Drexel Biddle, scion of the Philadelphia Biddles. The late Douglas Fairbanks Jr. once told me that in the 1920s and 1930s, two men monopolized the top rungs on everyone's best-dressed list: William Rhinelander Stewart (the family's Rhinelander Mansion hosts Ralph Lauren's flagship store) and our man Biddle. Behold American style at its most patrician in one of my all-time-favorite fashion candids.

Although Biddle's male confrere relies on his suit jacket to double as a sport coat, Biddle brooks no such backsliding. Tony Biddle was not only a prominent socialite; he also was one of those rare barometers of male fashion who could single-handedly realign its boundaries. Following a strenuous workout, Biddle bundles himself up with his towel-cum-neckerscarf, lobs a seersucker sport coat over his tennis sweater, and exits the court in full-cut loose-cuffed tennis whites astride bespoke spectators.

No longer the new kid on the block, the sport coat became the centerpiece around which the city's leisure wardrobe was assembled. Now found in most better urban wardrobes, a well-blended gray and maybe a morning or travel jacket in a country homespun look were relied upon for less formal occasions, such as an afternoon's social call or a few rubbers of bridge in the evening.

ABOVE:
Brooks Brothers pleated-back jacket.

LEFT:
*Henry Fonda in action-back tweed
and sport-detailed flannels.*

BELOW:
Clark Gable in a shirred-back design.

THE ODD JACKET

The term "odd" for a sport jacket was not occasioned only by its lack of a matching trouser; the word also fits because of the garment's individualized detailing. In 1926, the outstanding sport coat at Palm Beach was the solid tan gabardine sport coat. Ushering in the fancy-back jacket era, here's another of the Brothers Brooks' many contributions to permanent fashion, their classic pleated-back gabardine sport jacket, with a stitched belt across the back waistline and four pleats above and below it.

In the photograph above, a very youthful Henry Fonda comfortably furls his lanky frame on the stage, courtesy of his jacket's "bi-swing," action-back design. Functional bellows pleats run from the back's belt up to its yoke, freeing the arms' movement while facilitating the rotation of his shoulder. Notice the consorting of his

tweed jacket's edge-stitching with his flannel trousers' correspondingly jauntier open lap-out side seams.

The most popular fancy-back jacket of the time was the shirred-back design with one piece of material between the yoke and belt. When Clark Gable walked across the screen wearing one, this model catapulted to the front of the pack. At first, this back treatment was confined to gabardine, but as it grew in acceptance, other fabrics such as Shetland wool, linen, and tweed soon saw action.

Likewise, offbeat pocket treatments were frequently employed to inject a bit of social pluck into the odd jacket's rusticity. Based on the way Hollywood film director George Fitzpatrick is upholstered, you'd expect him to be a chap of casual but eccentric bonhomie. Certainly his splayed shirt collar and foulard cascading from his one-button jacket's inverted pleated breast pocket would support such a hypothesis.

Another pocket permutation playing to gentle pretense is Master Gable's asymmetrically angled and gusseted breast pocket. While merging form and function, it also seems to have resolved the challenge of how to accommodate the bulk of both a pocket square and pipe.

It has been said that the horse actually invented male sports clothes. As a result of the British sportsman's passion for all things equestrian, the cloth coat was forced to be cut away at the front for freedom of movement, eventually influencing the tailoring of suits worn in town. By the mid-thirties, the hacking jacket moved out of the fields and into the city, showing the influence of riding clothes in its extra length and flair, slanting flap pockets, and twelve-inch side vents. Straight from the horse's mouth, here's an early Brooks rendition of the classic English riding rig.

The thirties also witnessed the civilian adoption of military apparel identified with the Commonwealth's colonies in Asia and Africa. The first of these was the mid-length safari jacket, inspired by the summer uniform of the English army during the First World War. Fastened by a row of buttons, it featured a yoke in front and back, four gusseted pockets, a belt, and long sleeves with cuffs. Different design offshoots of this garment have enjoyed periods of revival, and with the new business-casual mode taking hold,

ABOVE:
Film director George Fitzpatrick's very "oddly" detailed sport jacket.

BELOW:
Clark Gable with pipe and pockets to go.

TOP:
Brooks Brothers classic hacking jacket.

ABOVE:
*Safari or bush jacket—
the alternative sport jacket.*

RIGHT:
*The stripe sport coat as favored
by Princetonians.*

a simplified version of the classic safari jacket could very well be in the offing.

Although World War II put a damper on new sport coats, when the war ended, the first article of apparel to reflect a sense of celebration was the patterned sport jacket. Back in mufti and extremely sports-minded, the fashion-conscious man had no intention of letting his new sport coat be mistaken for a suit jacket, and therefore bold-patterned jackets returned stronger than ever.

In the late forties, primarily on Ivy League campuses, the exuberant striped Shetland jacket loomed as heir apparent to the bold plaid. About the same time, authentic madras plaids were making their way into the fashion lexicon of the college and country club set. With *Esquire*'s "Bold Look" of 1948, the American male seemed destined to wear clothes that would express his new optimism. However, no one could have predicted the conservatism of the fifties, when the gray flannel suit practically became a state of mind.

From the seventies onward, designer-driven exploits subjected the sport jacket to more experiments and manipulations than any other piece of tailored men's clothing. The recent interest in alternative business attire has reinvigorated the tailored sport jacket, investing it with a new fashion importance.

THE BLAZER

Just as the fancy-back sport jacket was reaching its peak of popularity, the burgeoning appeal of the plain-back blazer loomed on the horizon. The overwhelming acceptance of the blazer marked the decline of the fancy-back jacket, and by 1938 the plain-back jacket became the leading odd jacket style.

The first blazers had been part of English cricket club scenery as well as other sporting environs since the 1880s. These sport jackets were customarily decorated with stripes in the club's colors. Some were so bright that they became known as "blazers." Solid serge or striped blazers with flannel trousers and straw boaters became a familiar Edwardian sight. They were subsequently joined by versions of the English navy's reefer jacket in double- and single-breasted models with gilt buttons and club badge on the breast pocket.

*A few English lads soak up America's swing music between races. Both the Cambridge and Oxford crewmembers sport
their colors atop Oxford bags while the chappy on the right opts for the updated reefer blazer.*

A roundup of some of America's early blazers as pictured on Palm Beach's older and younger denizens.

With blue and white as the imperatives of nautical dress, navy blazers and white trousers made a dashing sports outfit for the wealthy American man of the 1920s. Being class-conscious, he adopted it as another means of distinguishing himself from the masses. Whether in a solid color and piped at the edges or in bold regatta stripes, the lightweight blazer became a summer sensation.

By the thirties, the blazer began to be seen in different solid colors. The standard shade of dark blue so long associated with white trousers was now being overshadowed by brighter and gayer shades such as robin's-egg blue, deep medium blues, or purplish blues. Whether in one of the new blues or its second-running favorite, dark green, the blazer became the bridge between workaday and weekend wear.

The blazer ranks in dressiness somewhere between a suit and a sport jacket, and its formality can be influenced by simple changes in modeling, detailing, or accessorizing. As the double-breasted blazer projects a slightly heightened aura of dress-up over the single-breasted model, so do flap pockets over patch, peaked lapels over notched, side or no vents over center, and dark trousers over light.

THE BLAZER BUTTON Emblazoned with its typical metal hardware, the navy blazer remains a hierarchical type of garment. While many men appreciate the gentility implied by the traditional gilt blazer button, in today's less ceremonial world some men feel uncomfortable with such conspicuous display. While the dark brown horn button is usually the first nonmetal alternative considered, its dullish character lacks the personality necessary to offset the dark jacket.

The most traditional blazer button is the brass or gilt variety. Unless your family has its own coat of arms or you are entitled to wear a distinguished club button, the classiest choice is the plain, flat, English gilt button with a shank that must be anchored into the cloth. Alternatively, men with gray hair or those planning to wear predominantly gray-toned trousers will often opt for the aforementioned button in a dulled nickel or silver shade. In the case of a brighter blue tropical wool or linen blazer, off-white mother-of-pearl buttons are always an option.

As to the ideal number of buttons for the blazer's front and sleeves, personal taste tends to defer to tradition. To begin with, the number of sleeve buttons is related to the coat front's button arrangement. With the most popular jacket model being the two-button single-breasted, four sleeve buttons are the norm, although two are equally proper. Three sleeve buttons on a two-button coat seem slightly out of balance, whereas with the three-button model, three or four sleeve buttons harmonize handsomely.

Judging the correct number of buttons for a double-breasted blazer is guided first by its styling, second by tradition, and third by personal taste. The classic double-breasted blazer with flap pockets is traditionally trimmed with six front buttons, two that button, two that don't, and two upper display or dress buttons, a formation that pretty much demands four sleeve buttons, as illustrated by a preening Prince Charles.

The well-selected navy blazer offers an almost chameleonlike versatility. Whether in the country or traveling around the world, with long or short pants, flannels or jeans, ascots or neckties, short sleeves or French cuffs, the classic navy blazer remains man's most accommodating tailored companion.

Prince Charles practices his Napoleonic pose in a classic navy blazer.

THE ODD TROUSER

By the early twenties, the odd trouser had established itself as an essential part of every well-dressed man's wardrobe. However, in 1925, American college men vacationing in England were confronted by voluminous pantaloons worn by the Oxford and Cambridge undergraduates to camouflage their knickers, which were not allowed in the classroom. With pleated waistline, baggy knees, and bottoms measuring from 22 to 26 inches, the Oxford bag ignited a fad that swept the country in the space of a year.

*England's answer to America's
Fred Astaire, fashion plate
Jack Buchanan in Oxford bags.*

Although their popularity went into decline the following year, the Oxford bag initiated a vogue that would last forever—fuller-cut trousers. With Anglomania at an all-time high and the Ivy League student a major source of fashion innovation for America, these pajama-width bottoms left the style-conscious young American in favor of wider-cut slacks. Here's the soon-to-be exemplar of English fashion, Jack Buchanan, taking a pair of bags out for a spin.

As the thirties began, many young men began ordering an extra pair of trousers to match their tweed three-pieces of jacket, vest, and plus fours, or knickerbockers, a style that flourished on the golf links. When the trouser was donned with the vest and jacket, the ensemble could be used for business and then split up for sport or other leisure pursuits. This development resulted in many young men reverting to odd trousers for casual wear because they were more serviceable than the sport-only knickers.

The new trouser fitted close at the waist while hanging freely and easily over the hips. Two generous pleats were fixed into its high waistband to give extra fullness across the front, while the trouser leg was long enough to break slightly over the instep. It was thought that the cuffed bottom and crease fore and aft had significantly improved the line of a trouser, abolishing baggy knees and fringed hems.

Along with tweeds, flannel became a leading bottoms fabric during the interwar period. It was first used in the nineteenth century strictly for underwear, but by the 1880s, flannel was worn for golf, cycling, and tennis. In the twentieth century, flannel was recognized as a stylish cloth, and in the late 1920s, the woolen mills in the west of England created skillful mixtures of black, gray, and white that added light and dark highlights to the plain gray cloth, establishing the gray flannel trouser as a worldwide commodity. Among the young blue bloods from British society, gray flannel slacks came to be known as "grayers."

Charcoal flannels dealt the sporting knicker, or plus fours, an early blow, while colored and striped flannel pants relegated it to chasing golf balls over the countryside. By the late thirties fashionable Americans abandoned knee-length bottoms both on and off the golf course, and the knickerbockers went into full eclipse.

Gray ultimately loosened white's stranglehold on the upper-class weekend regiment, because it looked more appropriate in winter than white. As a result, it was not long before the gray flannel pant found its principal role as the companion for any type of sport coat. Here's a 1940s French menswear magazine's depiction of this "trouser of trousers'" virtually unlimited choice of dance partners. Ranging in texture from tweed to corduroy, in pattern from solid to

Men's ready-made flannel trouser swatches from Brooks Brothers

Surrounded by friends, the gray flannel trouser is the blue blazer of cool-weather dress slacks.

fancy, and in color from green to fawn, the medium gray worsted trouser is the blue blazer of odd dress slacks.

Today's less tradition-savvy male is sometimes confused when the services of a medium gray dress trouser are recommended for a non-gray solid or patterned sport coat. Although the blue blazer has long been paired with gray trousers, somehow the inherent stylishness of such a combination loses its relevance when the non-blazer jacket and trouser ensemble is being considered. No doubt, such an oversight is occasioned by the pragmatic but instinctively female approach of marrying the pants color to an exact match found in the jacket. Unfortunately, this sensibility often leads to the less sophisticated colonization of the sport jacket with a navy or dark brown dress suit–trouser shade. This is one of those times where the obvious is not always the more tasteful. Should you be considering a new sport jacket and are having difficulty visualizing it with a medium gray trouser, move on.

ABOVE:
David Niven luxuriating in gabardine trousers.

OPPOSITE TOP:
The gentrified corduroy sport trouser.

OPPOSITE BOTTOM:
The Duke of Windsor nursing his pipe and baby cords.

The first alternate to the classic charcoal gray dress trouser for the blazer or odd jacket is either a slightly lighter shade of gray or a representative from the tan family in a wool covert, gabardine, or cavalry twill. Because tan produces slightly more contrast than gray under the average sport coat, it registers a slight drop in relative dressiness. Various shades of corduroy or classic olive drab chinos follow next on the dress-down meter, with blue jeans residing somewhere below.

One trouser fabric that gave both the white and gray flannel a run for its money back in the thirties was wool gabardine. The silky, smooth gabardine offered a textural change of pace to the rough, woolly flannel. Still regarded as one the most luxurious lengths of worsted ever to grace a male thigh, it's shown here on a man with the legendary gift of "gab," the well-lighted David Niven in rustic dishabille.

With the 1930s university man donning sport jackets and slacks almost every day for class, it's little wonder that the college campus pioneered many of the new dress trouser fashions. In the early thirties, Glenurquhart plaid slacks gained popular acceptance among university students. When worn with solid jackets, they marked an emphatic change in the balance of pattern between the traditional tailored sport ensemble of solid bottom and patterned top.

In 1933, having gained acceptance at Yale and other Eastern college campuses, covert cloth started the trend for sturdier, more rugged types of slacks fabrics. As another tan alternative to the omnipresent gray flannel, covert's gray-green hue worked well with most tweed jackets, and especially well with the blue blazer. Initially tailored from topcoat fabric that proved too heavy for comfort, covert cloth's enduring popularity was assured when it was fabricated into lighter-weight trousers.

Already familiar with the ribbed hardiness of Bedford cord and cavalry twill in the saddle, the paddock set champed at the bit for any opportunity to sport the cord trousers on terra firma. In regular weights and variegated ribs, cotton cords were perfect for campus or outdoor activities. Here we observe two of the faithful considering which suds to sample first on a Saturday afternoon's tailgate gathering.

Following on the heels of the wider-wale corduroy's popularity, what better way to step up its warm-weather comfort level than to step down its weight? The Duke of Windsor keeps score on one of Arnold Palmer's golfing nemeses, South Africa's Gary Player. While always resplendent, the Duke tones down not only to avoid any backswing distraction but also to accord with his light-color complexion. Details worthy of note are his low-fastened tweed sport jacket with short side vents (very Fred Astaire), cuffed baby cords; and monk-strap shoes.

With the college man returning to classes after military service, the arrival on campus of a

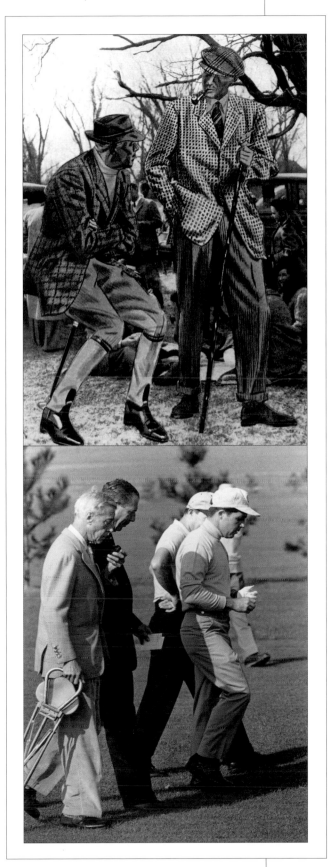

military type of work fabric in the fall of 1945 came as no surprise. Chino cotton trousers in olive drab became the new uniform, remaining an integral part of the collegiate man's wardrobe for the rest of the forties and into the fifties. By the mid-fifties, gripped by the emerging gray flannel conservatism, sport slacks gained a back strap but lost their pleats, cuffs, and swagger, tapering down to 17½ inches at the bottom. The plain-front model maintained a dominant position throughout the next several decades, courtesy of a series of fashions that pushed the trousers' waist down to the hip: the fifties Continental look, with its low-rise pant; the sixties hip-hugging blue jean; and the low-slung suit trouser of French designer Pierre Cardin's seventies silhouette.

Ironically, the century's last two decades witnessed the return of the tailored trouser to nearly the height of its pre–World War II stylishness. With the drapey swathings of Italian designer Giorgio Armani and the 1980s mini-revival of the 1930s look, fuller-cut trousers made a comeback. And along with its softer mien, the sometimes suspendered, always longer-rise trouser resumed its classical positioning on the male's natural waist.

As the new millennium picks up pace, men's tailored trousers are dividing into two camps: the "updated classic" as represented by the fuller-cut, pleated-front form; and the "moderne," as configured by the harder-edged, plain-front, trim-fitted shape. The modernists' slack "de sleek" reflects their preference for pared-down, uncluttered simplicity. For the fashion vanguard, this cuffless bottom's low rise and condomlike contour offer a sexy antidote to the loyalists' larger-volumed silhouette. For the fashion savvy, this dernier cri seems vaguely reminiscent of a former leg-hugging social equalizer, the blue jean, except that now its chic can be dispensed in any one of three shades of black.

CLASSIC ODD TROUSER MODELS

Most men's dress slacks are made with belt loops. While trouser waistbands and belt loop dimensions are not immune to fashion, those accommodating belt widths ranging from 1¼ inches to 1½ inches will always remain impervious to obsolescence. Along with the traditional plain- and pleated-front trouser models, several lesser-known odd slack models continue to curry favor with the better-slippered buck. Whether narrow or full cut, the following waistband treatments have maintained their fashion authenticity and insider currency since their inception back in menswear's prewar heyday.

THE DAKS SLACK   The Daks waistband was invented in 1932 by Alec Simpson, the eldest son of Simeon Simpson, founder of the English House of Simpson. As an avid golfer, Alec shared the irritation felt by fellow golfers when impeded by one's braces and disordered shirt in the course of a swing. Trained as an engineer, Alec decided that there must be a better way to

WITH THOUGHTS OF SUMMER in mind, we offer you a few suggestions from Simpsons' vast array of appropriate clothes. The left-hand figure seems comfortable in a double-breasted suit—worn without waistcoat—at £6.12.6. The saw-edge straw hat and the whangee cane add a touch of seasonable light-heartedness. Right, the Daks trousers are in hopsack (30/-); the striped sports shirt (30/-) being neatly topped by a foulard scarf.

The Daks Slack—the first self-supporting beltless trouser

construct a sport trouser and came up with the idea of a "comfort-in-action slack," the first self-supporting beltless trouser. In memory of his father, he named his creation Daks, an acronym combining "Dad" and "slacks."

First, rubber pads were sewn into the waistband to hold the shirt in place. Then, on either side of the waist, self-cloth tabs with buttonholes were designed to connect to a concealed band of elastic running through a tunnel loop around the inside back of the waistband. This permitted the tab on either side of the waist to pull forward and fasten on one of the two side waistband buttons, bringing additional tension on the waistband for support.

Although sport-inspired, the genuine Daks top waist design is expensive to manufacture and therefore typically found only on higher-priced ready-made or custom-tailored suit or sport trousers. Here's one of the earliest ads for Simpson's beltless classic.

THE SELF-BELT Between the wars, the demand for lightweight sports clothes encouraged innovations in beachwear. The self-belt design removed the bother of having to pack a separate waist rigging. When cotton slacks with matching tops sauntered into vogue for resort wear during the late twenties, the convenient and easy-to-fasten self-belt pants model gained further acceptance, eventually infiltrating general sportswear and dress trousers. A matching

separate or attached half self-belt was usually provided with either a plain or covered D–ring, as modeled here by actor Errol Flynn.

THE HOLLYWOOD WAISTBAND

The popularity for higher-waisted trousers in the fifties spurred the re-emergence on the West Coast of a model initially created in the thirties. Aptly termed the "Hollywood," this longer-rise model featured a one-piece front and back with narrow belt loops positioned below the trousers' top. Modeled here by "Ol' Blue Eyes," the Hollywood's nonwaistband design and lowered belt loops necessitated narrower belts, which were believed to help it conform more closely to the wearer's natural waistline. One variation on this theme was for style avatars such as Leslie Howard to sport his belt buckle off to the side, purportedly for comfort but probably also for swagger.

TOP:
Errol Flynn wearing a self-belt tweed trouser.

LEFT:
Frank Sinatra surrounded by a Hollywood-style waistband.

RIGHT:
Leslie Howard sporting his self-belt stylishly to the side.

THE ODD WAISTCOAT

Other than coming upon an odd "postboy" languishing about one of London's antiquarian men's emporiums, the last time anyone spotted the genuine odd waistcoat for sale on American shores was back when Brooks, Chipp, J. Press, and Triplers still basked in Madison Avenue glory. The odd waistcoat was one of the chromosomal WASP's trump cards in his former days of peacockery.

A cursory survey into this American tradition begins in 1928, the Gatsby era, with a linen waistcoat in pastel shades of tan, gray, and blue. It was apparently in such favor that the trade paper *Men's Wear* decreed that "the linen 'odd' vest is an important item in the wardrobe of every man who makes any pretense whatever at following the fashions." By the mid-thirties, smart country attire spawned a new waistcoat, the single-breasted tattersall vest, its colors chosen to harmonize with the accompanying horsey jackets. Younger men who had never worn the odd waistcoat before were cautioned to remember that the louder its hue, the quieter its style should be. "For instance," wrote a *Men's Wear* editor, "the tattersall check is almost invariably seen in the single-breasted model, while the plainer, more conservative colors may be sported in the double-breasted model."

By the 1940s, a semi-sports outfit was not only acceptable for city wear but according to *Esquire*, "it was smart to be sporty." The new detailing of semi-sports clothes was an outgrowth of hunting and riding togs. Unfortunately, despite the separate vest's national sponsorship, the waistcoat per se was waning. During the war years, it was dealt an insurmountable blow when the War Production Board decreed that double-breasted suits could no longer be manufactured with vests. While the checked, plaid, or brightly toned solid odd vest remained a fixture on many Ivy League campuses up through the sixties, the Peacock Revolution ushered in the shaped suit, effectively killing it. By the early seventies, the peacock had distanced himself from the postboy.

Even though the current workplace has activated the sport jacket for dress-down duty, unless the four-in-hand is similarly mobilized, the separate vest is not likely to be seen storming the front lines of men's fashion anytime soon. This is a shame, because the snappy odd weskit could always be depended upon to inject a bit of whimsy into the wardrobe.

The tattersall waistcoat emsemble.

*T*he shirt, more so than any other male garment, has served to distinguish a man's wealth and social class. Up through the nineteenth century, the white linen dress shirt was considered the epitome of male elegance. A man with an immaculate collar and cuffs clearly did not work with his hands, and in the days when a large portion of the populace was impoverished, wearing white imparted prestige. The century's most famous dandy, Beau Brummell, who dictated the main lines of men's fashion to all of Europe for more than one hundred years, advanced the maxim "fine linen, plenty of it, and country washing."

"Since you asked, sir, I recommend a plain white shirt with that suit and a no-nonsense tie."

7

THE DRESS

SHIRT

Throughout most of the nineteenth century, all gentleman's underclothing was made of linen. The word "linen" became a generic term for a man's underwear. The dress shirt functioned exactly like the modern T-shirt by keeping sweat away from the outer garments while protecting the body from the coarse outerwear materials. However, propriety demanded that only its collar and cuff be visible, hence the term "showing linen" meant that white linen at the neck and hand was a sign of gentility. As recently as the late 1940s, it was as shocking for a man to expose his dress shirt in polite society as it would have been for a woman to walk into a restaurant wearing nothing over her brassiere.

The modern dress shirt's shape developed during Victorian times as men donned tight waistcoats, forerunners of the modern vest, thus rendering the full-cut shirt obsolete. Once the current dress shirt's body shape was established, the collar became its most distinguishing and fashion-sensitive feature. In 1820, a housewife in Troy, New York, changed the face of men's fashion. Hanna Montague was the wife of a fastidious blacksmith who insisted on a clean shirt every evening to attend his civic engagements. Vexed by the daily drudgery of laundering, she liberated both the shirt and herself by cutting off the collars, binding the edges and neckbands, and attaching strings to hold them in place.

At first, Mr. Montague was disturbed by his detachable collar, but the idea caught on among his friends, and soon Troy housewives were snipping away. The owner of a general store recognized the commercial possibilities of this simpler shirt and started manufacturing some in his back room. Almost overnight, Troy abounded with shops clamoring to turn out the detachable collar. In fact, American shirt-making giants such as Cluett Peabody and Phillips Van Heusen first began as separate-collar manufacturers in the Troy area. Separate collars rose to the pinnacle of fashion in the years preceding the First World War, when the commercial artist J. C. Leyendecker created the male equivalent of the famous Gibson girl, the legendary Arrow Collar Man.

As sportswear came into being during the second half of the nineteenth century, so did the separate double, or turned-down, collar. However, war forever changed its destiny. With five million men serving their country in government-issue soft attached-collar shirts, the war dealt a blow to the separate stiff collar from which it never recovered. By the 1920s, critics lamented that the United States was alone in its espousal of the collar-attached shirt for town wear. By the early 1930s, soft double collars were accompanying the new dinner jacket, a development that sparked considerable debate. Advocates of the stiff collar regarded it as the keystone of classical male elegance, the last bastion against slovenliness.

A youthful Anthony Eden (*preceding page*) dons a dress shirt with a stiff, attached straight-point collar. Notice how tightly knotted and therefore, small, the knot had to be to fit into its starched environs. The knot's positioning up, into, and directly out from under the stiff collar's inverted "V" point became the criteria of smartness for the emerging soft-collar fashions. Just as the tailcoat mentored the dinner jacket's evolution, the older stiff-collar's design abetted that of the newer soft attached-collar decorum. Even today, a dress shirt appointed with a purposely tied necktie affecting a crisp knot sitting high in its collar is still an expression of an authoritative and polished practitioner.

PLAY YOUR BEST LINE

One of the most important but least understood functions of male attire is to lead the viewer's eye toward the face. Understanding the subtle balance that should exist between a man's most visible and expressive body part—his face—and the clothes that lead up to it is a prerequisite of fine dressing. By virtue of its proximity to the face and its configuration of angle, scale, and mass, no article of male apparel is better equipped to enhance a man's countenance than the appropriately shaped dress shirt collar.

The triangular sector formed below the chin by the "V" opening of a buttoned suit jacket constitutes the cynosure of a man's tailored costume. Several dynamics work to direct the viewer's focus toward this area. First of all, it is directly under a man's most animated feature, his face. Second, this triangular encasement is accentuated by contrasts between the darker jacket and lighter shirt, silken tie and dulled or matte shirting, etc. Again, keeping in mind that the face is that destination where one's dress should be escorting the attention of the beholder, think of the face as a picture and what surrounds it as the frame.

Whether or not the color or pattern of a dress shirt coordinates perfectly with an outfit, if its collar is too small, the head will appear large; if the collar sits too low on the neck, it will make the neck look longer than it is. The choice of a dress shirt should be guided first and foremost by the appropriateness of its collar to the wearer's face, rather than the vicissitudes of fashion or personal whim.

Choosing the appropriate shirt collar requires a bit of experimentation and a little common sense. A small picture requires a comparable frame, just as a smaller man with delicate features requires a collar of more restrained dimensions. Conversely, when the content is more expansive, the frame must enlarge to afford proper balance without distracting from the intended focal point. Just as large tabletops beg for ample pedestals, heavyset or big-boned men require more fully proportioned collars. For example, former President Clinton compensates for his larger jaw with slightly spread collars while balancing his full face with generously scaled,

THE CYNOSURE OF THE TAILORED
MAN'S PRESENTATION.

Founder of Black Enterprise *magazine, Earl Graves employs a long pointed full-scale collar to balance his lionesque visage.*

SMALL COLLARS MAKE A LARGE HEAD APPEAR LARGER.

long-pointed ones. Both Conan O'Brien and David Letterman possess pronounced jawlines and favor dress shirts with larger-proportioned collars on camera.

The length and spread of the collar points should complement the head's contour and size. Long straight-point collars, those 3 inches or more, with little spread between their points, will extend and narrow a wide countenance, just as the broadly spaced points of a spread collar will counterbalance a long and narrow face. Long-necked men require taller collars with wider neckbands that raise the collar's height, while short-necked men need lower-sitting collars with a more forward slope. The tab collar or other pin-affixed collars provide the additional height that can diminish a long neckline. The writer Tom Wolfe presents a fairly striking image with his Ichabod Crane–height collars, almost Victorian in their stiffness and grandeur, but they do camouflage his longer neck.

Collars should also counterbalance the facial structure by either softening its dominant lines or strengthening its weak ones. Long-pointed collars that are either pinned or buttoned down will help to countermand faces with angular features and strong lines. A full face that sags around the chin or cheeks demands a stiffer collar to counteract the effects of age and gravity. While soft button-down collars are classically stylish, they are too often favored by the double-chinned set, who should expressly avoid them in lieu of a slightly firmer collar.

Throughout 1980s and much of the 1990s, in an effort to give men a more casual air, fashion designers unfortunately tried to neutralize the dress shirt's traditionally dignified and ordered format. Dress shirt collars were shortened, lowered, and softened to such a degree that their original stylistic precepts were either distorted beyond recognition or lost completely. Abbreviated button-down collars could no longer roll, shortened straight-point collars lost contact with the shirt's chest, and spread collars sat so low on the neck from their diminished collar bands that they were sapped of all their inherent flair.

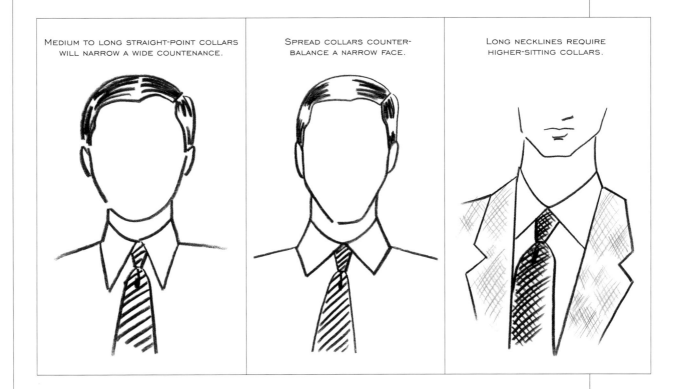

MEDIUM TO LONG STRAIGHT-POINT COLLARS WILL NARROW A WIDE COUNTENANCE.

SPREAD COLLARS COUNTER-BALANCE A NARROW FACE.

LONG NECKLINES REQUIRE HIGHER-SITTING COLLARS.

Other than the Jermyn Street or odd bespoke product, nowadays most men are wearing dress shirts with collars too small for their face that sit too low on their necks. And, with the spread collar's return to the fashion forefront, those men who have adopted the so called half- or full-Windsor tie knot have succeeded only in exacerbating the problem, as its bulbous mass invariably forces the collar's already truncated length points even farther off the shirt's chest.

Fortunately, toward the late 1990s, dress shirt aesthetics began to follow that of suits by returning to their custom-tailored roots. Fueled by an Italian revival of classical elegance and the emergence of artisan-made clothes, high-end menswear stepped into the new millennium on bespoke footing. A plethora of ready-made dress shirts are now beginning to feature collars that no longer have to apologize for their style-defining presence.

Tom Wolfe's tall collar camouflages his long neck.

ON THE FACE OF THINGS

Unlike other less visible accoutrements such as hosiery or shirt cuffs, the shirt collar is an integral and highly revealing gesture of personal style. All sophisticated dressers have arrived at one or more collar styles that best highlight their unique features while adding a bit of dash along the way. The following men illustrate how their physiognomy and sense of style influenced their choice of dress shirt collar.

THE STRAIGHT-POINT COLLAR

Because the straight-point collar was the collar shape gracing most military-issued dress shirts since WW I, it has long been the foundation of the modern man's dress shirt wardrobe.

As the most stylistically neutral of all collars, the straight-point collar can be worn with any kind of suit or sport jacket. Ideally, its collar points should finish between 2¾ inches and 3⅜ inches in length. The narrow opening between its points favors a rounder, oval-shaped face, rather than a narrow one.

Here is a man who chose to title his autobiography *It Took Nine Tailors*. As one of Hollywood's great early leading men, Adolphe Menjou was also one of its leading dandies. Here he is tailored to his own measure in a long-point collar with just the right amount of calculated disobedience to play the harried political boss in Frank Capra's *The Man Behind the President*. His collar's casual deportment not only defangs his aggressively striped bespoke suiting but also serves to elongate his oval contours.

If you were feeling uneasy that this collar presentation was overly ballyhooed, consider the next victim. Here's a dress shirt performance that is definitely laying an egg. England's Leslie Howard is pictured taking a stroll on deck as he returns to Europe aboard the SS *Berengaria* (and, let's hope, to a

good Jermyn Street chemisier). How he has managed to come up with exactly the wrong collar for his face is anyone's guess. Its long and very perpendicular lines pick up where those of his face leave off, rendering his already gaunt visage even more lank. If there ever was a prime candidate for a spread-collar shirt, Master Howard would be it.

THE SPREAD COLLAR

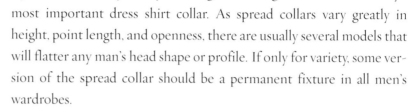

The spread collar has been the keystone of the English bespoke look since the double collar came to town during the early 1920s. Its introduction is widely attributed to the famous Prince of Wales, probably due to his alleged creation of the Windsor knot that was supposed to escort it. In fairness, it was really his younger brother, the Duke of Kent, who first popularized it.

Because of the spread's inherently dressy and elegant bearing, it has become today's most important dress shirt collar. As spread collars vary greatly in height, point length, and openness, there are usually several models that will flatter any man's head shape or profile. If only for variety, some version of the spread collar should be a permanent fixture in all men's wardrobes.

Although Prince Charles mars this perfect tableaux of royal shirtmaking by being caught with his finger in his ear, his collar architecture is spot-on (*top left*). The height, point length, and spread of his Turnbull & Asser glen plaid collar points are perfectly symmetrical with the contours of his face. Notice how the collar's points touch his chest while remaining tucked under his coat's front, even when his head is turned, one of the spread's practical advantages over other models. In addition, the dimple of his four-in-hand knot falls directly under the "V" point at the collar's top. And just for good measure, notice that his sleeve cuff has not receded from view, even when his arm extends, courtesy of its longer sleeve and close fit of its cuff around his wrist.

Because the majority of Italian men are smaller-boned, most fancy some version of the spread collar. Fabio Borelli, one of Italy's new generation of shirt-making scions, is no exception. As his face tapers down almost to a point, the spread collar is, in fact, the only possible design able to counteract such a contour.

Borelli has employed a higher-sitting spread collar to better frame his face while tinkering with tradition with typical Italian *sprezzatura* (*bottom left*). Don't think for a minute that his collar's slight bowing, the minutely skewed angle of his knot, or even the peaking of his tie's underblade happen to be coincidence. To the contrary, this demonstration of noblesse negligence is another reminder of an almost cultural predisposition by Italy's style cognoscenti to continually rework the canons of English taste. Who says that the male species is any less decorative-minded than the female? However, like most aspects of stylish habiliment, true elegance resides not in the clothes themselves but in how they are worn.

Here's the spread collar cum Windsor knot's most indefatigable champion, the late actor and author Douglas Fairbanks Jr. *(below)*. The moment this collar and knot team hit London, Junior immediately adopted it, eventually becoming its lifelong ambassador. Fairbanks's enthusiasm may have had as much to do with the large knot and collar's early acceptance by the beau monde as with its alleged instigator, the Duke of Windsor.

OPPOSITE:
Well-proportioned spread collars as worn by Prince Charles and Fabio Borelli.

LEFT:
Doug Fairbanks with spread collar and full Windsor knot.

THE ROUNDED COLLAR

The short, stiff round collar has been an obligatory part of the Eton school uniform since the mid-nineteenth century. Originally a separate stiff white collar that attached to a banded collar shirt body, early on the collar signified membership in one of the world's most exclusive male clubs, hence its moniker, the "club" collar. The famous Arrow collar ads in the early twentieth century helped to elevate this style of collar to the pantheon of classic dress shirt collars.

As a soft attached collar, the club collar became one of the 1930s' most popular collar shapes to be worn pinned. Its curves played particularly well under the decade's athletically chiseled visage. Although the club collar rarely cavorts among the masses, this holdover from Victorian society can occasionally be found hobnobbing with the custom-tailored set.

*Here's one of America's
most fashionable socialites,
Milton Holden, sporting an
early invocation, a short, stiff,
to-attach club collar.*

THE TAB COLLAR

The Prince of Wales is generally credited with introducing the tab collar to high society. Coming into its own during the late 1920s and early 1930s, it flirted briefly with fashion once again in the 1960s. Although its popularity has waned due to the inexorable casualization of male fashion, the tab collar remains a favorite of those seeking that extra nuance of nattiness.

The tab collar must be designed perfectly for the tie knot to rest comfortably in its opening. Special tabs fasten to each other under the tie's knot to hold the collar's points in place, thrusting the shirt collar and necktie knot higher up under the wearer's chin. Long-necked men welcome the tab's higher positioning, while the round- or square-shaped visage appreciates its longitudinal symmetry. Originally, a special brass stud secured the collar to the neckband while connecting the collar tabs. Today, with pre-attached tab collar dress shirts, a snap or a button and buttonhole apparatus is usually substituted. However, as with most old-world wearables, the original brass stud still projects a more polished sophistication than its less visual modern surrogates.

Britain's answer to the stylish supremacy of America's Fred Astaire was their own tony thespian and hoofer Jack Buchanan. To be called a "Buchanan" was a compliment, suggesting the recipient knew his way around a fitting room. And this Buchanan guy could outfit himself with the best of them.

Jack Buchanan, the always natty hoofer, and Britain's answer to America's Fred Astaire.

PINNED COLLARS

At one point during the 1930s, nearly half of all American men reportedly wore their dress shirt collars pinned. Today, it would be surprising to find one man in a hundred so appointed. Some men find the pinned collar fussy; most men are simply intimidated by its obligatory rigging.

Considered by many shirt savants to be the pinnacle of collared carriage, this is not neck trapping to hide behind. Unlike the cutaway or button-down, the pinned collar's stylishness rises or falls in relation to the skill of its execution. Wearing it with panache demands a little practice, some manual dexterity, and a bit of patience.

Functioning much like the tab, the pinned collar raises the tie knot up on the neck, shortening the long neck. The straight points' verticality work to counterpoint the rounded or oval contoured head or chin. Back in their heyday in the thirties, straight-point collars were finished at between 3 inches and 3½ inches long, making them natural candidates for pinning up. The most common apparatus was a plain gold safety pin; next was a sort of spring-loaded slide mechanism; while the aficionado used a bar with shaped ends that unscrewed to fit through specially made collar eyelets. The next step in such collar accoutrement was to acquire one decorated with a sporting motif such as a golf club, polo mallet, or riding crop.

Following the same principle of stylish neck rigging, the pinned club collar transports one quietly out of the ordinary. Fastening snugly beneath the tie knot, the rounded collar elevates the wearer's collar height, and its

LEFT:
*Saks Fifth Avenue's former chairman, the ever
elegant Philip B. Miller, donning his signature
long-point collar secured by a simple gold safety pin.*

IT'S ROUND · THAT'S THE POINT

...it's trim
...it's neat
...it's new

*Richard Merkin,
pinned to perfection.*

softer, rounder outline harmonizes particularly well with the square or angular jawline. With no points to curl up, bend over, or go askew, the rounded pin collar remains trim and tidy throughout the day. Artist, writer, and well-known New York toff Richard Merkin pins his collar to perfection (*right*).

THE BUTTON-DOWN COLLAR

Initially popularized by American sportsmen and Eastern university men during the 1920s and 1930s, the oxford button-down is America's sole contribution to the lexicon of permanent dress shirt fashion. Since World War II, European enthusiasts have descended upon the doorstep of its shrine, 346 Madison Avenue, to load up on this unique American classic. Until recently, no elegant male could unfurl his stripes without at least one Brooks Brothers pink oxford gracing his closet.

   With designer menswear helping to blur the distinction between disposable and permanent fashion, Brooks Brothers has further muddied the waters by abdicating its role as the protectorate of America's traditional fashion. As goes Brooks, so goes the button-down. The Ivy League look was the last patrician-inspired men's fashion to establish itself before the roots of America's upper-class taste were displaced in the upheaval of the 1960s Peacock Revolution. Were it not for

the vision and genius of Ralph Lauren, America's very own natural-shoulder style would have followed his alma mater, Brooks Brothers, into sartorial eclipse.

Traditionally clad Continentals have always appreciated the American original's innate classiness. Each year, a small coterie of French and Italian merchants offers up its own take on the Ivy League look, inspired by Old World images of American society at play in Newport or Palm Beach.

When hosting a necktie, the button-down collar projects about the same level of dressiness as the navy blazer or Weejun-style loafer, two of its more frequent coconspirators. Like the blue blazer, the oxford button-down can be dressed up or down, although it tends to consort more comfortably with like-textured fabrics such as flannel or tweed. In the button-down's salad days, all style was forfeited, should its points lack sufficient length to roll over and play casual.

ABOVE:
Sequestered amid its cronies, circa 1950, the button-down is flanked by other Ivy League bona fides, soft-shoulder tweed sport jacket, cuffed gray flannels, foulard four-in-hand, doeskin vest, and slip-on moccasins.

LEFT:
Speaking of those who like their fashion unbuttoned, observe Signor Barbera's sleight of hand. Not bothering to button his collar points, he seems to have turned a blind eye to those on his jacket as well. Barbera's stylish imperfection has been partly inspired by his country's own Signor of Style, Gianni Agnelli (see page 230).

SHIRT FABRICS
FALL

FINE-CHECKED BLUE BROADCLOTH

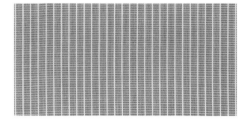

HAIRLINE STRIPE ON BLUE CHAMBRAY GROUND

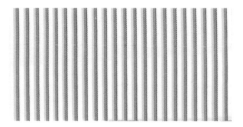

BLUE SHADOW STRIPE

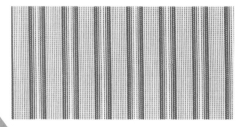

LIGHT-BLUE ANTIQUE TRACK STRIPE

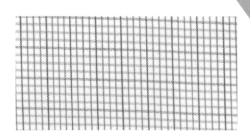

NAVY/BLACK FANCY CHECK

WEDGEWOOD BLUE BROADCLOTH

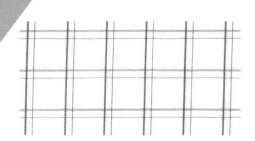

TWO-TONE BLUE GRAPH CHECK

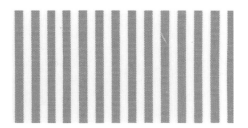

DELFT BLUE BENGAL STRIPE

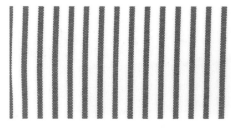

NAVY AND WHITE PENCIL STRIPE

Unless indicated, all dress shirtings are constructed from fine two-ply cotton yarns.

WINTER

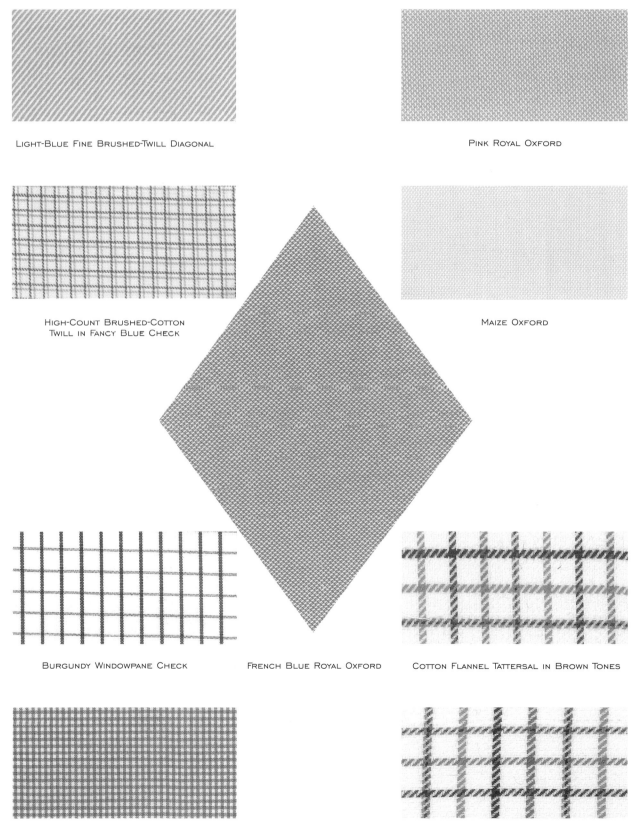

LIGHT-BLUE FINE BRUSHED-TWILL DIAGONAL

PINK ROYAL OXFORD

HIGH-COUNT BRUSHED-COTTON
TWILL IN FANCY BLUE CHECK

MAIZE OXFORD

BURGUNDY WINDOWPANE CHECK

FRENCH BLUE ROYAL OXFORD

COTTON FLANNEL TATTERSAL IN BROWN TONES

FOREST GREEN PIN CHECK

COTTON FLANNEL TATTERSAL IN OLIVE TONES

SUMMER

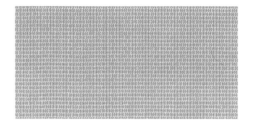

OPEN-WEAVE LIGHTWEIGHT
BLUE OXFORD

DELFT BLUE PENCIL-STRIPE BROADCLOTH

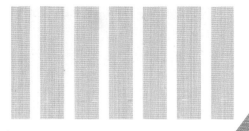

COTTON/LINEN PASTEL BLUE
MADRAS STRIPE

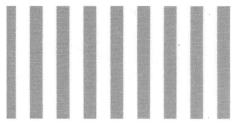

CAMBRIDGE BLUE CANDY-STRIPE BATISTE

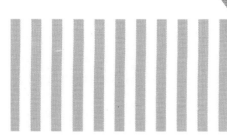

GOLD BENGAL STRIPE

CORNFLOWER BLUE
COTTON/LINEN POPLIN

CRIMSON HAIRLINE CHECK

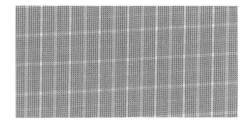

ROYAL BLUE TATTERSALL WITH GOLD ACCENT

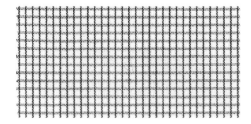

ROYAL AND RED FANCY CHECK

SPRING

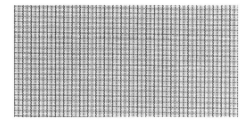

MICRO-CHECK BLUE BATISTE

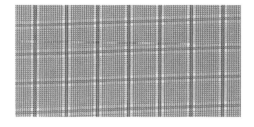

TWO-TONE BLUE CHECKERBOARD

ETON BLUE END-ON-END BROADCLOTH
WITH FANCY BOND STREET STRIPE

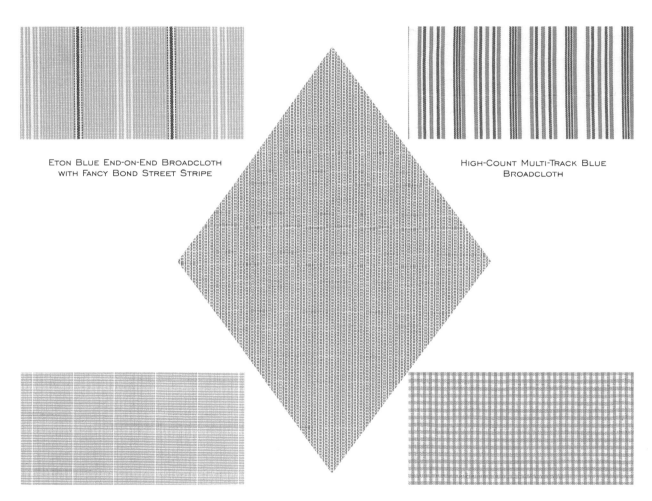

HIGH-COUNT MULTI-TRACK BLUE
BROADCLOTH

PINK CHAMBRAY GRAPH CHECK

LIGHTWEIGHT FANCY WEAVE
BLUE BATISTE

OLIVE MINI-CHECK POPLIN

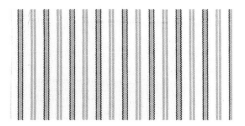

FANCY PINK STRIPE

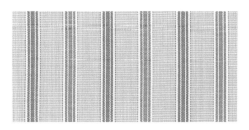

JERMYN STREET ALTERNATING BAR STRIPES ON
LIGHT-BLUE END-ON-END GROUND

FITTING THE DRESS SHIRT

With the exception of the Italians, who border on the fetishistic relative to the fit of their dress shirts, most men wear theirs too tight in the neck, too short in the sleeve, and too full around the wrist. The explanation for this is relatively simple: successive washings shrink the collar size and sleeve length, while most manufacturers allow enough cuff width for a large Rolex-sized watch to drive through.

Unless its collar fits comfortably, the best dress shirt is useless. With the top button closed, two fingers should be able to slide comfortably between the neck and the collar of a new shirt. Most fine shirt makers add an extra half-inch to the stated collar size to allow for shrinkage during the first several washings. Should the collar of a new dress shirt fit to perfection when first tried on, return it or risk being strangled before too long.

As the torso's second skin, the shirt should fit comfortably. At a minimum, it should be cut full enough to allow the wearer to sit without concern for whether its front will gape open. Even normal shrinkage or weight gain should not create tension across the chest or waist. The shirt's overall length should be such that you can raise your arms without it pulling out of the trouser top.

When a necktie is worn, the collar's points ought to be able to remain in touch with the shirt's body, no matter how the wearer turns his head. Semi-spread to cutaway collars should have no tie space above the tie's knot, with points long enough to be covered by the jacket's neckline. And finally, no part of the collar's neckband should peek out over the tie's knot.

Whether barrel or French cuff, the shirt must fit snugly around the wrist so that the additional length required to keep the cuff from pulling back when the arm is extended does not force it down the hand. Shirt cuff and hand should move as one. If the hand can slide through the cuff opening without first unfastening it, the cuff's circumference is too large.

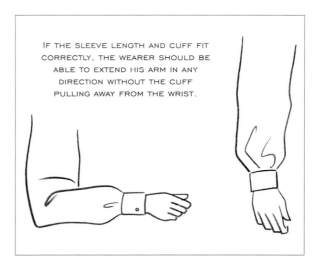

DRESS SHIRT MODES

Most men are taught to employ the dress shirt as a harmonizer of the suit and necktie. When the go-go eighties transformed the necktie into a riot of pattern, the dress shirt was forced to take a backseat. While the solid dress shirt provides a blank canvas on which to improvise, the accomplished dresser will frequently opt for the fancy shirt to serve as the ensemble's focal point, to which the necktie and suit jacket must then pay deference.

The English class system is responsible for this realignment of furnishings. In prewar times, most upper-class Englishmen typically wore only those neckties that they were entitled to by virtue of a public school, military regiment, or private club affiliation. As the typical English aristocrat enjoyed no more than a dozen or so of these associations, his cravat collection was therefore somewhat limited. To compensate, he took to diversifying his somber worsteds and predictable club ties with snappier-looking dress shirts. As he began accumulating more dress shirts than neckties, Jermyn Street, like Savile Row before it, became an entire street devoted to the craft of bespoke shirtmakers.

As these next pictures attest, the spirited dress shirt alternative can lend smartness to the tailored scenario without compromising the boundaries of good taste. Because this format relies on a high degree of counterpoint between suit, shirt, and tie, it tends to favor the higher-contrast complexion. However, affecting such a coordination is no more complicated than seating a few of your old wardrobe standbys next to different dinner partners.

Better-collared and looking quite sure of himself, the English actor Trevor Howard deftly saves a potentially flat presentation by casting his dress shirt in the leading role.

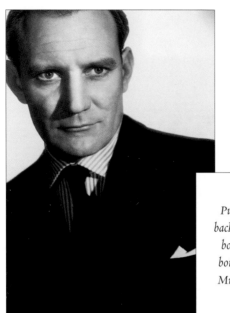

TOP:

Punctuating a plain backdrop, the shirting's bold stripe lights up both center stage and Mr. Howard's visage.

LEFT:

With a polka dot dress shirt and a breast pocket of patterened silk, Douglas Fairbanks Jr. trumps up his solid suit and tie.

DRESS SHIRT AESTHETICS

In addition to flattering the wearer, the dress shirt should type with an outfit's style and level of formality. While differing collar styles connote varying degrees of dress-up, so do certain shirt fabrics. The sophisticated dresser would not normally pair a sporty button-down with an elegant navy suit; nor would he mate a soigné dress shirt with contrasting white collar with a casual tweed sport jacket. Although the laissez-faire attitude of modern men's fashion has obfuscated many of those guidelines that safeguarded good taste, several remain that are still relevant in assessing whether a particular dress shirt will add or subtract from an ensemble's intended dressiness.

A shirt's formality begins at the collar, its most prominent and defining feature. The stiffer the collar, the more formal its intentions. The more open the collar's points, the dressier the presentation. A contrasting white collar automatically adds ceremony, while most tab or pinned collars heighten the average solid or patterned dress shirt's propriety. Softer collar configurations such as the button-down or unstarched long point rank lower on the formality scale.

The cuff also contributes to the overall effect. The formal shirt's stiff single cuff, which accompanies the white tie and tailcoat, presents the most formal arrangement. While the French cuff dresses the hand more than the standard button variety, the double-button cuff outranks the single-button in wrist decorum.

Fabric serves as the next indicator of formality. Smoother or more lustrous materials are dressier. White broadcloth ranks about equally with white-on-white broadcloth in formality, while white royal oxford runs a close second. White voile for summer inches out the white pinpoint, which does the same to the regular white oxford.

As for nonwhite solids, blue broadcloth registers below white-on-white but above the white oxford in formality. While blue end-on-end rates about equally with white pinpoint oxford, pink, particularly in broadcloth, is not far behind, followed by yellow or gold, tan, and then green.

The dressiness of a fancy shirting is determined by the amount of white in the design's ground. White ground patterns display a more fastidious air than a colored ground fabric, making them a step up on the formal ladder. In a two-color stripe or check where white is the ground, the bolder pattern denotes the less dressy garment. Finer stripes are more ceremonial if not more austere than widely spaced stripes, while the smaller the check or plaid in a patterned shirting, the dressier the effect. In general, a horizontal-striped shirt will read dressier than the same stripe running vertically.

THE SOLID-COLOR DRESS SHIRT

Although pure white has traditionally been the color of choice for a basic dress shirt, medium blue actually flatters more men's faces than white. Pure white can drain away what little natural color men exude. Television producers will advise male guests to don a blue dress shirt to compensate for the studio's strong lighting, which tends to flatten and weaken the complexion.

Just as a mahogany table lends a more expensive aura to the items placed on it, medium blue enlivens all men's skin tones. Any color or texture placed on or near a fine-quality medium blue dress shirt automatically appears warmer and richer. At least half of a man's dozen or so dress shirts should ideally be in some shade of solid blue or in a predominantly blue pattern; these provide the most versatile backdrop to coordinate a tailored ensemble. (See shirt fabrics gatefold.)

Naturally, some blue hues offer complexions more help than others, but there are at least several shades of medium blue that notably invigorate every man's skin tone and luster. The trick is to find the deepest shade of blue that highlights the face without distracting from it. And let's not be misled by those overcast, almost royal numbers that have been promoted of late with similar-toned solid neckties. They are yet another naive aberration from good taste and permanent fashion fostered by the industry's need for short-term novelty and profit.

A man with strong contrast in his complexion can enjoy a larger range of colors, including deep-tone blues like the Cambridge or Wedgwood shades found in fine two-ply broadcloth, royal oxford, or darker end-on-end cottons. Fair-haired men with muted complexions can balance their lighter tones with soft-hued blues such as end-on-ends, oxfords, and mini-checks, whose weaves use white to reduce the blue's intensity. With a summer tan, the depth of blue can be increased to play up the heightened color contrast between skin and hair.

Cream or tan can be complimentary, though these low-intensity shades do more for the muted than the contrasting complexion. Pink is sometimes viewed as too feminine a shade for men; however, the pink oxford button-down has been a linchpin of Madison Avenue lore for fifty years. Pink also flatters the rosy-cheeked visage. When bedecked with a contrasting white collar, and paired with a dark gray or navy striped worsted, the pink end-on-end dress shirt or broadcloth dress shirt continues as a perennial favorite of the Jermyn Street set.

Yellow or gold tones are highly desirable but similarly undervalued dress shirt colors. Unlike blue, they do have a drawback. Men with sallow skin need to steer clear of these shades. But their champagne sparkle can impart an élan and vitality to any suit from the browns through the grays to navy. Gold is frequently used as an accent color in many patterned neckties, so if a man has flecks of blond hair, echoing it under the chin is an opportune way to illuminate the face. In fact, the bold yellow or gold striped dress shirt and blue blazer with gilded buttons has been known to add spring to any man's gait.

THE PATTERNED DRESS SHIRT

Complexion also dictates the choice of pattern. Once again, the amount of contrast found in the complexion above will dictate the degree of contrast desired below. The hairline, pin, pencil, shadow, Bengal, and variegated striped settings enjoy long-standing popularity on the business circuit. In the check family, the pin, miniature graph, and small box tattersall are also highly recognized figures within the corporate boardroom.

While it's hard to own too many simple blue-and-white-striped dress shirts, the same can be said for those dressy mini-checks that effect a predominantly blue background. Because the small, fancy blue check appears like a solid from a distance, substituting the fine blue check for a blue solid shirt lends an air of sophistication with little risk of fussiness. Stripes or checks with red accents suit a ruddier complexion, while yellow or gold patterns favor the fair-skinned or blond man. Medium to bottle green stripes or simple green graph checks on white grounds are always stylish, especially under the classic navy or gray worsted suit.

With a white ground stripe or check, a contrasting white collar is always an option, and its historical provenance should not be ignored. The contrasting white-collar dress shirts hark back to the days of the separate collar. Today, only the rounded, club-type (preferably pinned) or the very open, almost cutaway model are stylish enough to hold their own when contrasted against a different color or patterned shirt body. Contrary to popular opinion, the contrasting white collar does not require a matching white French cuff to maintain its pedigree, although it does more to catch the eye. While the matching French cuff is always acceptable, a button cuff has no place at the end of a sleeve attached to a shirt with a contrasting white collar.

DRESSING THE HAND

Shirt cuff design usually evolves along with collar styles, and during the nineteenth century, cuffs and collars shared many features. Like the blunt, square single collar, the shirt cuff was rectangular and stiffly starched. The cuff could also be single or double, but it was the latter form that came to signify formality. Separate cuffs, like the detachable collar, could be reversed when one edge was soiled.

In the nineteenth century, the cuff was often left unbuttoned at the side and could hang about half an inch below the coat sleeve, a throwback to the days when the shirt was considered underwear and served as a protective layer against rougher materials. In principle, modern cuff canon follows its forebears' aesthetic, with the added caveat that a hint of shirt linen below can make the arm appear longer, provided the jacket's sleeve length is correct. A man with short arms should always exploit this "sleight of hand."

Since the hand gestures in accordance with a man's facial expressions for drama and emphasis, dressing the hand attracts its share of aesthetic focus and controversy. Here is Italy's most renowned dandy of the early twentieth century, the poet Gabriele D'Annunzio *(top)*, "shooting his cuffs." In immaculate repose, the stiff collar and cuff elevate his appendages to poetic perfection.

The debate between stiff, separate collars and soft attached ones had lost much of its steam by the time button-down connoisseur Fred Astaire appeared in this next picture. America's own master of stage, screen, and soft style liked his Brooks button-downs with just about everything: DB suits, dressy wedding ties, cardigan sweaters. He even pinned the collar down just to show it who was boss. Perhaps it takes one jaunty performer to appreciate another, as Astaire's folded-back shirt cuff plays the perfect foil to his collar's unpredictable roll *(center)*. Like the dancer's gait, his clothes always appeared in perpetual motion.

Think the shirt cuff was designed simply as a tailoring contrivance intended to join the sleeve to the wrist? Jean Cocteau didn't *(bottom)*. As his countryman Stéphane Grappelli did for the jazz violin, Cocteau elevated the ornament of the wrist to an art form, dressing his hand with the same creativity he invested in all matters visual.

THE SHIRT MONOGRAM

When laundry was first sent out of the home, the monogram was used to authenticate ownership. In the heyday of men's fashion, monogrammed braces, initialed belt buckles, and embroidered pocket handkerchiefs were popular gifts from grooms to ushers, while regarded as tokens of affection from the fairer sex. Today, some men consider the display of one's initials somewhat pretentious, while others appreciate its as a sign of individuality and quality.

Since the dress shirt was considered underwear until well into the late 1930s, most monograms were sequestered from view, either on the bottom of the shirt's tail or beneath the suit's vest. As the vest began to disappear and men began to remove their jackets in public, this little eye-cue began to acquire its own cachet.

Discretion is paramount to good taste, and large or conspicuously placed initials are indiscreet. Displaying one's monogram on a collar or cuff clearly declares the perpetrator's lack of savoir faire. As in most matters of male decoration, less is usually more.

For the shirt monogram to create a touch of class, lettering style should be simple and small, no larger than ¼-inch high. Most monograms should be situated about 4 inches to the left of the shirt placket's center. If the shirt has a pocket, initials are usually centered on it or positioned in the middle of its upper welt. Top-drawer initialing is done by hand, with the letters sometimes punctuated by tiny periods. Because of the marking's diminutive scale, it's frequently contrasted in either a darker shade or a different color from the shirting. If the fabric is fancy, the monogram usually echoes one of its component colors. Some men have a favorite color, such as gold or purple, which serves to delineate their personal style.

Tyrone Power's monogram is so minute (suggesting its handmade origin) as to become a point of curiosity. Its appearance reflects the English and American predilection for the more conspicuous pocket placement, about 9 inches down from the neck point. Alternatively, the European man's escutcheon espouses his penchant for disci-

plined understatement. Dropped just below the direct line of vision, the monogram's lower altitude usually appears roughly 14 inches from his neck point or 4 to 5 inches above the trousers'
waistline. Of the two addresses, this locale is definitely the more subtle, if not chic.

When the Continental wears his single-breasted jacket unbuttoned, a waist-level duet
commences between the coat's open fronts and the necktie's ends. The necktie's unfettered blades,
in rhythm with the man's gait, fan across the shirt's front, permitting nothing more than a soupçon
of monogram to peak through. Without superfluous distractions, these small orchestrations take
on a symbolism all their own.

The English aristocracy has long
acknowledged its hereditary strain of eccen-
tricity. Fred Astaire hobnobbed with enough
of these valet-trained lads to observe such
form firsthand. Quartering one's initials on
the shirt's outer sleeve is either a custom
peculiar to show-biz types or another affectation of the privileged with too much time on
their hands. Whether such swank smacks
more of the titled than the theatrical, one
thing is for sure: hallmarking one's shirt sleeve
on its upper forearm certainly reinforces its
bespoke provenance, a proposition not likely
overlooked by those so inclined.

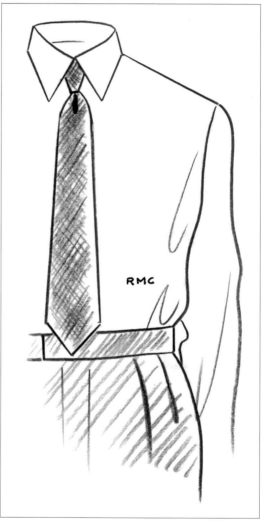

*D*espite three centuries of persistent attempts to loosen the necktie's grip on the civilized man's throat, this insignificant little strip of silk continues to hold on for dear life. Like a fighter punched silly for eleven rounds who stages a near-miraculous comeback in the twelfth, the tie finished the twentieth century on a high note. Dressy, full-bodied wovens along with all manner of sportier, highbrow four-in-hands returned from virtual fashion obscurity to the forefront of style.

Despite this curious little ornament's seemingly

"I intend to demonstrate that my client was temporarily insane from the time he attempted to push Mr. Bergrund out the window until the time he purchased that tie."

NECK

WEAR

implacable resistance to death by fashion decree, male neckwear faces its most serious challenge to date. While the workplace has traditionally been the necktie's foremost bastion, its rapid casualization is handing this former adjunct of male elegance its pink slip, inviting any number of less throat-constraining alternatives to apply for the job. It is increasingly common to see men in positions of authority without a necktie. In some office environments, the bare-necked executive has become the symbol of a new management style.

In an ironic twist, the necktie's longtime protector, corporate conformity, may now be its ultimate undoing. Whether this latest dip in the necktie's fortunes will permanently alter its destiny is hard to say. Without the tailored uniform to monopolize the corporate landscape, the necktie's role in contemporary men's fashion will certainly change. Its appearance will more than ever signify the wearer's desire to embrace a dressier, more authoritative image. Perhaps in time, man may come to regard the necktie as proof of his individuality, something that sets him apart from the crowd.

CRAVATOLOGY

Since a necktie should be agreeable to the touch, silk is undeniably the fabric of choice. Ideally, the tactile qualities of a fine silk tie should produce a sensation not unlike that of skin. The term that the industry uses to designate a fabric's weight, texture, and feel is called its "hand." Connoisseurs appreciate a beautiful hand.

The necktie's motif, or pattern, expresses the poetry, the sense of whimsy, the psychology of the individual wearer. Design motifs, called cravatology, began to flourish in the 1930s. Two great design families divide the patterned necktie kingdom: yarn-dye wovens and prints. In the case of the first, the jacquard loom weaves different color threads directly into the fabric, while in the second, colored patterns are printed directly onto raw or dyed silk.

WOVEN NECKWEAR

Because it allows for highly detailed motifs while providing an incomparable richness of hand, the woven silk tie is regarded as the ne plus ultra of male plumage. The weaving process tempers a color's innate brilliance by incorporating it into a complex surface interlacing, making the woven four-in-hand the dressiest of all necktie silks. Although wovens represent a small percentage of the total neckwear produced each year, they have returned to favor along with hand-tailored clothes and bench-crafted footwear.

Here's a classic example of how England came to set the standard in international men's style for the better part of the twentieth century. The Macclesfield necktie, a silk group of patterns made from small weaves of diamonds, squares, and circles, became especially fashionable among well-dressed British men in the early 1920s. These small geometrics were first made in contrasting tones of gray, black, and white, giving a marquetry effect across the surface of the tie. They were the specialty of the textile weavers from Macclesfield, a small town in Lancashire, northwest England.

Among the world's sartorial literati, the Macclesfield necktie continues to enjoy its longstanding reputation as the quintessence of upper-class English taste. Parenthetically, it is the only genre of traditional neckwear to retain its original metaphorical imagery. Referred to as a

The British are coming

"wedding tie" in certain circles, this silvery necktie began its venerable career as the obligatory long tie for formal day attire, meaning weddings and other daytime celebrations. As smart lounge clothes began to solicit its company, the dressy Macclesfield necktie found its elite services broaden to include the embellishment of other less formal ensembles.

From royalty to rodeo, here's a pictorial *histoire (opposite, below, and on the following page)* of the Macclesfield's rise to sartorial stardom, beginning with the Baron Nicolas de Gunzberg, socialite Anthony Drexel Biddle, and Hollywood's Robert Montgomery and Gary Cooper.

While there are a myriad of woven necktie patterns, only a handful have won time-honored places of correctness and affection in the gentleman's wardrobe. One of the most renowned is the Spitalsfield tie, yet another contribution of England's legendary Bond Street style to permanent neckwear fashion. Rising to prominence beside its silver Macclesfield confrere in the 1930s, this woven necktie was also named for the town that produced it, Spitalsfield, on the outskirts of London.

The Spitalsfield design originally distinguished itself from the Macclesfield by its slightly fancier and larger motifs, which were arranged in allover settings of two-, three-, or four-color combinations. This more versatile type of silk design constitutes the backbone of Britain's high-class woven neckwear. No longer made exclusively in this small London town, woven neckties of the Spitalsfield type are now manufactured all over the world.

THIS PAGE:
*Gary Cooper dressing up a sport jacket
with a Macclesfield necktie.*

OPPOSITE:
*Cary Grant crossed a button-down shirt
with a double-breasted suit and a
Spitalsfield necktie.*

*Dean Acheson wearing a
Spitalsfield-type necktie.*

Here, Dean Acheson relies on the firm hand of his attached tab collar to downplay his sagging neckline while the classiness of his Spitalsfield necktie plays up his diplomatic urbanity.

THE REGIMENTAL CANARD British by derivation, regimental stripes have been continuously used in tie designs since the 1920s. Before the days of universal khaki, all British regiments had a color scheme of their own, seen at its most typical in the mess jackets of the officers.

English regiments wore cravats decorated with stripes in their regimental colors. This gave rise to what is known as the regimental tie, which features colored stripes on the diagonal, a feature inseparable from British uniform design. After returning to civilian life, British men wore the ties of their former regiment, and, frequently, no other.

One point of long-standing contention between blades from the other side of the herring pond was the colonists' alleged sartorial violation of having their stripes run counter to those of the King's men. Following both historical precedent and aesthetic logic, English tie stripes ran from left shoulder down toward the right side. This direction coincided with the male jacket's traditional left-over-right fastening (thus preventing the coat's front from interfering with a soldier's unsheathing of his sword from his left side). One hundred years ago, when Brooks Brothers first introduced the English regimental tie to the States, in deference to the originals, they had theirs cut in the opposite direction (high right to low left). Apparently, Englishmen belonging to certain British regiments got very touchy about seeing their precious colors around the necks of American tourists. Here is F. R. Tripler's play on words over the "American Way" of its stripes.

At odds with the prevailing taste for whimsy, classic striped neckwear had been out of favor for some time. However, as a result of Italy's tie designers loosening up Britannia's conventional stripe arrangements and color combinations, striped neckwear is in a renaissance. Designer Luciano Barbera (*page 145*) could have chosen any type of necktie for this outfit, but

Famous Stripes . . . in the American Way
The unusually smart designs and actual color combinations of the English school ties, called "OLD BOYS," woven here especially for TRIPLER. And in all silk repp. Very handsome—broad range of patterns for blue, grey or brown suits. They just can't miss— they are tops for that gift. Let TRIPLER make your selection
WITH FOLDED SILK THROUGHOUT, $4.25 EACH
When ordering by mail state colors of suits. Early selection advisable
F.R.TRIPLER & CO.
MADISON AVENUE AT FORTY-SIXTH ST. NEW YORK 17, N.Y.

he opted for a stripe. One would be hard-pressed to find anything regimented, derivative, or predictable about its design, which is probably why he chose it. Note the proper direction of his stripes, high left to low right.

Another reason for the stripe's habitual presence under the better-arrayed chin is its diagonal dynamic. The smart dresser understands that any line that angles across the body also works to slim it. In the striped necktie's case, its oblique pattern magically chisels away breadth and softness from the face, an advantage much prized by its devotees.

There's another compelling illustration of why men of loftier social plateaus tend to lean toward the stripe: its infatuating swagger. Below, film actor Reginald Gardiner employs his stripe to punctuate his expanse of blue serge, while each of its forty-five degrees reinforces the diagonal symmetry of his double-breasted suit. Book-ending wife Benita on the left, Ronald Coleman engages the broad repeat of his necktie's stripe to harmonize with his sport jacket's oversized plaid.

STRIPED NECKTIES CHISEL AWAY BREADTH AND SOFTNESS FROM THE FACE.

THE PLAID TIE Whether printed or woven, silk or wool, the plaid necktie has always attracted the traditionalist by virtue of its rich Scottish heritage. The first plaid ties were made of wool, because of the motif's association with tartan kilts. However, the authentic Highland plaids were gentrified into dressier silk versions for town wear. What distinguishes the plaid from other necktie motifs is its multilayered boxlike design, which creates the illusion of dimension. When mated with a stripe or a different scale check, the plaid's depth of field produces a rich and nuanced nattiness. Here's a man who knows how to make a solid suit and dress shirt appear less plain. Power's high-contrast colored necktie also saves his own strong complexion (dark hair and light skin) from appearing less so.

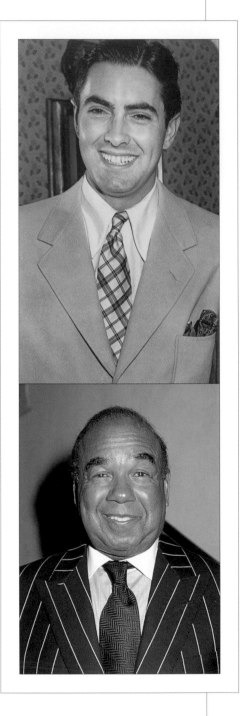

SOLID NECKWEAR This next statement might seem somewhat of an oxymoron, but the more sophisticated a man's tastes in clothes, the more solid neckties he's likely to own. Like the tuxedo's chic, which depends on only two colors, the solid necktie becomes virtually indispensable if one favors the quiet assertiveness of the simple two-tone kit. (See Douglas Fairbanks and Gianni Agnelli, chapter 1, "Permanent Fashion.") George Frasier, *Esquire*'s fashion pundit extraordinaire, had a personal love affair with the solid black grenadine necktie, as did former Barney's New York owner, Fred Pressman. You could make book on Pressman showing up in one of his classic gray flannel or tan gabardine ensembles accompanied by his ever-present black grenadine four-in-hand pinned just so askew into his blue dress shirt. The perennially soigné entertainer Bobby Short owns a collection of solid navy and solid black fancy woven silks that undoubtedly outnumber those of Porter, Gershwin, and Ellington combined.

The second rationale for a wardrobe replete with interesting solid neckwear is the pattern prerogative. As the aficionado ascends the pattern-on-pattern staircase, the solid necktie often becomes his best friend. Someone once facetiously described the British approach to male decor as that which employed the largest number of colors without clashing. For those men inclined to push the pattern envelope, the solid tie has saved many a neck from overly ambitious decoration.

WOOL NECKWEAR The Italians have interesting style karma. Empowered by their design virtuosity, with one hand they managed to inundate the tie-wearing world in a sea of intrusive prints, while with the other they managed to produce enough high-class neckties to keep from drowning in their own commercial effluvium. Besides rescuing the stripe from certain extinction, they can also be credited with the stylish male's current appreciation of luxury wool neckwear.

Fortunately for the outside world, each of Italy's cities contains pockets of socially prominent, style-savvy businessmen who happen to be passionate about apparel of exceptional quality and understated taste. Were it not for this discriminating segment in the Italian men's market, many non-Italian men would not be privy to such rarefied taste and wearables.

Not to be confused with the inexpensive wool country necktie of English notoriety, this is a totally different animal. Hand-sewn in 100 percent worsted cashmere or blends of cashmere and silk, this small-knotting, sinuous strip of tactile delight injects another layer of textured richness into the flannel suit or luxury sport jacket ensemble. Here we have the embodiment of Italian brio, Gianni Agnelli, who likes his herringbone wool tie so much that he wears it over his cashmere sweater. Looks perfectly kosher to me.

Long an advocate on this side of the Atlantic for this cool-weather neck regalia, the author weighs in with one of his early wool orchestrations. Fortunately, a groundswell of enthusiasts now understands the wool tie's textural cachet as well as its change of silken pace.

PRINTED NECKWEAR

The first printed fabrics actually showed up around man's throat in the form of formal silk mufflers sometime in the late nineteenth century. It wasn't until the early 1920s that the first geometric designs printed on a pure silk twill began to make the rounds of the culture's more fashionable necks. From there, the transition to neckties was almost automatic, if somewhat limited. In its formative years, the stamped or applied method of making patterned cloth was considered inferior to permanently weaving the design directly into the cloth's surface.

Because it is less expensive to produce than the woven and can accommodate decorative motifs of every conceivable variety, print neckties are the largest-selling category of neckwear. By the 1960s, the export of printed silks to the vast American market unleashed a veritable explosion in the quantity and diversity of fabric designs, which in turn prompted further innovations in the production process.

In the eighties, computer-driven technology presented the print designer with a virtual blank canvas on which he could record and instantaneously reproduce any or all creative impulses. Whether in the name of wearable art, entertainment, or simple shock, the net result was that after two decades of neckties as conversation starters, the printed necktie undermined itself as an adjunct of male elegance while debasing the neckwear taste of an entire culture. For the moment, should a man want to acquire a necktie with a reasonable probability of aesthetic longevity, the woven design tie would generally be the safer bet.

That said, there are still a wealth of figurative motifs and genres of print ties that transcend the vagaries of fashion. Like the well-cut gray flannel suit, these neckties retain their stylishness by virtue of their incontestable good taste.

CHARVET PRINTS With the affluent in the 1920s and 1930s spending more and more time on vacation, resort dressing became a principal source of fashion inspiration. The wealthy European embraced a summery-looking tie conceived by the famous Parisian shirt and cravat maker Charvet. This light and breezy necktie featured motifs that perfectly captured the holiday mood of its environs.

Meanwhile, in the late twenties, the white summer suit began to gain acceptance in Palm Beach and around several American universities. The neutral-toned suit demanded some strong contrast, and like their European counterparts, smart Americans took to the Charvet tie like ducks to water. Although the fashionable man generally avoided bold neckwear, this exception to the rule gained the favor of those well-dressed society men who ordinarily held closely to small and conservative effects in their neckwear. Its chic was in their unfussy, nonchalant bearing. To the delight of their many admirers, the Charvets' open settings facilitated blending with all kinds of fancy suits, from houndstooths to stripes to plaids of almost any size or design. The original Charvet prints became the first, and regrettably almost the last, bold-figured necktie to symbolize upper-class taste. With the exception of Emilio Pucci's large, all-over print ties in the 1950s, selected Hermès scarf ties, and the odd Ralph Lauren and Garrick Anderson necktie prints (two of America's best purveyors of the past), the preponderance of large-figured print neckties could probably be termed noisy rather than nice.

Radio personality and comedian Fred Allen hosting the famous Amos 'n' Andy team. Up to their neck in Charvets, these boys knew how to entertain millions with wit and intelligence, words that could aptly describe their neckwear.

DOTS AND OTHER ALL-OVER NEATS As the earliest print design used in menswear, the polka dot is supposed to have been a tribute to the Sun God. Along with small geometric shapes, dots were the first to enliven men's ties. Previously used exclusively for female dress, the polka dot's transformation into a man's motif owes a debt of gratitude to one Sir Thomas Lipton, a successful London businessman and inveterate yachtsman who always wore a navy bow tie with white dots of his own design. Polka-dot ties enliven all kinds of menswear ensembles, but they are on particularly friendly terms with stripes. A dotted tie is a natty foil to the chalk stripe suit.

THE PAISLEY Due to its origins, which date back to Babylonian civilization, and its association with English taste, paisley enjoys a special status in the world of male neckwear. In his controversial seventies book *Dress for Success,* New York image consultant John Molloy opined that certain neckties had that "Ivy League cachet," because they signified good breeding and education. Of all the loud neckties, he deemed paisley the only permissible one, because it was the "fun tie" of the upper-middle classes. Freud thought that a paisley-patterned tie symbolized virility, since it resembled sperm.

The paisley motif provides for rich opportunities of color nuance and formal invention and therefore can realize its full complexity only through the printed medium. Jimmy Stewart shows off his pattern-mixing prowess with a dress-down ensemble of striped shirt, glen check sport jacket, and foulard four-in-hand. (See also Dean Acheson's woven paisley tie, page 39.)

CLUB AND SPORTS In the introduction to his book *Ties,* the eminent English costume historian James Laver pointed out that the earliest recorded set of sporting colors belonged to the I Zingari Cricket Club, which was founded around 1845 by a group of young Cambridge University students who enjoyed both the game and amateur theatricals. They would rendezvous at the Blenheim Hotel on Bond Street. Sometime thereafter, a set of colors was adopted that could be printed on a flag and flown over the pavilion during their matches. They chose black, a carroty bright red, and gold, to symbolize "out of darkness, through fire, into light." In 1870, when they came to adopt a tie, it naturally embodied the same colors.

Another category of figurative motifs that began with a British inflection was the allover sport tie. First gaining popularity in the early 1920s, it was issued in small editions of subject-related patterns printed on wool challis. Each theme provided its devotees with an excuse to wear small sports figures that signified one's social status as a polo player, golfer, and so on.

It took the celebrated French designer Henri d'Origny, a passionate horse lover, to put the sports tie back in the saddle when he released his famous equestrian designs for Hermès in the 1950s. Today, the classic Hermès tie has branched out to other subjects, such as palm trees, elephants, and balloons, garnering a following around the world even among men who normally eschew any form of identifiable attire. In much the same way that the Hermès tie's narrow width defies fashion and most men's physiques, this icon's seemingly contrarian image works to its advantage. For the investment community and other "suits," its familiar Hermès design argot has made it the world's newest old-boy's club tie. (See also Prince Charles's tie, page 128.)

TOP:
Jimmy Stewart in a paisley necktie.

BOTTOM:
The sports motif four-in-hand.

NECKWEAR STYLES

THE ASCOT The ascot is the most formal type of necktie known. Its name derives from England's Ascot races, held annually in April since 1771. Although it adheres more closely to the earlier types of neckwear than the four-in-hand, the ascot still belongs to the genre that fills in the coat front. Worn specifically with formal day clothes, the ascot is frequently found in rich silks of subdued colorings and, incidentally, affords the gentleman who wishes to indulge in a display of jewelry the opportunity to wear a crested pin or a pearl.

Today, ascots are worn for formal day dress, especially weddings, and considered de rigueur at hunting outings. The pointed-ended blades are tied in a simple knot, with the ends crossed over the shirtfront to form a plastron on the chest, the whole secured by a cravat pin in pearl, preferably a real one. To quote from a 1913 *Gazette de Bon Ton,* society's high arbiter of Gallic *goût,* "For a man to wear the Ascot properly, along with the nobility of his manner, the authority of his gait, and the volume of his torso, an elegant bearing and much natural presence are likewise indispensable." So much for the average Joe being able to muck around in one.

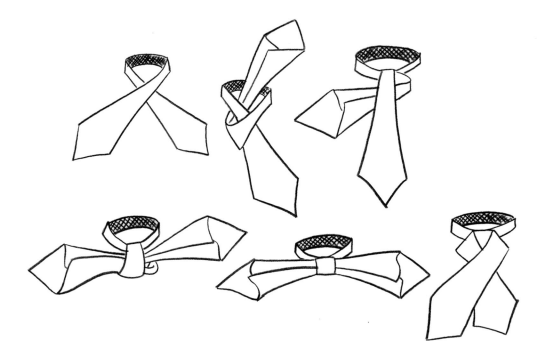

THE BOW TIE The bow tie derives from the centuries-old style known as the stock, a bolt of washable fabric wrapped many times around the neck and tied in front. Eventually, the stock was reduced to a single band around the neck with its ends tied up in the bow of today. At the end of the nineteenth century, there were at least two distinct models of bow ties—the butterfly and the batwing. The earlier butterfly style was characterized by broad "flared-shape"

ends whose wide bow tied up with a small knot. The famed English manufacturer Welsh Margetson, along with other English firms, called their butterfly bows thistle ties, which was a more accurate description of their form.

Later on, the butterfly was modified into a narrower shape with square ends and termed the "batwing." Although the effect was practically the same, it was attained with much less trouble. The butterfly's wings had to be made in different widths to accommodate varying collar heights, while the unshaped, straight ends of the batwing fit most collar sizes. In America, this style came to be known as the club bow. Although they can be worn interchangeably, the thistle ends should not exceed 2¾ inches or be less than 2¼ inches in width, while the batwing's tabs can range between 1½ inches to 2 inches.

Bow ties can be worn on both formal and informal occasions, day or evening, and are correct with either single- or double-breasted jackets. As they expose more shirtfront than the longer four-in-hand, it is not uncommon to find some form of waistcoat in attendance. The bow tie tends to be adopted by those men whose professions require them to lean over frequently, such as architects, doctors, and waiters.

In America, the bow tie reached its peak of popularity in the mid-thirties. Educated bow-tie fare for the college man went something like this: a foulard bow for a tweed jacket, a plaid butterfly for his single-breasted gabardine suit, and maybe a regimental batwing with his Shetland jacket and gray flannels. In the late 1960s, the bow tie acted as the perfect foil for the most imaginative and outrageous of color combinations and designs.

Wearing the Bow Tie In the hands of an experienced practitioner, the bow's final shape can end up influencing the outfit's overall image even more than its fabric. Neckwear should not distract from the face, and because it is usually the most prominent item of clothing, it must always be carefully presented. Here's the architect Le Corbusier (*at top*) fashioning his slip of silk to conform with its more ordered environs. Askew enough to reflect its benefactor's handiwork, the bow's formation suggests a man in control of his environment, of his own style. Alternatively (*below*), he is captured in less austere circumstances, reflected both in his facial expression and by his more casual collar and softer-rendered bow. Notice in each case the presence of a waistcoat, which helps to minimize the front's open expanse.

Le Corbusier tying his bow tie in accordance with his mood.

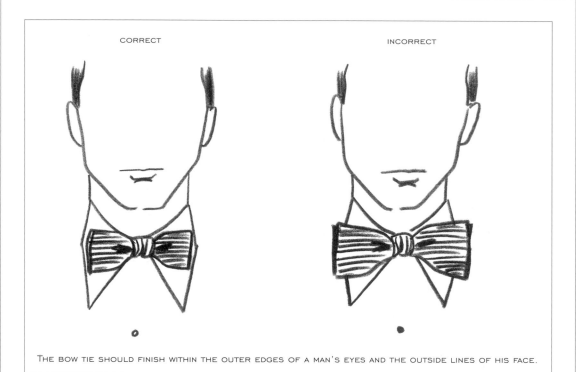

THE BOW TIE SHOULD FINISH WITHIN THE OUTER EDGES OF A MAN'S EYES AND THE OUTSIDE LINES OF HIS FACE.

To wear a bow tie stylishly, two issues should be considered. First, its width should not extend beyond the outer edge of a person's face, and definitely not beyond the breadth of his collar. As with other neckwear, the shirt's collar should frame the tie's knot. Button-downs with some roll or longer straight point or softer semi-spread collars will happily accommodate the average-size bow tie.

Ensuring that the bow's width ends up within the collar's outer edges is easily accomplished today, thanks to the graduated-band system that superseded the original exact-size bow tie. Don't purchase any bow tie without first trying it on, so as to be certain that it can be shortened enough to harmonize with your own facial features. This means that if after you have adjusted it to your exact neck size, its bow is still too wide (a common problem), check to see that it can still be made smaller to fit correctly.

The second issue concerns the tying of the bow. The bow tie was once described as a "garment that combines confident flourish with absolute respectability." There is no point in sporting the bow tie unless you plan on tying it yourself. Place a mathematically perfect, pre-tied bow under your chin and you forsake all individuality. The hand-tied bow's moody loops and unpredictable swirls give you that subtle insouciance, that desired aplomb.

Few men wear theirs with more sangfroid than the French boulevardier and actor Philippe Noiret. Here he fashions his club bow with understated élan. Tweed jacket, alpaca waistcoat, soft-collar shirt, mini-dot bow, spot of foulard at chest, and *naturellement,* the obligatory cigar, Gallic *goût* at its most succinct. Note: You are more likely to find men with real personal style from those who have lived long enough to have observed it and then appropriated it for themselves—in other words, the over-fifty set.

Philippe Noiret showing his Gallic goût.

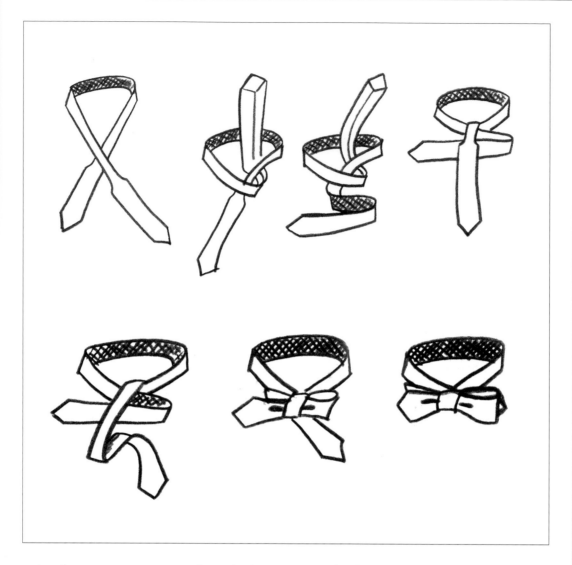

Tying the Bow Tie Learning to knot the bow tie is not the daunting task you might imagine; it requires no more skill than tying your shoes. One way to practice is to first try tying one around your thigh. Sit down and cross your legs. Wrap the bow around your thigh just above the knee. Now close your eyes and tie it as you would your shoelace. Opening your eyes, you should find that, although it may lack a certain aesthetic, you have manipulated the bow into a recognizable knot.

With it still wrapped about your knee, the bow can now be fine-tuned. Hold its left loop in your left hand and the right loop in your right. Pulling the two loops in opposite directions tightens the knot, while pulling the two tab ends reshapes and straightens the loops.

After familiarizing yourself with the process, now try knotting it around your neck but without a shirt. For novices, the shirt collar complicates the learning process. The big difference here is that in order to get each side of the bow to come out equally in width and length, one blade must start out four or so inches longer than the other. Which side you choose to make longer is really up to you.

THE FOUR-IN-HAND The term "four-in-hand" for the slipknot now worn throughout the world came into general use at the end of the nineteenth century. The exact derivation of the term is still unsettled. At one time, it was thought to be a reference to the Four-in-Hand Club, founded in England in the nineteenth century by young men who indulged in carriage racing and then adopted this type of knot for their ties. Or, it could have referred to the way one held the reins of a four-horse carriage. The new four-in-hand knot was quicker to execute, and considered more masculine than the decorous bow tie.

With its contrasts and harmonies, the necktie's design comes close to the art of painting; however, knotting it resembles the art of sculpture. The manner in which a tie is knotted offers the only true means of imposing one's individual stamp on it. Over time, this male rite should evolve into another manifestation of one's personal style. Most men were introduced to the discipline of necktie decorum by their fathers. Since the majority continues to regard this early indoctrination as somehow sacrosanct, few have ever revisited this procedure in a creative manner. Gentleman designer Luciano Barbera, one of Italy's most respected tastemakers, shares some thoughts on his relationship with the necktie: "The tie follows the culture. In the fifties, I wore a bow tie. In the sixties, I tried a Windsor knot. In the seventies, I went open-necked. In the eighties, I had a big aggressive knot that said, 'Don't mess with me.' Now I find that what I want is a less-fussed-over knot with a soft pleating. It is simple. It is declarative. It feels right. How will I wear my tie in the next decade? Who knows? Ask me then."

Although two knots, the Windsor and half-Windsor, still enjoy limited use, the four-in-hand remains the preferred knot for most facial types and for the world's most elegantly attired men. The four-in-hand's principal advantage is that it is the simplest knot to execute and its thinner frame fits into all shirt collars without pushing its points away from the shirt body, like the wider bodied Windsors. On a purely architectural basis, its conical form flatters more men's faces than the Windsor's horizontal geometry, which looks at odds under a tapered chin. The four-in-hand's slightly asymmetrical set also helps the presentation appear less fussy than the symmetrically static and triangular Windsor presentation.

Its hybrid, the half-Windsor, can almost be excused, if only to help a thin tie produce a larger knot. However, should a fuller knot be desired, it's better to use the Prince Albert version, basically a four-in-hand looped over a second time. This feature makes it particularly attractive to short men, because it results in an abbreviated tie length more consistent with their stature. When looping the tie over the narrow strip, care should be taken not to pull the knot too tightly; otherwise passage of the second loop will be difficult. Like the four-in-hand knot, the Prince Albert's asymmetrical set adds that salutary touch so important in conveying the look of nonchalance.

Regarding the appropriate width of a man's tie, the principal criterion has always been its relationship to the jacket lapel—once again, fashion must defer to the architecture of its practitioners. Widths between 3¼ inches and 4¼ inches will generally ensure longevity. A man with narrow shoulders has less chest to drape a lapel across, and therefore its narrower dimension dictates that the tie follow suit. Conversely, a man who has broad shoulders requires the

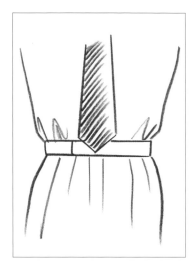

more generous services of a wider lapel line and thus a larger-scaled necktie.

With respect to the necktie's ideal length, the general rule of thumb holds that its widest point just above its tip should coincide with the belt's upper edge, as anything hanging much longer begins to take on phallic overtones. Following these guidelines, a corollary maintains that its narrow end should not fall below the wider one. However, both the Duke of Windsor (see page 226) and Agnelli, who is pictured here, knotted their ties so that the under-blade was long enough to slip through the loop under the top blade and tuck into the belt line, thereby holding the tie in place. This also solves the long tie–short man conundrum.

The Art of Knotting the Four-in-Hand Given the number of times a man will stand in front of a mirror positioning his tie into his dress shirt, it's amazing how few men manage to get it right. Unlike fastening a belt or rigging one's cuff links, tying a tie and positioning it into the collar is the only act of a gentleman's morning toilette that requires both manual and visual dexterity—there is a little art to it.

The most common mistake occurs right after the preliminary knot is formed, when it frequently ends up hiked into the collar while in the grip of the fat of the hand, much like one would hold an ice cream cone. Typically, it arrives looking like a car parallel-parked for the first time, dented and askew.

The secret lies in executing a knot compressed in such a way that it dovetails easily up and into the upside-down "V" of the collar points. If it is to remain there with a minimum of periodic fixing, it needs to be tightly knotted. To enhance its staying power, a dimple or inverted pleat should emerge from under the knot. The French call this a *cuillère*, which means "spoon" or "scoop."

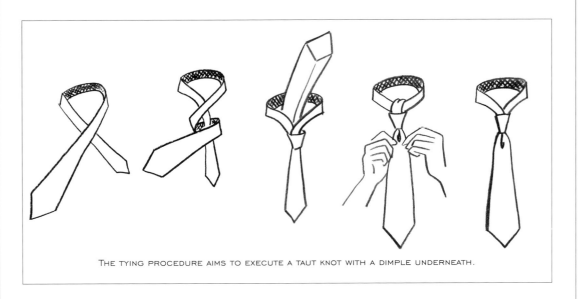

THE TYING PROCEDURE AIMS TO EXECUTE A TAUT KNOT WITH A DIMPLE UNDERNEATH.

Getting the knot to fold this way is important, because if is tightened properly, the two sides of its crease will deepen, blossoming out under the knot, anchoring it so that it resists loosening. It is particularly important upon first knotting a new tie to try to make the knot dimple properly, as the necktie's lining and silk encasement form a "memory" that will assist in the dimple's formation the next time out. This is another reason why more seasoned practitioners of this art tend to prefer hand-sewn neckties of woven silk. The woven silk's textured surface helps discourage undue slippage of the knot, and the genuine handmade article has greater resiliency. Thus more tension can be imposed on the knot without ruining the tie's fabric.

With the partially completed knot suspended from the neck, place both thumbs just below the knot under either side of top blade with the forefingers resting directly above. Pull down smartly. You will find that the tie's top blade will start to buckle in the middle just below the knot, forming a slight convex cavity. It will continue to do so as the upper blade is pulled tight. Gently guided to its final destination by the tips of the thumb and forefinger of one hand (as opposed to the fat of the palm) while the other hand holds the bottom blade in place, the knot arrives appearing fresher, more relaxed, and needing less final adjustment.

A TAUT KNOT LETS THE TIE ARCH OUT FROM THE COLLAR WITH MINIMAL PERIODIC ADJUSTMENT.

If the tying procedure is not executed with an eye toward producing a taut knot, the tie will not have the necessary spring around its knot to arch out from the collar, as if poised at attention. Instead, it will hang, like a dead fish, compromising the stature of the entire arrangement.. With the tie positioned smartly up into the collar, its dimple extending downward, the composition projects a subliminal authority.

THE NECKERCHIEF Since ancient times, a man has always felt the necessity to wear something around his neck. With the explosion of modern sportswear in the 1920s, the novelty of the open-necked sport shirt inspired a variety of new ways to appoint the neck. Long a popular fashion at European watering holes, the sports scarf was, and still is, closely identified with Riviera high style. As international travel accelerated the adoption of lightweight sportswear, it wasn't long before the new *tour de cou* began turning up around the necks of smartly turned out

FOLDING THE NECKERCHIEF.

FOLDING THE NECKERSCARF.

TYING THE NECKERSCARF WITH A LOOSE FOUR-IN-HAND KNOT.

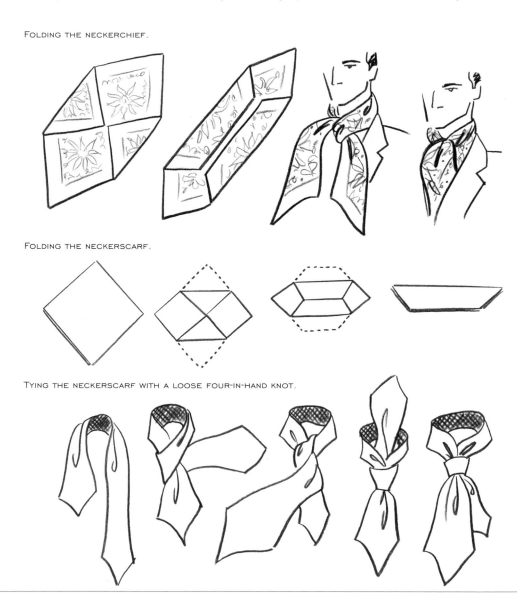

Americans from the south of France to the Caribbean's stylish strongholds.

Two basic models of sport neckwear began taking shape. The more common was the neckerchief, a solid color or patterned square of silk, cotton, or other material that was knotted or draped in ascot fashion around the neck (*opposite, top*). At one point in the mid-thirties, other than for a formal-wear layout, every Hollywood head shot of a male seemed to feature one version or another of these casual neckscarves. Take Cary Grant here. Okay, he has a head start in the debonair department, but drape a neckerchief in a throw-over style under a mundane knit polo and round-neck pullover and presto, instant chic.

The second scarf style was the neckertie, which was a silk square folded around the neck with its ends loosely tied in a four-in-hand style (*opposite, middle and bottom*). Other than the odd European, or especially Frenchman, sporting a foulard ascot, it's a rarity to find a man wearing a neckerchief anymore. For most men, tying something around the neck smacks of the fussy, the feminine, or both. This is a bit bizarre, since most middle-aged Americans grew up watching Roy Rogers and any number of John Wayne types swathed in neck decor as they rode herd on the bad guys.

Were the neckerscarf ever to stage a fashion comeback, the new mode in casual office attire might well become its logical sponsor. With all manner of tieless necks descending on the modern workplace, a variety of alternate neck treatments might provide a welcome relief from to what promises to be an era of relatively bland business-body covering. (See page 272.)

ABOVE:
Cary Grant wearing a neckerchief.

BELOW:
*Animating the open neckline
with a scarf tied like a four-in-hand.*

*F*rom hat crease to instep, the art of male habiliment can be divided into a series of individual yet related portraitures. To the north, the focal point of the tailored ensemble is the triangle formed under the face by necktie, shirt collar, and jacket lapels. To the south lies another tableau created by the rendezvous of trouser, sock, and shoe. One way for a man's outfit to add up to more than the sum of its parts is to have these two sub-portraitures bracket the body much like the first and last sentences of a paragraph.

9

HOSIERY HARMONIES

The color and pattern of a man's hose are the sartorial syntax that can connect these two textural outposts. By reiterating at floor level a color or pattern found near the face, the silhouette's upper and lower zones begin to network with each other, prompting the viewer is to take in the whole picture. Few artists captured Manhattan's café society with as much wit and stylishness as Peter Arno, so it is no surprise that he knew how to employ the vertical line for optimal effect. He's employed quite a few here, but we will focus on those clocked numbers colonizing his ankles.

*In striped tie, dress shirt, and hose,
artist Peter Arno relaxes in linear repose.*

Here's the classic navy dress suit enlivened by a whirlwind of navy and white accessories. Add a red carnation and you could host your own afternoon wedding. Although solid navy dress hose would be the vanilla of choice for such a feast of formality, without a pattern below the waist to integrate the costume's two halves, the bottom half is left in relative eclipse.

Implementing such a relationship is not such a daunting task. To begin, hosiery should match the trouser rather than the shoe. Footwear and hosiery that are perceived as a unit ultimately separate themselves from the trouser, stopping the eye at the pant-leg bottom instead of escorting it all the way down to the floor. With a navy suit and black shoes, navy socks appear richer than black. With a dark gray suit and brown footwear, charcoal hose would the more stylish color. While appropriate for formal wear and practically obligatory for those swathed head to toe in regulation black, black hose should be avoided at other times. "Hose noir" transforms the ankle into a black hole, diminishing that which it could beautify

Patterned hose help integrate and enliven the top and bottom halves of his ensemble.

THIS PAGE:
Sacha Guitry in silk dress hose and crocodile lace-ups.

OPPOSITE:
The sheen of Dean Acheson's and Averill Harriman's hose connect their dinner clothes to their formal shoes below.

A man's hose also needs to be compatible in dressiness with its two neighbors, the upstairs trouser and downstairs shoe. As a general principle, the more formal the ensemble, the finer or more sheer the hose.

Silk dress hosiery, with its inherent shimmer, therefore, continues to be the ankle embellishment of choice for the cognoscenti of after-six chic. Take note of the hose worn by Sacha Guitry, one of the great boulevardiers of the French stage. Few contemporary men don hosiery of this sheerness or opalescence, but it does complement the subtle luster from his crocodile shoes. Likewise, observe Cardinal Spellman as pictured here with two prominent and well-dressed statesmen of their day, Dean Acheson and Averill Harriman. Beginning with their silk-faced lapels, traveling down their trouser seams, and culminating with their socks and shoes, an unbroken yet unobtrusive stripe of light hyphenates each section of the outfit with the next. Notice how Mr. Harriman's hose escorts the sheen from his trouser seams down to his patent leather evening shoe.

*As with Luchino Visconti's and Frank Sinatra's thick hose,
for the sock to effect a stylish transition between
trouser and shoe, it must share some of their physical properties.*

The bulkier the outfit, the more one must step up the sock's thickness. Gossamer cotton lisle hose would appear lost with a pair of heavy flannel slacks and a tweed sport jacket. Weighing in beneath the great director Luchino Visconti's flannel trousers are wool hose in wide, chunky ribs, demonstrating again how the agency of texture can join different portions of an ensemble. Likewise, not only does young Frank Sinatra's sporty hose link his flannel trousers' coarser texture with that of his informal blucher lace-ups, but his argyles swing to the same beat as his necktie.

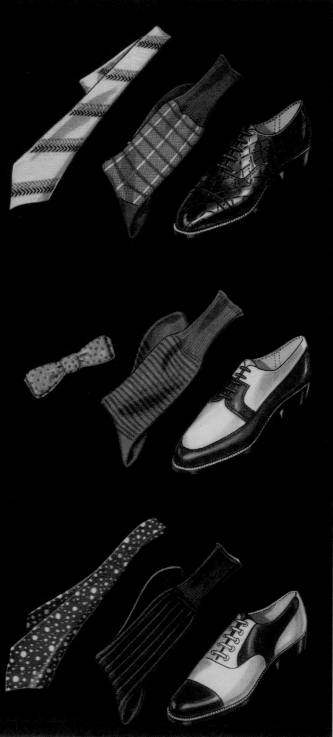

As mentioned previously, the best-dressed men look upon accessories as comrades in the struggle against sartorial mediocrity. Whereas hosiery has long fulfilled its hygienic responsibilities as a guardian of the ankle, it took some time before it could develop into its secondary role as a harmonizer of apparel. The sophisticated man of the 1930s was accustomed to coordinating his headgear with his footwear. With this precedent in place, why couldn't hosiery's varied colors and patterns also promote harmony between different sectors of an outfit? When neckwear motifs such as polka dots, stripes, and Spitalsfield neats began to appear in fine-gauge wool dress hosiery, men were further inspired to take full advantage of this accessory's increasing potential to enhance the entire ensemble.

ABOVE:
Gary Cooper dons complementary hose and four-in-hand.

Bogey uses his sport jacket to direct his hose's character.

By the end of the 1940s, fancy hose accounted for 60 percent of all men's sock purchases. Now cast as a principal character, the sock's role expanded beyond the simple exchange of dialogue with the necktie, its usual collaborator, and took center stage alongside the other ensemble players.

The next pictures profile this newest celebrity and its leading costars. After the necktie, the hose's most frequent stage partner is none other than the dress shirt. As the shirt is frequently solid, the hose is free to play off the shirt in color or pattern, as these next two illustrations demonstrate.

With hosiery now enjoying its newfound standing, other bit players wait eagerly in the wings, hoping to join the show. An odd sport jacket can sometimes improve some of the more improbable routines. Here's Bogey, relaxing in a mélange of Scottish woolens, his hand-woven wool hose feeling bonny comfortable playing opposite a tweed jacket from the same highland.

The conservative 1950s sounded a death knell for sophisticated men's hosiery. First, the gray-flannel man tried his best to look anonymous, suppressing any inclination toward fashion or individuality. Then the synthetic one-size-fits-all sock engaged the practical side of the American man's brain, and soon everyone's plat du jour was a choice between black, navy, and brown stretch socks. Some East Coast colleges even initiated the insider's fashion for dispensing with socks altogether. Some southern campuses even had "sockless fraternities," but as "cool" as it was to get dressed up and bare your ankles, few guys actually enjoyed wearing sweaty Weejuns or tassel loafers.

The dress shirt and hose execute a pas de deux.

A few words concerning the wearing of socks with shorts. Unless you can play basketball like the New Jersey Nets power forward Keith Van Horn, calf- or knee-high sport hose is uniformly unattractive. However, with tailored shorts finishing at different heights above the knee, their bottom openings require more mass than just footwear at the base of the body for proper balance. Other than losing the sock altogether, the only stylish alternative is an ankle sock with either a rib top that can be rolled over or a loose-fitting pair of bulky half socks with the tops folded down. (In fact, anklets look pretty stylish under long trousers, providing the trouser features a full and casual cut.) Worn here by Noël Coward (*opposite*) and pictured in different periodicals from the thirties, the anklet is still the most chic way to team socks and shorts. Unfortunately, the sports anklet was another in a long line of stylish hosiery casualties.

RIGHT:

The Duke of Windsor never missed an opportunity to parade his colors, or in this case, his stripes. Here he shows them off with pinwale cord trousers and one of his typically audacious window-pane affairs directing traffic.

OPPOSITE:

America's former ambassador of men's fashion, Neiman Marcus's own menswear expert, Derrill Osborn. Even the grandeur of the Taj Mahal cannot humble this man's dedication to personal adornment. A more spectacular example of harmonizing headwear, hosiery, and heart we have yet to see.

George Frazier, Esquire *magazine's legendary fashion columnist in the 1960s, pretty much summed up the pecking order of a man's ensemble:* "Wanna know if a guy is well dressed? Look down." *In fact, one theory muses that any man who respects quality footwear is likely to achieve success, because he understands the value of working his way up from the bottom.*

While shoes clearly articulate a man's sense of style, as well as his social position, taste in male footwear rests on a paradox: the more imagination and effort one brings to the enterprise, the more subtle the outcome should be.

"No one will ever take you seriously with those tassels."

10

FOOT

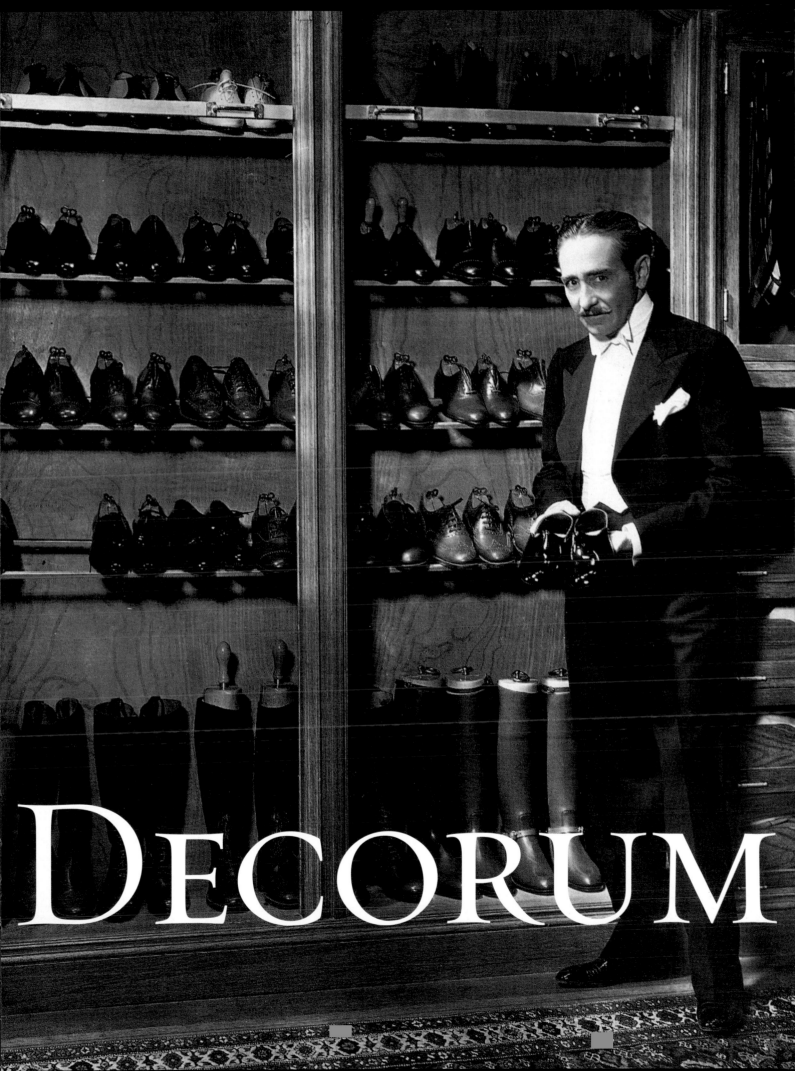

DECORUM

SOLES OF COMFORT

The first shoes were little more than soles, constructed from leather or wood. Roughly shaped without designation to the right or left foot, they were secured by straps or similar fastenings that kept them from falling off. Leather proved durable, readily available, and more pliable than wood. When shoes became enclosed, leather's prominence increased, because it was one of the few coverings that allowed air to circulate while affording the foot maximum protection against the elements.

Though the early male shoddings were exposed to rigors unknown to all but the most adventurous of modern men, durability in modern shoes is still a key feature. A well-made and properly looked after pair of leather dress shoes can provide several decades of fine service. Top-drawer footwear has uppers (the top part of the shoe) made from skins no more than twelve weeks old. These hides have a fine grain, taking a high polish. The outer sole, also made of leather, should be "welted" to the rest of the shoe. Welt construction dates back to the fifteenth century in Western Europe and consists of sewing a strip of leather in between the edge of the sole and the turned-in edge of the upper. This process yields an elegantly durable shoe in which the sole can be removed and repaired repeatedly with minimal damage to the shoe's upper.

The soles of the best shoes are vegetable-tanned for longevity and coolness, their stitches hidden in a specially cut channel around the sole. Insoles and linings should also be constructed of leather, because they absorb perspiration without conducting heat, allowing the foot to breathe and the shoe to mold to its shape. Well-crafted heels are made from layers of leather nailed together with brass pins, a sandwiching effect that provides the greatest cushioning, support, and strength. Finally, the shape of the first-class shoe should follow the foot itself—straight on the inside and curved on the outside, with the instep pointing toward the big toe rather than the shoe's centerline. If the shoe's last (the wood form on which the shoe was crafted) fits the wearer's foot well, there will be little need for the ritual breaking-in that is usually associated with the new-shoe experience.

In his lifetime, a man may walk as many as 115,000 miles. No wonder that Leonardo da Vinci, an artist of epic importance and a master of anatomy, called the foot "a masterpiece of engineering and a work of art." It's impossible to spend too much on a finely crafted, perfectly fitting pair of shoes. Unlike man's own two cuffed works of art, these new artifacts will improve with age.

PREVIOUS PAGE.
Adolphe Menjou in front of his footwear stable.
Given his expanse of custom-made shoes, not to mention
his collection of riding boots, whoever coined the term
"clotheshorse" must have had him in mind.

STEPS IN TIME

The look of modern men's shoes has always borne a direct relationship to the cut of the trousers. At the turn of the twentieth century, high shoes with sharply pointed toes perfectly complemented the cuffless, narrow-bottom, pegged trouser. By 1905, cuffed trousers paved the way for the oxford shoe with its round, bulbous toe.

By 1919, newly liberated servicemen gave the oxford shoe a tremendous boost, opting for its comfort after stomping across Europe in suffocating combat boots. According to *Esquire's Encyclopedia of 20th Century Men's Fashion*, "The well dressed man of the postwar period became as comfort-conscious as he was clothes conscious." When the popular knickerbocker suit demanded equally modern and more comfortable footwear, the high-top shoe went the way of the stiff, high-fitting shirt collar.

Plain-bottom trousers and slim-fitting benchmades.

The English still regard the aristocratically slender trouser leg and its equally fastidious narrow, plain bottom as the sovereign of all trouser silhouettes. With such diminutive dimensions sheathing the ankle, anything less spartan than a pair of chisel-toed, imperially slim benchmades would constitute sartorial suicide.

Between the two world wars, a tidal wave of male fashions was unleashed as footwear stepped to the forefront. The majority of today's classic shoe models were first created for individual customers by one of Britain's own custom shoemakers. Just as the English Savile Row artisans established the benchmark for tailored men's fashion during the 1920s and '30s, London's West End cobblers set the standards for high-class footwear. By 1929, shoe manufacturers and retailers agreed that the way to sell shoes was through "styleage rather than mileage." This fluorescent period of men's fashion produced the half-brogue oxford, the cap-toe blucher, the plain-toe monk front, the wing-tip buckskin, the Norwegian lace-up, the correspondent shoe, the white buck, the Weejun slip-on, and a variety of casuals for sport, spectator, and evening wear. Although the latter half of the century contributed a few more entries to the classic footwear omnibus, like men's fashion in general, authentically fashionable male footwear encountered a series of detours and dead ends.

In the fall of 1948, *Esquire* magazine previewed the new head-to-toe "Bold Look." This contrived but masterful retail promotion proposed that the conquering American war hero manifest the new world order by wearing bolder-proportioned and -colored clothes. Naturally, in order to keep in step, men's footwear had to step up in both scale and design. From then through the latter half of the 1950s, the American fashion plebe often walked around in straight-hanging, natural-shoulder suits anchored by gunboat-size brogues with heavily detailed wing tips.

As the veterans visited Europe, they began taking notice of the Italians' new, lithe, "columnar" look. This tight-fitting silhouette contrasted sharply with the shapeless sack suits of Madison Avenue. Over the next thirty or so years, American men began their flirtation with clothing and footwear designed to make the male body and foot appear not only smaller but leaner. With its lower vamp, pointier toe, and slipperlike platform, the lightweight Italian-crafted shoe was the logical conclusion to the era's narrow-legged bottom. Not until the mid-eighties, when Giorgio Armani introduced his fuller slouch suits, did men's shoe design begin to revisit the larger proportions of its forebears, the welt-constructed Anglo-American dress shoe.

While the sixties Peacock Revolution spawned a plethora of creativity, especially for those collectors of pop culture kitsch, other than Pierre Cardin's "blunt-toe" boot of 1968, which served as the inspiration for Gen-X's "pilgrim-toe clunkers," those years and the next twenty were a wasteland of male shoe design. However, with the dawning of the new century, male footwear finds itself treading on familiar terrain. Following closely in the footsteps of those hallowed custom shoes created in Edwardian England, more fine men's stores today sell classically proportioned, hand-lasted footwear than at any time since the tradition-toppling sixties.

COLOR

While black dress shoes have always been considered de rigueur for dark dressy suitings, dark brown offers equal refinement, if not superior style. Regardless of their luster, black dress shoes will always lack the antiqued brown's deep patina and changing highlights. Just as any article placed on a polished mahogany tabletop immediately acquires an expensive aura, top-quality brown leather shoes invest all fabrics with an intangible richness.

In 1936, the leather antiquing process was finally refined to the point where it spurred acceptance of the dark brown shoe for dressy worsted wear. Here is the editor's response to a reader's query from a 1936 *Apparel Arts* magazine on the correctness of coordinating brown shoes with navy suits:

> DEAR MR. E.: *It was customary years ago to wear only black shoes with a dark blue suit. In recent years there has been a decided trend toward brown shoes, not the light tan, but the dark antique brown shade. Since these are almost as dark as a pair of black shoes, their adaption for wear with dark blue suits became quite general.*
>
> *At the present time, dark brown shoes are considered correct and satisfactory for wear with a dark blue suit. Light tan shoes are not considered appropriate.*

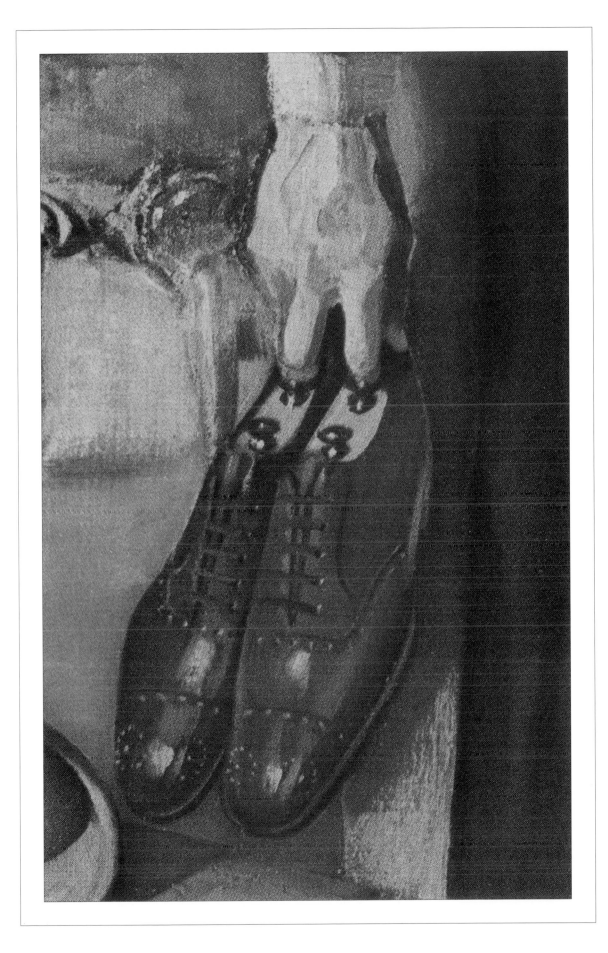

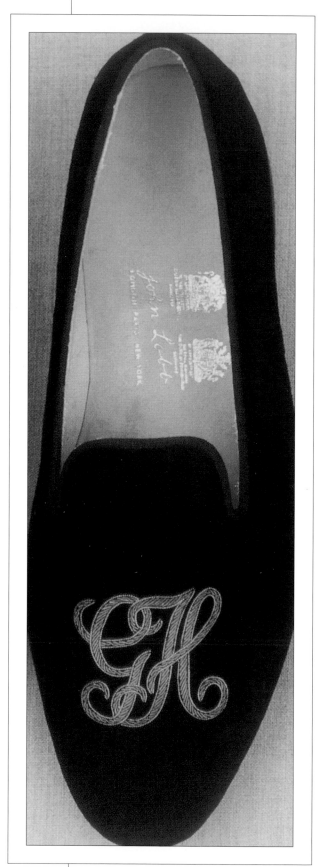

The Boston Brahmins have long appreciated the eccentric yet classy habit of mating brown cap toes with navy or charcoal suits. And the Milanese male, considered by present-day style arbiters as the most sophisticated dresser in the sock-wearing world, is almost fanatical in favoring brown lace-ups over black. He is vigilant that his saddle-tanned business bench-mades are bone-polished for the week's work, reserving his brown suedes for the more leisurely activities of the weekend.

It's difficult to explain why burgundy, navy, or gray leather shoes for men never connoted much class or taste. Perhaps it's because such dyed, shiny colors appeared artificial and showy next to the natural saddle-leather shades. Only when a classic shoe design, like the Belgian or Gucci slip-on, acquires an iconic or insider status can alternate-colored footwear on men come off looking refined rather than contrived—and then only when in the rich nonreflective textures of suede or velvet.

The genesis of such fanciful footwear can be traced back to the English aristocracy's penchant for dressing in black tie for dinner accompanied by their favorite bottle green, burgundy, or navy velvet smoking jacket with matching toned and monogrammed Prince Albert slippers. Once the titled started sporting their dress-down dinner regalia outside the home or private club, the smoking lamp was lit for men's colored evening, and then daytime, footwear.

PUTTING YOUR
BEST FOOT FORWARD

THE OXFORD SHOE The oxford shoe derives from the Oxonian, a half boot with side slits that first gained popularity at Oxford University in 1800. The side-slit soon developed into a side-lace that eventually moved to the instep as students began to rebel against knee-high and ankle-high boots.

 The plain cap-toe oxford lace-up is the basic shoe style for smart, though not strictly formal, town wear. Designed to meet the demand for a more stylish, lighter-weight shoe than the full brogue oxford shoe, this oxford was one of the early styles to take the place of boots. The toe cap's punched holes are sometimes replaced by two narrow rows of stitching. With a round or slightly square plain toe or with a medallion decoration, it is the staple of many business wardrobes. This town shoe's smart line is enhanced by its beveled "waist," the center portion of the sole that joins the front with the heel, a feature of all lightweight shoes as opposed to the square waist used for more stout types such as the monk or Norwegian.

THE WING-TIP BROGUE The low-heeled oxford trimmed with perforations, stitchings, and pinkings known as the brogue comes from Ireland and the Scottish Highlands. Centuries ago, it had no heel and was made of thick, untanned deer hide with the fur intact. The word "brogue" comes from the Gaelic *bróg*, which meant to push an awl through, as was done in the stitching of leather. Modern brogues haven't borrowed much more than the name from the ancient style, except for the punchings that are known as broguings. The imitation punchings that decorate today's brogues once were actual holes or slashings made to let water drain out of these early Scottish shoes, which were often worn while fording a stream or crossing marshy land.

The traditional wing-tip dress shoe is slightly less formal than the plain or decorated cap-toe model. Its complete broguing produces a slightly bulkier, less sleek appearance, and its larger proportions allow for a more harmonious match with heavier-textured fabrics such as flannels, cheviots, or tweeds. The wing tip takes its name from its toe cap shaped like the spread wings of a bird, pointed in the center and extending toward the rear with heavily perforated side seams.

THE BLUCHER   When Prussian general Gebhard Leberecht von Blücher, one of Napoleon's more formidable opponents, decided that his troops needed better shoes than the low-cut ones they wore with gaiters, he commissioned a boot with side pieces lapped over the front. They had a loose inner edge and lacing across the tongue. Whether or not this footwear gave his infantrymen an advantage is debatable. But Blücher's well-shod forces did help Wellington trample the French at Waterloo.

Success begets imitation, and after Blücher participated in Napoleon's famous defeat, the shoe bearing his name was adopted by armies throughout Europe. During the 1850s, the blucher evolved into a trendy sporting and hunting shoe, but it wasn't until the turn of the century that it debuted as a low shoe for town affairs. Distinguished from earlier shoes by the forward extension of its quarters over the vamp, the blucher often has a tongue cut in one piece with the forepart.

The modern blucher is a basic model for town, sports, and leisure shoes of oxford height. Because its side straps lend a slightly heavier appearance than the closed throat lace-up, the blucher is a step down in dressiness from the oxford. Men with higher insoles tend to favor its open-throat front fastening, which permits more give over the instep than with the closer-fitting bal-type (short for Balmoral, the Queen's castle in Scotland) oxford.

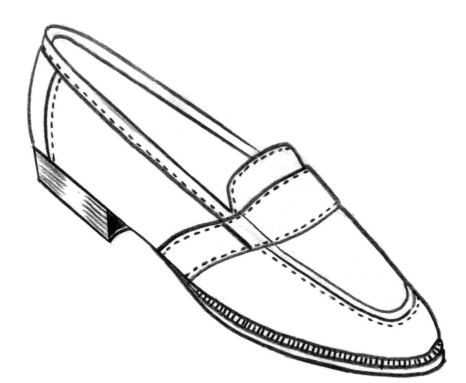

THE DRESS SLIP-ON Back when a man's choice of clothes was dictated by degrees of formality, pairing a slip-on shoe with dress clothes would have been frowned upon as a faux pas. But with current men's fashion fueled by convenience and comfort, the slip-on nowadays enjoys an equal footing with the lace-up for tailored business clothes.

The introduction of the lower-cut, lightweight Italian footwear in the mid-fifties hastened the lace-up's slide from style supremacy. The pairing by the American businessman of his natural-shoulder suits with black Weejuns in the sixties presaged the gilt-buckled Gucci loafer's infiltration of Wall Street's boardrooms in the seventies. In the eighties, the sock-revealing low vamp slip-on reached a kind of dubious ubiquity.

A tassel loafer of any shape, design, or color was originally a casual shoe, and therefore never intended for donning under the cuffed sobriety of the dark navy or gray worsted. However, certain slip-ons can stand side by side with the typical business brogue in the ankle propriety department. These hybrids are usually appointed with the following lace-up-like features: welt-soled bottoms for better foot scale and stature, dressy, bespoke-inspired vamp designs, and overall decorative understatement.

THE SIDE-GUSSET SHOE J. Sparkes Hall, boot maker to Queen Victoria, devoted much of his life to designing footwear that was easy to put on and take off. In 1836, at the Queen's urging, he invented a shoe with inserts of elastic fabric on either side. Made with stretchable gores of rubberized cloth that presented a trimly fitted ankle, his feminine boot was described by one of the Queen's ladies as "the comfort of my life." As he developed this new branch of shoemaking, the style spread to America, becoming known as the "Congress gaiter" or "Boston boot."

Today, the elastic-sided men's shoe is generally confined to the rarefied world of the custom-shoe aficionado. A longtime champion of this traditionally bespoke style of shodding, the former dean of English shoemaking George Cleaverley loved this model, because he felt no other design produced a better-fitting slip-on. Trimming the exposed elastic side gussets with small leather panels is one way of further refining it. For those in the know and fortunate enough to come upon a good pair, the side-gusset slip-on is a very stylish solution to the business-shoe conundrum of comfort versus correctness.

THE MONK-STRAP SHOE   One of the few articles of apparel to earn its name honestly, the monk-front shoe was actually patterned after a type of footwear worn for centuries in European monasteries. Legend has it that the style originated among friars in the Italian Alps in the fifteenth century. A visiting English brother was supposedly so impressed by the simplicity of the monks' shoes that he was presented with a pair. He took them back to England, where the style was readily adopted.

The modern monk-front model is a low-fitting strapped shoe with an upper composed of three leather pieces. A broad strap across the instep fastens through a saddle buckle on the shoe's outside. The monk-strap's tongue is broader than those used in most low shoes where a closer fit is desirable, thus enabling a more comfortable fit around the ankle than the typical lace-up shoe.

Devotees appreciate the monk's superbly proportioned smartness and offbeat panache as well as its intermediate formality, registering somewhere between that of a slip-on and a lace-up shoe. Essentially plain-toe, the monk model can handle some broguing, if desired. From black calf to brown reversed calf, the monk's economically eloquent front enables it to gracefully escort a diverse range of trousers.

THE SUEDE SHOE It is generally conceded that the first U.S. sighting of male extremities swathed in something other than polished leather occurred during the 1924 International Polo matches at Long Island's Meadowbrook Country Club. There, astride the regal feet of the Prince of Wales, American society was treated to the first flannel-suit and brown-buckskin-shoe ensemble. Though the sovereign-to-be's sartorial proclivities were already legend on both sides of the Atlantic, fashion observers were aghast at his supposed breach of good taste in sporting "reverse calf" (as suede was then termed) oxfords, with a suit, no less.

Style scouts called the Prince's fashion risk "a mark of great effeminacy." Many men initially questioned the shoes' fashion pedigree, sidestepping them because of their fear that such lackluster footwear appeared delicate and unmanly. Others called them "brothel-creepers."

The Prince astride brown suede lace-ups.

Brown suede or buckskin shoes can be worn all year round.

Retailers found the reverse calf shoe too radical. Because the suedes mostly came in shades of brown, clothing salesmen were hesitant to try to sell tenderfoots on the correct clothes to wear with them. However, fashion arbiters adopted the suedes immediately, although it wasn't until almost a decade later that the laity finally saw the light.

When the suede shoe fashion finally did hit, it arrived in conspicuous plenitude—perforated cap-toes on town-lasts for business suitings, rubber-soled bluchers for the country, and ankle-high, two-eyelet tie models for spectator sportswear.

By 1932, the brown buckskin shoe had so infiltrated English sporting circles that no well-dressed Brit considered his wardrobe complete without at least one pair. On the opposite shore, the society sportsmen at Meadowbrook and Piping Rock Country Clubs on Long Island were so enamored of the brown-tweed-jacket and gray-flannel-trouser combination that he who "really belonged" invariably finished off this ensemble with a pair of the new buckskin shoddings.

While this timeless symbol of aristocratic British taste makes anything worn with it appear more stylish, the brown suede shoe also happens to be suitable for all seasons, perfectly shaded for light-colored spring clothing, and rich in not-so-shiny refinement for winter-weight worsteds and flannels. Once smitten, many aficionados have a tough time returning to the shiny surfaces of conventional male footwear.

THE CROCODILE SHOE   The first crocodile leather shoe for men was introduced in the spring of 1935, courtesy of one of London's better-known boot makers. It met with instant success among well-dressed Englishmen, who adopted it for resort and informal town wear. Many Americans visiting England brought the shoe back home to inaugurate the fall fashion season.

   Like the brown buckskin shoe, crocodile leather in a dark honey tone affords versatility. Whether in a monk-strap model for the weekend, plain cap-toe lace-up for town, or tassel loafer for the nineteenth hole, the small-scaled crocodile shoe offers the normally matte-shod sophisticate a rare opportunity to cosset himself in sybaritic sheen.

THE NORWEGIAN   By the mid-thirties, well-dressed Americans had adopted two leisure-inspired shoes: a slip-on moccasin or Weejun and a lace-up model with moccasin front called the Norwegian. Distinguished by its split-toe design, the Norwegian features a vertical hand-stitch down the center of its toe. With heavy leather uppers and thick country soles, the rugged Norwegian was built for the outdoors. Today, the most famous purveyor of the Norwegian street shoe is the French shoemaker J. M. Weston. When the broader-shouldered clothing of the late eighties first caught hold, Weston's black semi-chassé lace-up was one of the few quality shoes capable of balancing the fuller-scaled fashions.

THE SLIP-ON MOCCASIN   When fish were less than forthcoming, Norwegian fisherman would pass the time by stitching together peasant shoes. Some of these "Norwegians" were exported for sale to Great Britain, and during the 1930s Americans touring London discovered the Oslo import—a casual slip-on with a moccasin-style front.

Strangely, it was the Norwegian and not the Indian who gave the moccasin its big boost as a casual fashion. Previously, the Indian moccasin appeared mostly as soft-soled camp footwear or a beaded bedroom slipper. Norwegian designers were the first to copy the Native Americans' idea of inserting a plug of leather to cover the forepart of the foot and then hand-stitching it to a combination sole and upper.

With the help of the local fishing industry, the Norwegians began producing leisure slippers that turned up at smart Continental resorts and selected European cities. Visiting American manufacturers brought them home and re-adapted the original American Indian invention. Here's a man who rarely stood on ceremony, the well-heeled Jimmy Stewart, loafing about in a pair of Weejuns.

In the mid-thirties, the G. H. Bass company registered the name "Weejun," which, along with its moccasin toe and diamond cutout pattern, became one of the most recognized models of this popular new genre, also known as penny loafers. Initially worn as a summer shoe in and around the home, the Weejun-style slip-on became the year-round workhorse of many men's casual shoe wardrobe. Today boot makers J. M. Weston and John Lobb produce renditions that come as close to "pennies from heaven" as possible.

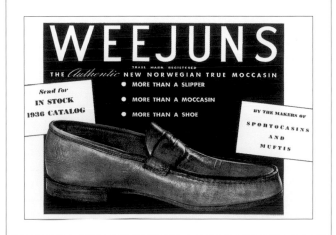

THE TURF OR CHUKKA BOOT This style
of footwear has inspired many offshoots; however, it is
presented here in its original form, the two-eyelet
ankle boot. Originally brought to the West from India
by the British Raj, they dubbed it "chukka," after the
playing period in polo. Often unlined and fitted with
a leather or rubber sole, this field shoe can frequently
be found ensconced under a pair of flannels or cords,
in either a smooth tan calfskin or a russet shade of
suede. Kitted out in Tyrolean chapeau, Scottish Shetland sport coat, and English moleskin trousers, this
tastefully attired toff reaffirms the chukka's international ranking.

THE GUCCI SLIP-ON Just as the red heels of Louis XIV and his courtiers exuded an air of nobility, the famous Gucci loafer trimmed with a bit of gilded-horse regalia continues to resonate chic. Whether in brown leather for the cosmopolitan's gray flannels or black suede with lug sole for the downtown urbanite, the Gucci loafer is still one of the softest, most comfortable casuals in or out of town.

In 1966, the House of Gucci single-handedly revived interest in their famous slip-on, which has spawned more imitations than any other style of male footwear. By the early seventies, Wall Street investment bankers took to appointing their corporate chalk stripes with Turnbull & Asser spread collars, Hermés four-in-hands, and Gucci leather slip-ons. Very few male shoe designs survive the vagaries of high fashion, but more than thirty years later, Gucci's buckled soles of comfort have style mileage to spare. Douglas Fairbanks Jr. poses in this icon of Italian craftsmanship.

Douglas Fairbanks Jr. in Gucci loafers.

*Famed Hollywood costume designer Adrian,
cosseted in the classic white buck shoe.*

THE WHITE BUCK No article of footwear better typified the postwar trend toward relaxed style than American white bucks. Their slightly scuffed appearance lent them that lived-in character so characteristic of the country's natural-shoulder fashion. Uniquely American in their understated temperament, the white buckskin oxford lace-up with its red rubber soles first served as comfortable summer accompaniment to resort clothes worn in the early 1930s. Later on, resourceful commuters discovered that these comfy suedes comported themselves equally well on steamy summer pavements under lightweight gabardine, seersucker, or tropical worsted suits.

Brothers Brooks used to make the sine qua non of white bucks in England. They were the perfect companion to the trad's well-worn khaki pants or madras Bermudas. Unfortunately, the Brooks' British original is yet another casualty of the company's rush to divest itself of its old-guard heritage. Here is Hollywood's famed costume designer Adrian enjoying the soft-spoken luxury of his worn-in bucks.

THE SPECTATOR The famed English boot maker John Lobb claims to have designed the first spectator shoe for cricket around 1868. It's probable that the shoe's contrasting dark leather areas—its counters, tarsal strap, toe cap, and facings—were initially designed this way, because they had to withstand the most wear during the rigors of sport.

In the jazz age, the shoe was known as "the correspondent," its two-toned tenor associated with those shady characters who sometimes acted as correspondents in divorce cases. It was originally designed in brown willow calf and white buck or reverse calf suede, with black box calf often substituted for the brown leather. An essential part of the thirties yachtsman or holiday sports wardrobe, this two-toned lace-up's unusual contrast of texture and color eventually became known in the States as "the spectator."

Today, the real McCoy can be acquired only through the auspices of the bespoke shoemaker. Courtesy of modern commerce, manufacturers have replaced this pedigreed shoe's authentic white suede with a cheap and shiny synthetic leather, effectively eliminating the class from this summer classic.

George Gershwin and Irving Berlin winging it in "corresponding" spectators.

THE DRESS SLIPPER It's hard to pinpoint the exact time or place when a David Niven type might have ventured outside his home or club swathed in a pair of elegant house slippers. Such an occasion must have followed closely on the heels of the modern dinner jacket's early public excursions.

Unlike other apparel originated by royalty or high society, dress slippers for men never caught the public fancy. Aside from the cost of such a one-of-a kind furbelow, the ornamented Albert slipper rarely crossed paths with the average man. Part of its club-elegant appeal was its insider chic. One also needed confidence in one's own taste: ankling about unsympathetic taprooms in a pair of these elitist trappings could test the depths of any man's machismo.

A slipper is a generic type of shoe, not a particular style, including a wide variety of footwear for many uses. Slippers, which end below the ankle, are slipped on and held by the foot without any fastening. The pump is a slipper, as is the Oriental babouche with turned-up toe.

To break away from the old-fashioned house-slipper association, some manufacturers called the indoor-outdoor type a slip-on.

Here's Cecil Beaton and hostess extraordinaire Elsa Maxwell making merry at the Antibes Ball in the south of France circa 1935. Young Beaton's ensemble is worth examination, as it vitiates more dress codes than it follows. Like one of his legendary photographic sittings, where he would imbue a member of the beau monde with a heightened aura of glamour, Beaton has done much the same thing here, dressing down three normally unrelated wearables of unimpeachable taste: a bespoke suit, a classic T-shirt, and a pair of black dress pumps. The future Sir Cecil transcended time, place, and vogue to become like much of what he touched, permanently fashionable.

LEFT:
Cecil Beaton tweaking convention in opera pumps, T-shirt, and suit.

OPPOSITE:
David Niven with two gorgeous children and monogrammed slippers in toe.

*L*ord Chesterfield once described dress as "the style of thought." If that is true, then accessories act as punctuation, sometimes providing a point of exclamation, other times signaling a transition from one colorful phrase to another. Just as no serious writer undermines his prose by neglecting essential commas and dashes, no true elegante ignores the opportunity to better communicate his own style. Here's a Gallic character trying to get a leg up, in this case, two legs, on the competition. Let's hope the femmes appreciate his joie de vivre as much as he seems to.

11

ACCESSORIES: THE MAJOR

IMPORTANCE
OF MINOR THINGS

THE POCKET HANDKERCHIEF

In May 1957, *Apparel Arts*, the men's fashion bible, declared the pocket handkerchief "an index of fashion change." In other words, when elegance periodically returned to the forefront of men's fashion, so did the puff of pattern in man's breast pocket. As with other artifacts of sartorial polish, like French cuffs or a collar bar, the jacket's chest handkerchief adds a finishing touch to the ensemble.

During the early Renaissance, handkerchiefs were considered an essential and functional accessory. As the sixteenth-century intellectual giant Erasmus noted, "To wipe your nose on your sleeve was boorish." Handkerchiefs gradually became more ornate, eventually serving as tokens of a couple's love for each other. Every respectable male carried a handkerchief, and to this day, it is considered a symbol of gentility and social rank.

In eighteenth-century England, the popular snuff habit and its concomitant art of containing a sneeze brought men's hanks into the drawing room. By the nineteenth century, the ordinary American farmer in the Deep South was mopping his brow with a cotton version of the original silk print imported from India. The tradition for colored handkerchiefs gradually galloped southwest along with the cowboy.

The Roaring Twenties saw a sharp rise in decorative handkerchiefs as the Prince of Wales endorsed the fad for bright silks. The more stylish dresser harmonized his hank and tie but did not match its fabric or color. By the thirties, well-dressed men carried two of these apparel staples.

Immediate access to a handkerchief is crucial, whether to head off that unexpected sneeze or to mop up spilled champagne. During World War I, uniformed officers with tightly flapped pockets cached their handkerchiefs within their coat sleeves. As the lounge jacket with its breast pocket supplanted the frock coat, the "one for blowin'" was safely tucked away in the unflapped rear trouser pocket while the "one for showin'" was permanently displayed in the jacket's breast pocket.

Since the advent of the men's lounge suit in the late nineteenth century, all traditionally tailored coats have featured an appro-

From the 1930s right up to today, pocket handkerchiefs remain symbols of sartorial gentility.

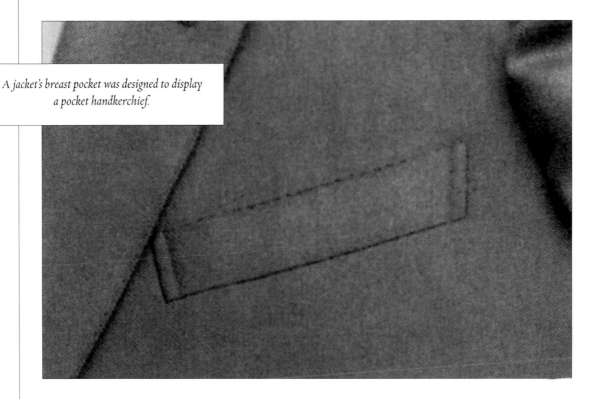

*A jacket's breast pocket was designed to display
a pocket handkerchief.*

priately angled chest pocket not for cigarettes or a pair of reading glasses, but to display a bit of finish. Without some form of pocket rigging, an outside breast pocket appears superfluous, and the outfit incomplete.

In the halcyon period of male elegance, one would be hard pressed to find a photo of one of the "boys" without a properly dressed chest pocket. For each of these Promethean dressers, the pocket hank afforded yet another opportunity to express his own individuality. The pocket handkerchief is part of the minutiae of male style that conveys more than just tradition; the manner in which it is displayed can be as distinguishing as its selection.

On the following page, the Duke of Windsor's sublime chic resided in the ease and naturalness with which he wore clothes, pocket decor included. Though the Duke folded his neatly, he wore them at odd angles within the breast pocket. Other famed fashionables added their own twist: Cary Grant moored his so discreetly that its one corner slants toward his face, contrary to its customary angle pointing out toward the shoulder. Fred Astaire liked to wear his silk squares in a puff fold that he allegedly invented. Gary Cooper sported his as if an afterthought, which hobnobbed happily with his curled-up collars and casually askew neckties.

Male habiliment is a daily intimacy that publicly transmits inscrutably private messages. While permanent fashions like the shepherd's check necktie, the camel-hair polo coat, or black-calf opera pumps are a few of this stylistic language's better-known eye cues, so is the simple white handkerchief. Today, most men avoid donning one, fearing that they will do it incorrectly, badly, or both. Images where the handkerchief is so conspicuous that it appears ready to balloon into space or poised as a table napkin reinforce the average man's dread of the potential faux pas. To the less sophisticated man, the pocket square may seem an effete flourish, yet a casually folded

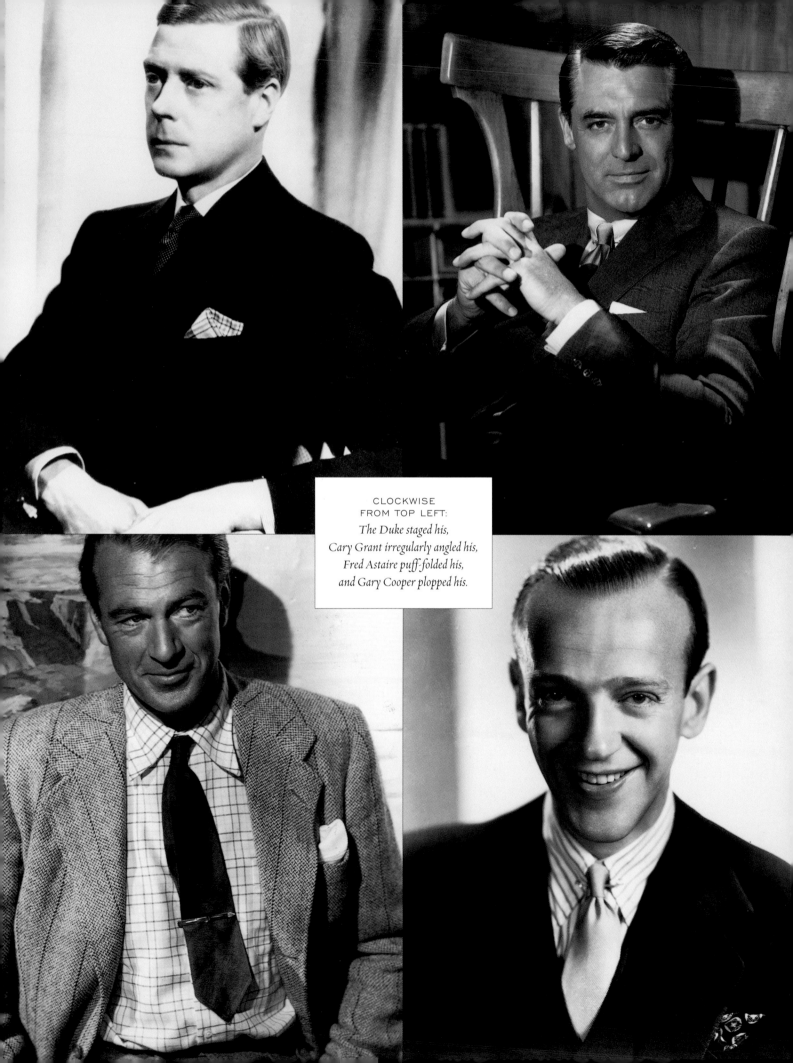

CLOCKWISE
FROM TOP LEFT:
The Duke staged his,
Cary Grant irregularly angled his,
Fred Astaire puff-folded his,
and Gary Cooper plopped his.

white handkerchief offers the quickest and least expensive way to lend a mediocre suit a more expensive look.

Since most dressy suits are paired with solid white, blue, or white ground-patterned dress shirts, this color format affords the simple white handkerchief ample opportunity to provide all the basic pomp needed. Therefore, the first order of business is to learn how to properly sport one of these white numbers.

Though the folding of a hank requires mindful care, like the tying of a bow tie, the most important thing to remember is that its deportment should appear unstudied, effortlessly contributing to the overall aplomb. Particularly because of its stark counterpoint to the dark suit, the white linen square needs to be irregularly arranged, with its points neither mathematically exact nor flattened as if pressed with a rolling iron. Like a good haircut, the best-folded squares are those that do not draw attention to themselves. One way to encourage this lack of contrivance is to angle the hank slightly outward toward the shoulder. This positioning not only reinforces the diagonal lines of the jacket's lapel but accentuates the chest's "V" shape and shoulders' breadth.

Although long considered somewhat passé, the square "TV" fold gained popularity back in the 1950s when several of America's television celebrities began to crease theirs in such a manner. Though President Harry S. Truman, a former haberdasher, adopted the same style, the trend failed to endure, probably because its purposeful symmetry contravened the art form's underlying spontaneity.

The best size for the pocket handkerchief is the 16-to-18-inch square, and, like the subtle hand-stitched edge of a finely tailored jacket lapel, its exposed points and edges need to be rolled and stitched by hand for genuine refinement. Here are a few ways to fold the solid linen square.

*Conspicuous pocket decor
detracts from the whole.*

The stiff "TV" fold.

While the white handkerchief will always be available to fall back upon, let's move on to the solid-colored hank. Although the pocket handkerchief can take its coordinates from several components within the tailored composition, the tie's color and pattern usually determine its choice. Because clothes should help escort the observer's eye toward the face, overtly coordinating, or worse, matching a tie and handkerchief is not only a sign of an unsure dresser but also a sure way to lead the eye across the body and away from the face. Following this logic, a solid-colored handkerchief should only be mated with a patterned necktie, and it ideally should not be of the same color as the ground shade of the necktie. On the opposite page is an editor's informed response to an *Esquire* reader's query, circa 1936.

Mating ties and hanks of different textures also helps keep them from appearing to bracket the chest. As a general rule of thumb, a tie's silken luster calls for a matte pocket square like linen or cotton. Conversely, a wool or linen necktie with a dulled surface requires the upbeat luster of a silk foulard. A foulard hank should fit comfortably into the pocket without

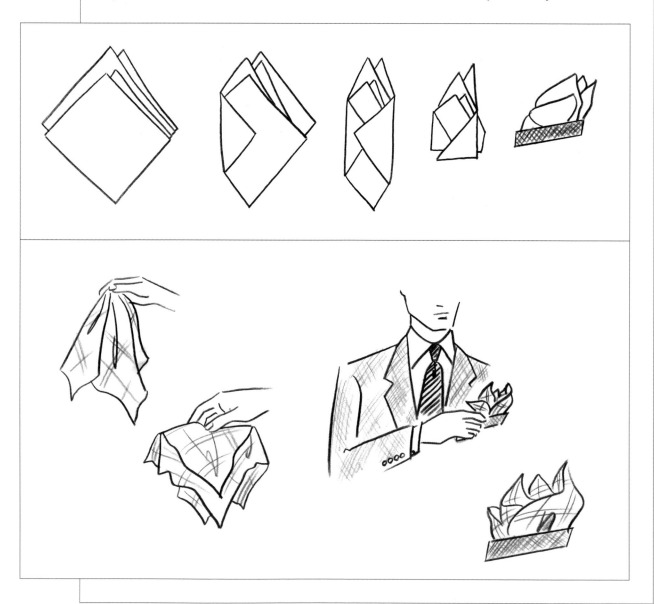

Wearing a matching handkerchief and necktie is a sure sign of an unsophisticated dresser. A solid pocket hank should echo a color in the necktie, shirt, or jacket.

FORMULA FOR HANDKERCHIEFS

Gentlemen:

Kindly suggest colors and designs of handkerchiefs (dress) to wear with combinations of plain color white, blue and brown shirts; with blue and white vertical stripe; with wide light brown stripe on white; and with solid color brown suit; grey suit (dark); or with a sport combination of unmatched coat and linen trousers.

Very truly yours,
Denton, Md., I. F. C.

Breast pocket handkerchiefs may be of similar shade to either the tie worn, its background color, or the colors of its figures or stripes. Alternatively, it may be of a similar shade to the shirt worn, or its stripes or patterns.

If it is possible to secure a handkerchief which contains colors that are both in the shirt and tie, this frequently makes a smart combination.

It is undesirable to match the colors exactly, as this looks studied.

sagging or bulking it up. Before buying one, you might want to test its volume by first plumping it in your breast pocket.

To affect a natural look, the smoother silk squares require a bit more diligence in furling than the perky, stay-at-attention linens. When kitted up in some version of the puff fold, with or without its points showing, the foulard handkerchief should rest in the breast pocket on a slight angle. As with its linen confrere, a diagonal setting fosters a less calculated , more jaunty swank.

Signor Barbera has cleverly configured his printed foulard to stay put. Here we see the maestro of mix first fold it rectangularly in the TV manner before tucking it over once more. This arrangement creates the extra volume and shape needed to remain upright while allowing the patterned border to fall properly to the pocket's outside.

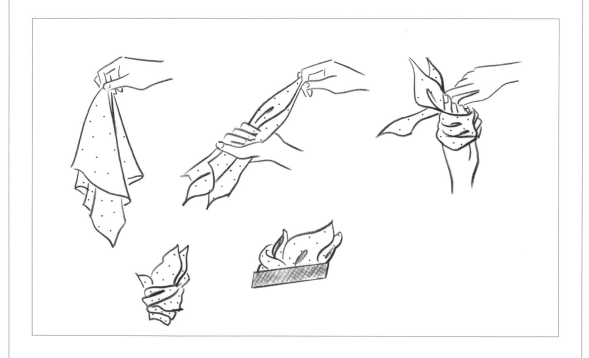

OPPOSITE TOP:
Contrast textures:
dry tweed jacket, wet silk hanky.

ABOVE:
Luciano with friend and pocket hanky
folded his way. (See also page 145.)

And to conclude this pocket pontification on a celebratory note, legendary social critic Lucius Beebe toasts café society's most famous parade ground, El Morocco, by sporting its signature leopard motif.

BELTS AND BRACES

Suspenders have long evinced an air of superiority over belts, like the slight arrogance felt by a man proud to declare himself a golfer but sheepish to admit he likes bowling. The Dandies favored them over the cruder belt, which they considered a Gothic invention; they liked their pantaloons tightly drawn and ultra-trim. France is generally credited as the birthplace of the "gallus," or modern suspender, originally made from fine silk ribbon in a multitude of colors and patterns.

The ancient rivalry between suspenders and belts gave rise to very distinct periods of suspender supremacy. Suspenders were among the first wearables to be ready-made in America, being fashioned and vended to the early colonists by traveling peddlers. Once they no longer seemed to be an artifact for paunchy old men, suspenders, or "braces," as the English called them, reigned supreme in the United States during the years prior to the First World War. However, according to *Esquire's Encyclopedia of 20th Century Men's Fashion*, "The doughboy of WWI wore a coarse yarn belt with his khaki uniform, and when he returned in 1919, he was decidedly belt-conscious." Nevertheless, braces continued to dominate menswear throughout the twenties with the consensus that high-rise, full-cut trousers with pleats draped best when held up by braces.

Despite their overwhelming acceptance, a gent revealed his suspenders only to his valet and the woman he brought home. Exposed braces were a source of embarrassment for men in mixed company, as they were still considered male underwear, a vestige of the Victorian era. However, as lightweight attire emerged during the daring Jazz Age, young men began removing their vests and donning belts. According to *Esquire's Encyclopedia*, during summer months in the late twenties, sales of belts outnumbered suspenders four to one.

During the 1930s, the success of the draped suit coupled with the influence of Savile Row formality returned suspenders to favor, but the time had come for the well-wardrobed man to own a selection of belts. The decade's full and looser-cut trousers encouraged manufacturers to equip them with belt loops. The popularity of knickers and knickerbocker suits also proved a boon to the belt industry. And, as a result of the interest generated in reverse calf footwear by the Prince of Wales, the world's undisputed fashion leader, coordinating shoes and belts soon became the vogue, with chamois and suede belts made to coordinate with this newly fashionable suede sport shoe.

World War II abbreviated the production of both belts and braces. In 1947, *Esquire* magazine, along with some American manufacturers, launched the Bold Look, an attempt to galvanize the American man to coordinate himself from hat to heels in a husky, confident manner. This look featuring large-scale proportion and strong color marked the beginning of the end of England's hegemony over American male dress and America's own descent into the morass of fashion mediocrity. Suspenders soon followed suit.

During the 1950s, *Esquire* followed with another fashion promotion termed "Mr. T." In contrast to the former, more egregious display of self, the Mr. T look was lean and conservative. Men now opted for conformist, anonymous apparel featuring dark and narrow dress belts to support their slimmer, plain-front trousers. This undistinguished style helped to quietly propel the American man into the gray flannel era. As men returned from the war accustomed to the services of a belt, suspenders took a fashion hiatus that extended for thirty years. The hip-held trouser of the Continental, Carnaby Street, Peacock, Pierre Cardin, and Blue Jeans eras relegated braces to the private bastions of the Savile Row aficionado and those remaining enclaves of the East Coast WASP, particularly Wall Street.

The 1980s brought the slow but inexorable return of men's trousers from their lowly positioning on the hip to the sanctuary of the man's waist. A confluence of events conspired to replace the skintight fit of the post–Peacock Revolution with fuller, longer-rise, pleated-front trousers. In the Hollywood movie *American Gigolo,* fashion designer Giorgio Armani introduced his looser, more casual silhouette to the fashion public, making it cool for men to look interested in their appearance. The worldwide success of Ralph Lauren's transplanted Anglomania also helped to educate men in some of the verities of old-world taste.

American men's fashion has slowly begun to reconnect with some of its prewar heritage. Michael Douglas won an Oscar for his portrayal of Gordon Gekko, the reptilian inside trader who favored resplendently striped English braces along with other Savile Row livery, in the 1986 film *Wall Street.* Following Douglas's lead, a new generation of men became enamored of the suspender's inherent smartness, along with cuff links, pocket watches, and all manner of classic male dress ornament.

THE BRACE/SUSPENDER   Oscar Wilde once stated, "Clothes should hang from the shoulder, not from the waist." In this, he is completely correct. A belt can never match the suspender in allowing the pleated trouser to fulfill its aesthetic function. By securing the pant's rear on either side of its back seam while anchoring the trousers' front directly above its two

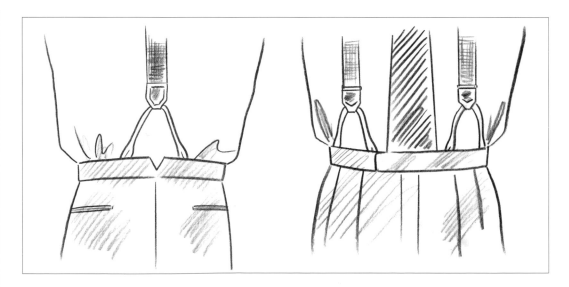

main pleats, suspenders allow the natural pull of gravity to keep the pant's front and back crease taut and in place. The trousers' vertical lines appear more defined and elongated, while the trousers' positioning on the waist imbues the overall look with more elegant proportions.

Originally, braces, like belts, were made in exact sizes such as 32, 34, or 36 inches. A controlled length allowed the suspender's back fork and adjustable front levers to be correctly positioned according to the wearer's height. The front levers are meant to rest in the hollow created by the chest's protuberance and the taper of the waistline. If set above the bottom half of the chest, the double layer of ribbon bulks up the torso, while the gilded buckles wind up distractingly close to the wearer's face. Today, most braces are sold in one size to accommodate taller men, leaving those under 5 feet, 10 inches with buckles up around their necks. However, if a retailer can't accommodate you, a shoe repair shop has the proper machinery to shorten them.

Suspender-worn trousers should have two rear brace buttons equidistant from the trousers' center seam and four in front, two lined up with each of the main pleats (the ones closest to the fly) and another two positioned just forward of the side seam. When suspended correctly, the trousers' main pleat lies smoothly while the front crease retains its knifelike line. Buttons set too far to the side of the trousers' main pleat not only fail to anchor it properly but reduce the tension on the shoulder straps, which then slip from the shoulder. Trousers should always be worn larger at the waist so that they can actually be "suspended" from the shoulders.

Depending on personal taste, brace buttons may be worn on the inside or outside of the waistband. In the early years, when protocol dictated that braces be concealed, the vest or buttoned jacket accomplished that deed handily. Naturally, it was more comfortable to secure them to the outside of the waistband, away from the body. In this portrait of Gary Cooper on the following page, his are affixed to the outside of his waistband, probably because he was wearing a vest. However, when men started going "vestless," the suspender buttons were moved out of sight to the inside of the waistband.

Needless to say, belts should never be worn with suspenders, and belt loops should not accompany trousers with suspender buttons. Even though some men like to alternate a belt or suspenders with one pair of trousers, suspendered pants with empty belt loops is one of those dodges, born of convenience that thwarts both convention and good taste. If suspenders are going to be worn, ideally the pant should be made with an extension waistband, to smooth over the trousers' open front, along with some kind of adjustable side tab for additional waist tension when worn without suspenders. While most rules of dress are made to be bent, this doesn't happen to be one of them.

The finest-quality suspenders are made of rayon, replacing yesteryear's silk. The straps are cut in 1¼-inch or 1½-inch strips. Any narrower and they will bind; any wider and they will feel cumbersome. Braces with clip ends are probably okay for farm work but not under a suit of clothes. Those of necktie silk can be comfortable but are neither authentic nor durable. Any patterns gracing a suspender strap should be woven rather than printed, as only the woven design possesses the strength of character to convey this appurtenance's utilitarian lineage.

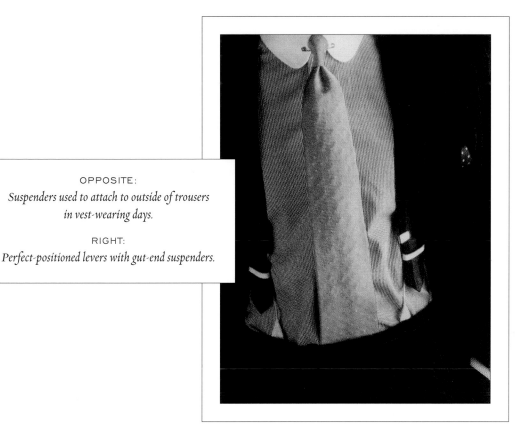

Suspenders with knitted ends work well with formal wear; they are softer, more pliable, and less bulky under a waistcoat or cummerbund. Quality braces are customarily made with machine-made ends in an effort to moderate price. However, England's Albert Thurston still turns out the Rolls-Royce of trouser suspension, especially if you happen to find its hand-finished specimens in white catgut. The white eventually turns cream, imparting an aged patina. Like working-sleeve buttonholes, old-fashioned white catgut is one of those sartorial bona fides connoting an educated palate. Note the correct positioning of this English brace's levers.

BRACE AESTHETICS Since braces share the same vertical plane as the tie, these two elements are coordinated first, followed by the dress shirt and trouser. The experienced dresser will use the brace's color or pattern to frame the ensemble's composition. Solid or striped braces afford more versatility than a patterned pair. As the majority of men favor patterned neckwear, the solid or simple striped ribbon can pick up one of the tie's colors without competing with the tie's design.

Patterned braces (nonstriped) coordinate better with the solid or striped necktie. In this case, they can either repeat one of the tie's colors or look to the trouser or shirt for companionship. However, since suspenders are hidden under the vest or jacket, they enjoy tremendous freedom to complement any, all, or none of the torso's accessories, depending on the practitioner's personal skill and taste.

THE DRESS BELT The choice of dress belt should be dictated first by the shoe's color and then by the hue of the jacket and trouser. Avoid mixing leather colors such as a brown belt with a black shoe and vice versa. Generally, dress belts should be of an equal or darker shade than the suit. A darker belt imparts a dressier look. The more the contrast between belt and trouser, the sportier the result. When well chosen, the color of the dress belt minimizes the transition at the waist without interrupting the linear flow of the coat and trousers'.

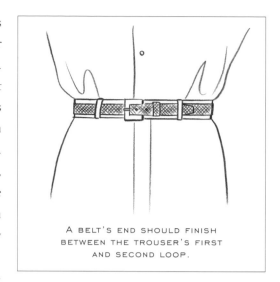

A BELT'S END SHOULD FINISH BETWEEN THE TROUSER'S FIRST AND SECOND LOOP.

Both the dress belt's exterior and underside should be constructed of a fine-grained leather in a width varying from 1¼ inches to 1½ inches. When buckled, its end should be long enough to finish through the trousers' first belt loop without running past the second. Buckles should be simple in design, in either silver or gold, depending on the color of the accompanying jewelry. A monogram, if desired, should be discreet and your own.

Dress belts are distinguished either by the smooth, dulled surfaces of fine-grained leathers, such as pinseal or baby calfskin, or from the subtle luster cast from the luxurious skin of a lizard or baby crocodile. However, here's the Duke using a gilded D-ring buckle to dress down his alligator waist pageantry into a semi–sport belt that accords more with his patterned ensemble's informality. Take note of how by keeping the necktie's top blade short, its underblade has enough length to tuck through the top's underloop and secure the whole arrangement neatly into the waistband. As usual, the Man has managed to turn the ordinary into a mini-portraiture of beauty and personal style.

The Duke appointing his waist as only he could.
(See also the bottom of page 166.)

JEWELRY

Since Victorian times, stylish men have tended to avoid all but the most discreet and useful accessories. With the exception of the finger ring, man's jewelry has been fathered by function—the money clip, tie clip, collar pin, key chain, cuff links, shirt studs, and wristwatch are utilitarian first, decorative second. However, a gentleman can still wear quite an array of jewelry without taxing the limits of good taste.

In pre–World War I days, a hip flask and cigarette case were considered essential accessories for a generation that believed a drink before and a cigarette after were two of the three best things in life. The demise of tobacco has stigmatized even the most stylish of smoking implements, while the flask has gone the way of the swizzle stick. (For the moment, sex is still in fashion.)

The 1980s revived those few sanctioned items of self-embellishment that could signify the wearer's business and social status. With the return of cuff links, suspenders, the collector's wrist- or pocketwatch, and select writing instruments, more men became collectors of vintage jewelry than in any other period of the century.

THE FINGER RING The ring on the male finger began its civilized career among the Egyptians, who linked them together into a necklace as a form of currency. The Greeks and Romans used theirs as official seals, and by the end of the Middle Ages, rings became so popular that there were laws forbidding gentleman with little or no property and men below the rank of knighthood to wear one. During the late Renaissance, the art of heraldry introduced a whole raft of signet rings crested with the family coat of arms. Today's fraternity pins and school rings carry on this tradition. Before World War II, the double-ring wedding ceremony was a rarity, but by the middle 1950s, nearly 90 percent of American husbands had revived the old-world custom of wearing gold or platinum bands.

As for finger jewelry, less is usually more, especially on younger men, who should stick with simple, understated adornment. More ornate, nonmarital finger rings have always been considered gauche and associated with men who make a living by commission.

Organizational rings, class rings, or signet, family crest, and military rings can be worn on either hand. The signet ring is one stylish alternative to the simple wedding band or jeweler's ring. When engraved with the wearer's initials, it suggests that one could hail from that side of the tracks where his forebears called upon their own seal to notarize correspondence or parcel out land.

Bogart in double-ringed understatement.

CUFF LINKS AND DRESS JEWELRY The golden age of jewelry workmanship spanned the mid-nineteenth century to the beginning of the First World War, with the later art nouveau and art deco periods also producing some extraordinary design and craftsmanship. Today, a pair of Edwardian cuff links or an early Cartier tank watch affords a man one of the few opportunities to actually sport an ornament of beauty and antiquity without eliciting the disapproving look of his cohorts. Recounting some fanciful tale tracing the item's origin or recalling its celebrated owner only enhances the mystique of a secondhand collectible.

It has been said that watching a gent undo his cuff links is every bit as sensual for a woman as for a man to hear the zipper slide down the back of a dress. Regardless of its effect, no form of shirtsleeve closure dresses a man's hand better than a well-fitted French cuff accented by the subtle glamour of its buttonhole-covering link.

The most prized examples of cuff-link art have always relied on all four sides to convey their craftsmanship and lineage. To fully exploit the cuff link's decorative potential, each side should bear a design and connect with a chain or link, the reason it is so named. Wearing cuff links that clip on one side exposes the superstructure, and suggests you could afford only the gold or gemstone on the outside. Though it is admittedly easier to link French cuffs with a bar that pushes through its four buttonholes, only half of each hand ends up embellished.

Around 1931, along with the new backdrop of Palm Beach's white dinner jacket, dress studs and matching cuff links with colored stones created a stir. Cuff links with bright, colorful rubies, emeralds, or sapphires are still considered too ostentatious for day wear and reserved for after-dark ceremonies. Sooner or later, every well-dressed man should acquire an antique set of studs. A proper dress set of jewelry includes a pair of double-sided cuff links, two or three matching shirt studs, and no fewer than three waistcoat buttons.

An American invention, the tie holder, or clasp, adds a touch of controlled flourish. A tie clasp keeps the tie under control, preventing it from flapping in the breeze or acting as a napkin while dining. In addition, affixing the tie to the shirt's front helps to maintain the tie's arch in the neckband. Tie bars also add a measure of panache for those shorter men who must tuck their four-in-hands into their trouser tops, à la Fred Astaire. Many aficionados cant theirs downward to affect a more casual air.

In the sixties, tie clasps went into decline, because the stylish wider tie was thrown off center when clipped to the shirt. Today, necktie bars should be simple and understated, though a whimsical one can add a bit of irreverence to the highbrow ensemble.

ABOVE:
Canting the tie clip downward effects a casual élan and an eccentric charm.

OPPOSITE:
Cary Grant in well-fitted French cuffs.

TIMEPIECES AND WRISTWATCHES

Fortunately, we have moved beyond the Victorian taboo on public displays of a timepiece (a true gentleman's concerns were not supposed to include the passage of time). On the "other hand," the actor Peter O'Toole may have carried things a bit too far. When queried as to why he sported a watch on both wrists, he replied, "Life is too short to risk wasting precious seconds glancing at the wrong wrist."

Early etiquette required the pocket watch to accompany the tailcoat, while a thin dress watch was deemed appropriate for dinner clothes or dressier day wear. The attached key chain and pocket watch achieved even greater visibility during the thirties as it became the uniform for both day and evening wear. (See chapter 12, "Formalwear: Black-and-White Etiquette.")

One measurement of a timepiece's quality and dressiness is its thinness. Unfortunately, many men wear Dick Tracy–scaled wristwatches with business suits (along with dress shirts whose cuffs are either too short or too loose at the wrist). Oversize watches do little for the man's overall stylishness and such encumbrances invariably accelerate the fraying of the shirt's cuff.

Of course, the Italians have their own agenda when it comes to wrist decor. Although they don't generally favor the French cuff, they do like their barrel cuffs to fit snugly at the wrists, leaving little room for anything but the most slender wristwatch. Italy's own "Duke of Windsor," Gianni Agnelli, crowned the "Rake of the Riviera" back in the 1950s, has been contravening protocol, sartorial and otherwise, for as long as anyone can remember. "Avocado" resolved this conundrum by sporting his watch over his shirt cuff—after which, all Italy took note.

The unbuttoned Agnelli-style watch over shirt cuff.

THE BOUTONNIERE

In polite society of former days, the wearing of a lapel flower was a symbol of gracious living, a tribute to the lady on your arm, as well as to your host or hostess. Years ago, it was nothing exceptional to see a man wearing a boutonniere. Today, other than flavoring the odd lapel of an "old boy" at "21" or some other elite taproom, coming upon this former grace note of male refinement is a rarity.

A few blades about town still insist on maintaining the old standards by not appearing in coat and tie *sans fleur*. New York artist and dandy Richard Merkin is one of the holdouts. Just as the suit's welt breast pocket was designed to hold a pocket handkerchief, the lapel buttonhole was made to accommodate a flower. Although a boutonniere is no longer expected or even conventional today, more times than not, the man who favors one usually fulfills the promise of gentility suggested by such custom.

Richard Merkin as Himself.

Like the concealed collar button, the stem of the lapel boutonniere should be invisible. Top-drawer clothes are finished with those tailoring details required to properly stage the lapel flower's presentation: a working buttonhole on the jacket's left lapel of not less than 1 inch in length and a loop of thread to hold the flower's stem on the lapel's underside. Resist pinning a flower to the outside of your lapel, regardless of the social occasion. It not only makes you look like an usher at a wedding; it appears as if the flower is wearing you. If your jacket cannot properly accommodate the boutonniere, there is no sense going out of your way to demonstrate it.

Because the boutonniere naturally attracts the eye, its form should be defined simply and distinctly. The best flowers are those that provide a particular spot or button of contrast, like the mini-carnation or the cornflower. The small carnation's base fits into most lapel buttonholes, while its flower is not so large as to overwhelm the average-width lapel. Because its base can sit in the buttonhole without its stem having to be secured in the buttonhole-guard, it can rest flat against the lapel.

There seems to be an impression that the wearing of both a pocket square and boutonniere is the equivalent of gilding the lily. This aberrant notion is supported by neither sartorial tradition nor historical practice. It is perfectly proper to wear both a pocket handkerchief and a flower, as evidenced by many of the gentlemen in this book.

If a man's suit ranks as his most articulate garment during the day, his formalwear should bespeak eloquence at night. When worn knowledgeably, the classic white- and black-tie formal kits present all men at their debonair best. Their black and white formats were intended to act as a foil to the woman's more glamorous, colorful finery.

Fashion has yet to establish surrogates for either of the medleys of male elegance that follow. While the tailcoat and white-tie regalia may no longer be in common use, the dinner jacket accompanied by correct black-tie regiment continues to justify an honored place in the well-stocked city wardrobe.

12

FORMALWEAR:

BLACK-AND-WHITE
ETIQUETTE

TELLING TAILS: THE HISTORY

The modern tailcoat was inaugurated by the famous George Bryan "Beau" Brummell. While other gay dandies of his day wore colorful coats and breeches for evening, the eminent Mr. Brummell donned a navy blue swallowtail coat, black breeches, white waistcoat and shirt, along with a white neck cloth and a 6-inch starched collar of his own invention. Near the end of his reign as the dandy definitive, all Londoners turned to somber clothes and haven't looked back since.

The tailcoat has changed very little since it originated as a riding coat during the latter part of the eighteenth century. Because its long fronts proved cumbersome for walking as well as riding, its double-breasted model was cut back. The modern tailcoat does not button in front and still retains three buttons on either side of its shorter front with a vent and buttons on the back, a vestige of a time when they were used to attach a sword or button back the bottom of the coat when walking or riding.

As the quintessential symbol of the Englishman's famous formality, this garment represents the extra standard set by the British gentleman for male elegance. All that was needed was for the tailor to apply its proportions to the wearer's frame, and presto—average men turned into movie stars like Adolphe Menjou, one of Hollywood's leading paragons of fashion.

THE TAILCOAT

Tailcoats were once akin to Fords: it was a point of pride that the model seldom changed. Cut on a straight line to the knee with the front finishing about the hipbone, the tailcoat fits snugly to the chest as if it were buttoned. A man of average height looks best in a tailcoat featuring some fullness across the chest. Its obligatory peaked lapels should not be skimpy in breadth and should be faced in either silk grosgrain or satin with a cloth collar. The jacket's back length should rest about an inch below the bend of the knee. The sides of the coat curve slightly over the hips, running down to the tails with nothing but the tailor's masterful yet unobtrusive art to hold them to the figure.

The coat's collar should cover the shirt collar's rear stud and the rear band of bow tie while revealing at least a ¾ inch of the wing collar. When one is dancing with elbows raised, the evening coat must not pull up to reveal the waistcoat's side baseline. The dress coat's front points should finish below the natural waistline so that no part of the white waistcoat extends below it. The tailcoat's sleeves are cut narrow, yet not so tapered that they cannot accommodate the width of the formal shirt's starched single cuff. Their length should be short enough to allow the shirt's cuff to extend about a ¾ inch. The jacket sleeve carries four closely set buttons.

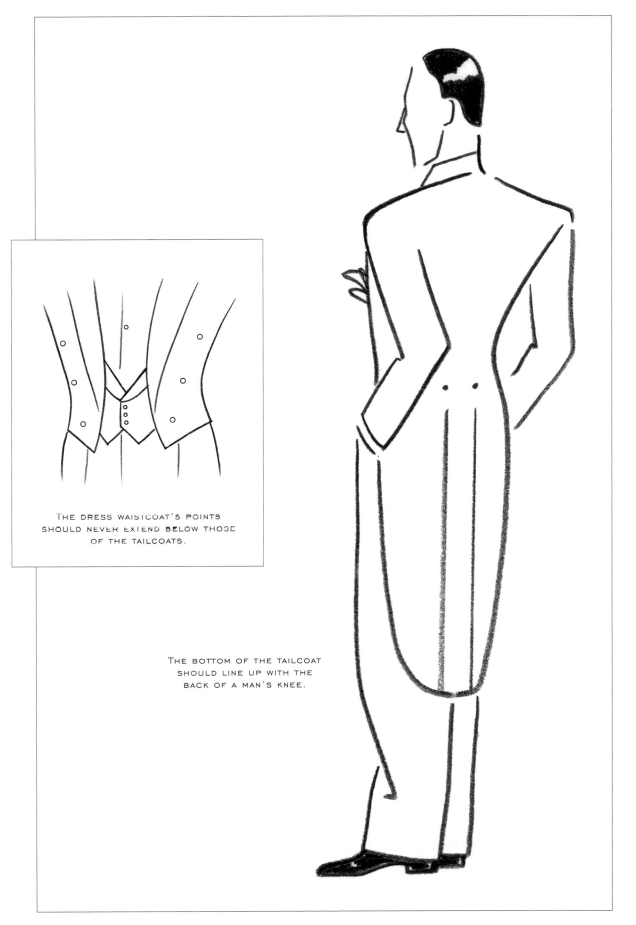

THE DRESS WAISTCOAT'S POINTS
SHOULD NEVER EXTEND BELOW THOSE
OF THE TAILCOATS.

THE BOTTOM OF THE TAILCOAT
SHOULD LINE UP WITH THE
BACK OF A MAN'S KNEE.

Fred wears a dress vest designed originally
for the Prince of Wales.

THE FULL-DRESS WAISTCOAT

Formal dress dictates a starched white bird's-eye backle (piqué) waistcoat in either single- or double-breasted design. The most traditional model is the single-breasted shawl collar with three-button closure. The bottom edges of the dress vest's lapels can either be square, rounded, or blunted, with the front generally ending in two symmetrical points, though there is some flexibility here, as demonstrated by Mr. Top Hat, White Tie, and Tails himself, Fred Astaire. Here he sports a replica of the model that the royal shirt maker Hawes and Curtis had done up especially for His Highness, the Prince of Wales, which, as legend goes, they politely refused to make for Master Fred.

The dress waistcoat's deep "V" opening must be cut to perfection for its narrow front to cover the shirt's bib-front bottom and trousers' waistband without its own bottom extending beyond the tailcoat's end points. To prevent the vest from pulling up, the correctly tailored version provided a fastening tab that buttoned to the trousers' inside waistband.

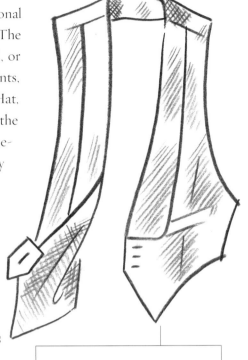

Fine dress vests have a tab that attaches to the trousers.

Nothing so quickly gives the well-dressed man an attack of the vapors as the sight of the waistcoat showing beneath the fronts of a tailcoat.

FULL-DRESS TROUSER

ailored from matching cloth, the dress trouser requires a longer-than-normal rise and suspenders to sit properly under the high-cut tailcoat and short-waisted dress vest. It wasn't for nothing that Menjou titled his autobiography *It Took Nine Tailors*. Observe the height of his waistcoat, which helps sets the stage for the costume's sublime proportions. High-class dress trousers usually angled their pleats toward the fly to distribute the fullness forward with vertical on-seam side pockets so as not to disturb the coat's line should a man choose to thrust a hand into one. Full-dress trousers are cuffless, break slightly at the instep, and should be trimmed with two narrow plain braids set close together.

THE FORMAL DRESS SHIRT AND BOW TIE

he formal dinner shirt is another item that brooks no deviation from tradition. Designed to further refine the wearer's visage, it features a stiff (preferably separate to attach) high-standing wing collar, a stiff bib front that accommodates either one or two studs, (depending on the wearer's height), and starched single cuffs.

The width of the shirt's bosom, a biblike design in boiled plain linen or stiff piqué, is not to extend under the suspender straps, while its length needs to stop short of the trousers' waistband. If its starched front extended into the trousers' tops, when a man sat down, it would billow like a sail in full wind. Like the dress vest, the well-made formal shirt has a tab that affixes to a designated button on the trousers' inside waistband.

The set of the wing collar and bow tie is key to this ensemble's preordained elegance. Designed to sit high on the neck, the dramatic wing collar needs to show ¾ inch above the tailcoat's rear collar, or ¼ inch more than the semi-formal turndown collar shirt. Whether in single semi-butterfly

The height of the tailcoat's waistline is the linchpin of this ensemble's distinctive elegance.

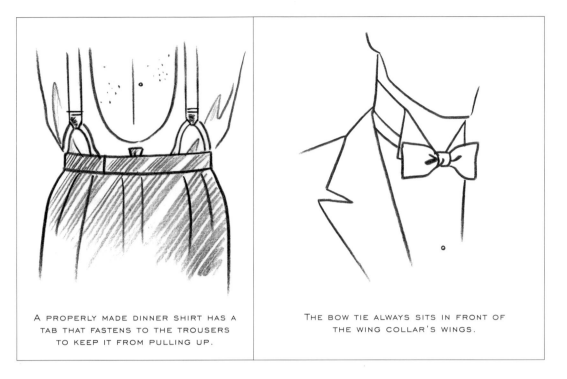

A PROPERLY MADE DINNER SHIRT HAS A
TAB THAT FASTENS TO THE TROUSERS
TO KEEP IT FROM PULLING UP.

THE BOW TIE ALWAYS SITS IN FRONT OF
THE WING COLLAR'S WINGS.

or batwing shape, the white piqué bow's ends are always worn in front of the wing-collar tabs, never behind them. Aside from the fact that the stiff wings of the original separate collars could never have fit over the knotted bow, the tabs' spring helped to push the bow tie forward.

Since these studs, straps, and buttons need to be precisely lined up, the white-tie kit might seem to be some form of Victorian bondage. To the contrary, when appropriately tailored, the outfit is surprisingly comfortable. And, not having to worry about the clothes staying put, a man can relax and concentrate on more important things, such as the location of the bar.

STUD SENSE

Investing in a matching set of antique dress studs crafted during the late nineteenth or early twentieth century in mother-of-pearl, 18-karat gold, or other precious materials for the dress waistcoat, formal shirtfront, and cuff would be money well spent. A slim gold pocket watch with fine key chain would augment any formal presentation. Completing the picture, dress hosiery should be black, above the calf, in silk or a fine-ribbed cotton lisle with or without clocks. For formal footwear, opera pumps or plain-toe oxfords in black calf or patent leather are mandated.

Headwear options include the collapsible silk opera hat or top hat paired with a single- or double-breasted dress chesterfield overcoat in black or midnight blue, with matching velvet collar.

Obviously, any coat worn for formalwear must be long enough to cover the tailcoat's bottom, which is why the longer the man's coat, the dressier it tends to look. Perhaps the most soigné of all formal coats is the slightly shorter-length, A-shape, single-breasted, fly-front model with raglan shoulders, peaked lapels, and velvet collar. With white braces underneath and corresponding white silk muffler, gloves, linen handkerchief, and mini-carnation, swellegance is never far behind.

SEMI-FORMALWEAR

Adolphe Menjou was once asked whether he thought the dinner jacket would endure. He replied, of course it would, since this last vestige of upper-class dress was a symbol of gracious living that paid tribute to the lady on your arm as well to the evening's host.

As the name suggests, the early dinner jacket was exactly that, a less formal dining ensemble worn in the privacy of one's home or club. The original design was created during the latter nineteenth century at the request of the English Prince (later King) Edward VII, who wanted a more comfortable alternative to dine in than the swallowtail evening coat with its bothersome tails. Here is royal tailor Poole's ledger recording the Prince of Wales's original order for the first dinner jacket.

The consensus is that the first model of this cutoff tailcoat was single-breasted with a roll collar (shawl) in black worsted wool with black silk facings on the lapels. This same jacket model had been sported as a separate "smoking jacket" in silk velvet by the English gentry. Its silk facings were lifted from the tailcoat's lapels. Victorian ladies did not smoke and insisted that their husbands confine this noxious activity and jacket to another room. From that time through the early 1920s, black-tie attire was deemed acceptable in the privacy of one's home or club, whereas the tailcoat remained obligatory for polite society in public.

For the low-down how the King's personal toilette managed to acquire the name "tuxedo," please refer to the glossary. However, the term "tuxedo," often abbreviated to "tuck," or even worse, "tux," is thankfully confined to the United States. Generally, it is correctly termed the dinner jacket both here and abroad, and rarely called a tuxedo, even in Tuxedo Park, New York.

The 1920s produced menswear's first unofficial designer, the Prince of Wales, later King, and eventually the Duke of Windsor. Clothes-conscious and a bit of a maverick, he was determined to throw off the court-ruled stuffiness of his father's generation. Even before his abdication in 1936, the Prince had sworn off the boiled-front evening shirt and separate stiff wing collar for the more comfortable pleated-front dinner shirt with soft, attached turndown collar. He also pioneered the backless formal waistcoat for wear in warmer climes. By the end of

		From folio		188	17	2	—
12	No 2926	A blue silk Smoking Jacket lined silk Sandringham Silk Collar & Cuffs		ac 181	13	8	.
		A pair " " Trousers lined silk		"			
		Packing Case		"	.	3	.
		Altering repairing & pressing Pea coat	m/ ad 55				
		New Silk breastfacings		"	1	15	.
		" " Velvet Collar					
		Altering repairing, cleaning & pressing frock coat	m/	"		5	6
		New cloth collar, Altering reps, cleang & pressg Frock coat		"			
		New Silk breastfacings			1	15	.
		Altering & pressing frock coat	m/	"	—	5	6
		" " " "	m/	"	—	5	6
		Finedrawing & pressing Blk Trousers	/	"		3	6

the 1930s, with the Prince's coterie of royal swells legging around in the latest semi-formal trappings, the dinner jacket began to replace the tailcoat.

No other era could have produced such a sartorial success. Each step of the dinner jacket's evolution was measured by the perfection of the outfit it intended to replace—the grandfather of male elegance, the tailcoat and white tie. Since the culmination of the dinner jacket's design in the late 1930s, men's fashion has yet to improve upon the genius of its original design or the unimpeachable refinement of its accoutrements. The new dinner jacket projected a level of stature and class equal to that of its starched progenitor, albeit while providing considerably more comfort.

Henry Pool's ledger recording the first order for a dinner Tuxedo jacket.

DINNER JACKET DOGMA

As the direct descendant of the tailcoat, the single-breasted dinner jacket with upward-sweeping peaked lapels invests all men with prominence and height. With only one waist button to fasten, it necessitates a waistcoat or cummerbund to cover the trousers' exposed waistband.

For those who don't object to wearing their jacket buttoned, the double-breasted dinner jacket offers equal distinction while dispensing with the additional layer of a waistcoat or cummerbund. Flanked by two of café society's more soigné souls are satin-revered husband Cole Porter (*right*) with his wife, Linda, and Doug Fairbanks Jr. in grosgrain finery.

While the shawl-collar dinner jacket conveys a somewhat more old-world image than the peaked lapel, the curve of its lapel tends to favor the more angular physiognomy. Noël throws architecture to the wind as he affects that old-boy panache.

Early off-the-peg English tuxedos were faced in glossy satin. At one point, the Savile Row establishment decided that the dulled ribbed silk grosgrain conveyed a more custom-tailored pedigree. However, as long as one opts for a single- or double-breasted model trimmed in satin or grosgrain, with either shawl or peaked lapels, permanent fashion is assured.

Dinner jacket models that deviate from these four classic archetypes or boast such informal embellishments as notched lapels or flap pockets devolve into sartorial oxymorons, convoluting both the form's aesthetic logic and its promise of timeless elegance. The whole idea of a formal suit is to distinguish itself from the notch-lapel business suit, not replicate it.

The balance of the proper dinner jacket's detailing remains fairly straightforward: a welt breast pocket for a white linen handkerchief and a working buttonhole on the left lapel to hold a boutonniere. Double-besomed (jetted) hip pockets can be either plain or trimmed in the same silk as the lapel. Like the tailcoat, the single-breasted dinner jacket takes one waist button and four closely set

ABOVE:
The S.B. dinner jacket with peaked lapels.
OPPOSITE:
*Cole Porter and Doug Fairbanks Jr.
in D.B. dinner jackets.*

Noël Coward in a shawl-collar suavity.

sleeve buttons, which can either be simple black horn or covered in the lapel's silk facing (either grosgrain or satin to match).

Since most formal affairs are held in climate-controlled environs, a finished or unfinished mid-weight worsted ($9^{1}/_{2}$ to $10^{1}/_{2}$ ounces) should take a man comfortably through three seasons of the year. Like the tailcoat, dinner clothes are trimmed in facings of varying degrees of luster; therefore, so as not to over-state the sheen quotient, the dinner jacket's base cloth should be in a dulled or matte finish. Subtle textured weave effects such as baratheas and mini-herringbones, or quiet variegated effects avoid affectation while adding surface interest to the formal ensemble.

When it comes to color, the base worsted cloth is limited to black or midnight blue. In the 1930s, midnight blue began to replace black, because under artificial light the dark blue retained its richness while black sometimes gave off a rust or artificial cast. The term "midnight blue" conjured up images of the shank of the evening, when romance and rambunctiousness were in full swing. While midnight blue dinner coats originally took matching facings, black grosgrain or satin trim-mings have been worn since the thirties.

Back in the days when the bon vivant required more than one dinner jacket, it was not unusual to find him donning a lightweight version in mohair or silk. Today, the dulled sheen of baby mohair and fine worsted wool is one of the few tasteful exceptions to the rule that normally consigns shiny clothes to the parvenu side of the tracks. Here is Italy's Gianni Agnelli swathed in silkenlike mohair dinner wear.

ABOVE:
Midnight-blue formalwear.

LEFT:
Signiore Agnelli shines.

DINNER JACKET ALTERNATIVES

As one ascends the social ladder, with its increasing demands for dress up, the odd or separate dinner jacket surfaces. Paired with the conventional formal trouser, this nonmatching jacket surrogate is often a variation on the velvet-smoking-jacket theme and traditionally reserved for less grand affairs. So long as its design conforms to one of the four classic models mentioned earlier, its fabric can flirt with adventure. Escorting the Duchess of Kent from his London house to her awaiting chariot, our man Fairbanks sports a satin-faced velvet smoking jacket and monogrammed slippers in toe.

Affecting an offbeat aplomb that only the genuine English toff can muster, artist and photographer Cecil Beaton squires Lee Radziwill to the English premiere of *Coco*. Between Beaton's own formal garniture and their matching velvet frocks, the couple radiates glamour.

LEFT:
D. Fairbanks in velvet smoking jacket and monogrammed slippers.

RIGHT:
Cecil Beaton dressing for himself.

THE BLACK-TIE WAIST

The underpinning of high-class dinner clothes was originally designed to be invisible. Dress studs hid the evening shirt's stud holes, and silk bands covered the formal trousers' outside seams. Following in the tailcoat's footsteps, the single-breasted dinner jacket requires the services of the dress vest or cummerbund to conceal and smooth over the edges of the shirt's bosom and the exposed trouser waistband. The faux-waistband dress trouser not only undermines the form's integrity but looks "bush league," to borrow a phrase from the days when this novelty originated.

The single-breasted dinner jacket with peaked lapels, like its tailcoat predecessor, synchronizes better with the dress waistcoat, since the vest's lower points echo those of the coat lapels above. While the shawl-lapel dinner jacket can accommodate either style of waist decor, the cummerbund's curve harmonizes particularly well with the lapels' rounded shape. In order to keep theater tickets at the ready, better-quality cummerbunds have a little pocket stitched behind their deepest pleat, which is why the cummerbund is always worn with its folds pointing upward.

Originally, the matching black waistcoat was imperative with a dinner jacket. Once that royal tweaker of tradition decided to toss one of his white-tie weskits into the formal ring, the rest, as they say, is history. Naturally, the Prince's imprimatur brought overnight acceptance to the white-waistcoat and black-dinner-jacket combination.

Proust once said that elegance was never far away from simplicity. The novelty of an odd-colored waistcoat or patterned cummerbund is to be encouraged, so long as it's limited to this single flourish. Injecting more than one contrasting accessory into the two-color format fragments its formal integrity into smaller, less important pieces. Furthermore, since the black-tie regiment already borders on the predictable, donning a bow tie and matching vest or cummerbund imposes on the wearer an even more contrived, prepackaged look.

By limiting your selection to only those components predominantly bordered by black, such as the waistcoat, cummerband, dress shirt, or pocket square, you have ensured that this single dollop of dissonance remains a part of the whole. However, when the contrast bow tie is thrown in under the chin, without being framed by a dark color, it stands out on its own, making the

*Curved cummerbund with
soft pleated dinner shirt.*

neck look gift-wrapped. It also distracts from the desired focal point—the face. Some aficionados embrace colored or patterned hosiery as their personal badinage, a practice recommended for only the more assured dresser.

The tonalities capable of enriching this already dramatic, high-contrast composition are those registering an equal degree of pluck and richness, such as plum, bottle green, scarlet wine, and gold. If a pattern is chosen, it should be a simple two-color design in which one color is either black or white, like a classic black-and-white polka dot or a burgundy-and-white houndstooth.

Injecting more than one contrasting accessory into the two-color format dilutes its formal integrity.

FORMALWEAR TROUSERS

Dinner jacket trousers adhere to the same principles of proportion and styling as full-dress trousers, with one exception: a slightly wider single decorative band replaces the formal trouser's two small strips on its outer leg seams. If the jacket's lapel facings are satin, the texture of the trousers' side trim must follow suit. However, if the jacket's lapels are trimmed in grosgrain, a matching grosgrain or a slightly narrower band with a raised-rib effect are equally correct. Like the tailcoat trouser, its bottom is never cuffed. The Fred Astaire–Ginger Rogers movie *Shall We Dance?* contains an amusing depiction of the cuffless tradition in which Astaire's band members try to side-track his wedding by convincing him that the latest fashion requires that dress trousers be cuffed.

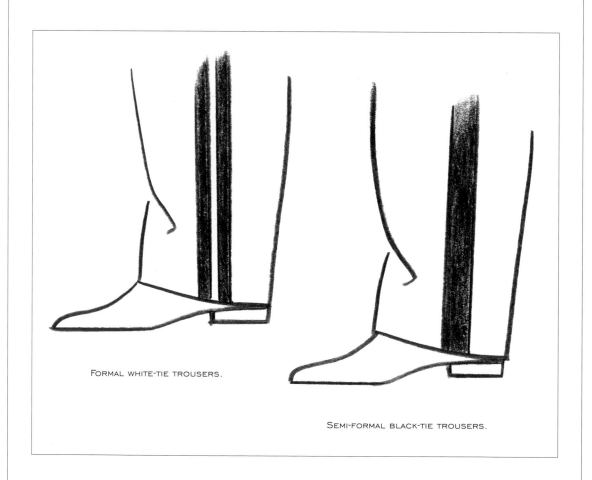

FORMAL WHITE-TIE TROUSERS.

SEMI-FORMAL BLACK-TIE TROUSERS.

THE BLACK-TIE DRESS SHIRT

There are two equally correct genres of dress shirts for the black-tie ensemble. The first and more formal is the white-tie evening shirt with starched wing collar, as described earlier. The second is the unstarched, turndown collar shirt with soft pleated fronts and double cuffs, yet another sartorial contribution from the "Prince of Wales."

While either formal shirt does justice to the four classic dinner jacket models, the wing collar's high starched points harmonize particularly well with that of the single-breasted, peaked-lapel dinner jacket. Like the full-dress formal shirt, top-drawer turndown-collar evening shirts, whether pleated or marcella fronts, are constructed with a bib-type design. Turndown-collar dinner shirts always take French cuffs and two or three studs, the correct number dictated by the wearer's height.

In spite of the wing collar's recent resurgence, most of today's ready- or custom-made versions make their wearers look like mad scientists; with one twist of the head and the collar's limp, diminutive points tend to roll over the bow tie. Originally, the stiff wing collar came separately, offering a variety of different heights and contours that ensured its broad-winged presence framed all men's faces in regal splendor. Unfortunately, once fashion mandated ready-to-wear versions, its attached collar became homogenized for broader appeal, thus forfeiting most of its function and all of its individual refinement. It's no wonder that several years back, the wing collar's emasculated remains were pushed aside to make way for the transient and frivolous collarless formal shirt with a fancy button closure.

Bottom right is an example of another mixed metaphor, a pleated front dinner shirt with a wing collar—a mutt of a garment if there ever was one.

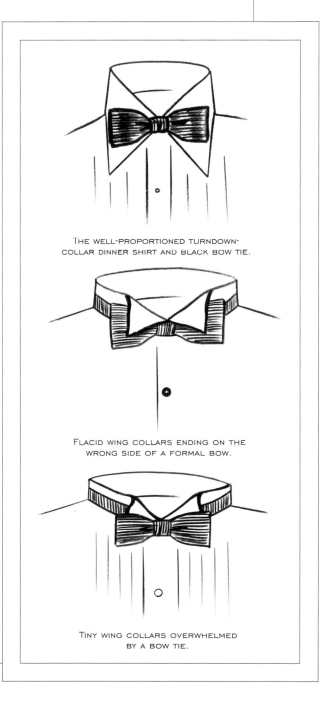

THE WELL-PROPORTIONED TURNDOWN-COLLAR DINNER SHIRT AND BLACK BOW TIE.

FLACID WING COLLARS ENDING ON THE WRONG SIDE OF A FORMAL BOW.

TINY WING COLLARS OVERWHELMED BY A BOW TIE.

*The authentic Windsor knot—
the Duke's own personal style.
The beau's own bow.*

THE BLACK BOW TIE

The semi-formal black silk bow's texture is governed by the jacket's lapel facings—a satin bow for satin facings, a ribbed or pebble-weave variation for grosgrain facings. Its butterfly or batwing shape is a matter of personal preference. While most men cringe at the thought of having to knot their own bow tie, it's rare to come upon a well-turned-out gent who cannot. A lack of geometrical perfection in the finished knot is both desired and important, humanizing the ensemble and making it look more individual. (See the section on bow ties in chapter 8, "Neckwear.") The bow's width should not extend beyond the collar's wings, the spread collar's perimeter, or the man's face. If a special Windsor knot could be correctly attributed to the Duke, it would be the one he employed for his bows rather than the bulbous confection for long ties erroneously credited to him.

FASHIONING THE FORMAL ANKLE AND FOOT

The formal shoe is as distinct from other male footwear as the dinner jacket is from a suit. Like other validations of white- or black-tie gentility, the formal shoe must imbue the dress trouser with a certain swank while affording the foot enough lightness and comfort to help dance the night away. Sometimes shiny, sometimes appointed with a silk bow, yet always appearing more like a slipper than a shoe, the formal shoe is the only appropriate way to finish off the formal ensemble.

As a vestige of male court dress, the opera pump remains the sole item of men's fashion to enter the twenty-first century pretty much as it left the nineteenth. With ribbed-silk bow, the opera slipper strikes the less sophisticated as somewhat effeminate. This is unfortunate, since it has been the foundation of formal footwear since the turn of the previous century. The more soigné tend to choose the dulled calf version over its patent leather peer.

Although the more conventional of the two classic formal shoes, the patent leather low-cut oxford did not make its debut on the dance floor until the early 1930s, well after the evening pump's entrée. With its plain toe, closely cropped soles, delicately beveled waist, and glovelike fit, this formal lace-up is both elegant and practical for dancing. Notice this bespoke shoe's silk laces, an old-world furbelow rarely seen today.

The more one finds himself donning dinner clothes for private occasions, the more likely he is to adopt several alternative styles of footwear. The club-elegant opera pump and Albert slipper models have long been used as formal shoes. The most classy version of the latter are those made in a dark velvet color and embroidered with a monogram of the wearer's initials or a family or club crest. (See page 192.) The ideal ankle wrappings to augment all this polish are of solid black silk, a fine-ribbed, over-the-calf cotton-lisle, or garter-assisted hose with either a self-color or contrasting clocklike design.

Classic opera pumps and classic formal hose.

Patent dress oxford with silk laces.

BLACKOUT FOR EVENING

The white mess jacket represented the first radical change in male evening wear and received such broad national acceptance that it was immediately adopted for the uniforms of bellhops and orchestra members. While it resembled a tailcoat cut off at the waistline, the mess jacket was not flattering to many figures, particularly those that didn't happen to resemble that of Adonis.

The American male was ripe for something along more conventional lines that retained the comfort and color of the mess jacket. In 1934, *Esquire* turned the nightmare of warm-weather formality into a midsummer night's dream, unveiling the white dinner jacket with shawl collar. Presented in both single- and double-breasted models, it received accolades from habitués of exclusive resorts everywhere.

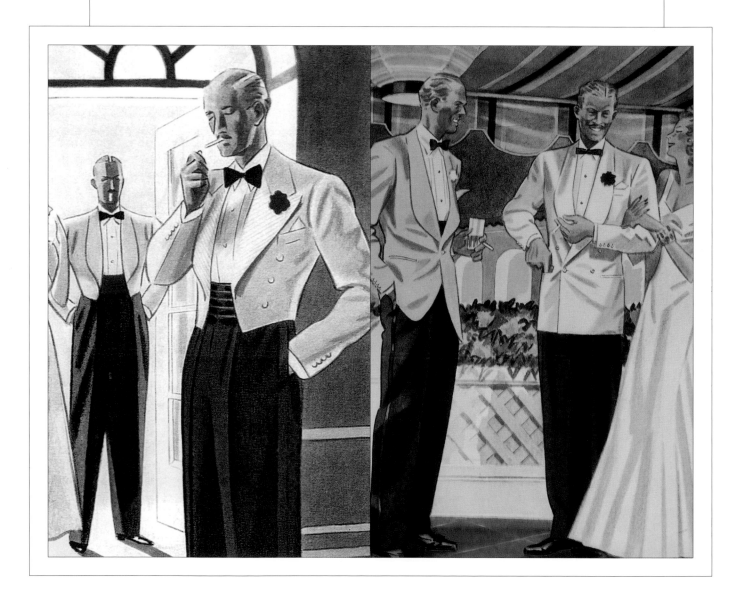

Once white broke the color barrier, other colored dinner jackets soon followed. Tan first gained popularity in a new color called "bisque," as seen here in the company of this blond-on-blond consortium. With men back in town now wanting to show off their recent suntanned complexions, the new colors were welcome additions to the cause, as the artist Leslie Saalburg's rendering *(above left)* of masculine formal elegance on the French Riviera brilliantly portrays.

We will never know whether this blazer-trimmed tuxedo *(above right)* was inspired by the artist, *Esquire*'s fashion staff, or an actual Palm Beach *elegante*. What an extraordinarily stylish idea! Reversing the white top and midnight blue bottom was the next logical step in evening wear's informal march.

Occasions calling for the cutaway and its attendant accessories are few and far between. More relevant might be to suggest the proper dress for a wedding or ceremonial outing, when formal attire is optional. As the fellow congratulating the serviceman already knows, turning up for such an occasion clad in a solid navy suit, white dress shirt, navy-and-white shepherd's check tie, white handkerchief, and black calf shoes was—and still is—a pretty safe and stylish bet.

Non-black-tie ceremonial attire.

Getting dressed for business used to be a no-brainer. You showered, shined, and slipped into your suit, one of three or four navy or gray, solid or striped, time-honored ensembles. The option was yours. It was hard to make too big a fashion gaffe donning a suit.

But in this era of workwear glasnost, the rules have loosened up. The allure and quick riches of the Internet start-ups in the nineties encouraged the Eastern Establishment to begin taking their fashion cues from Silicon Valley rather than Savile Row. Business dress standards that had endured for generations all but vanished, creating a patchwork of appearance standards never before seen within the American workplace.

13

BUSINESS

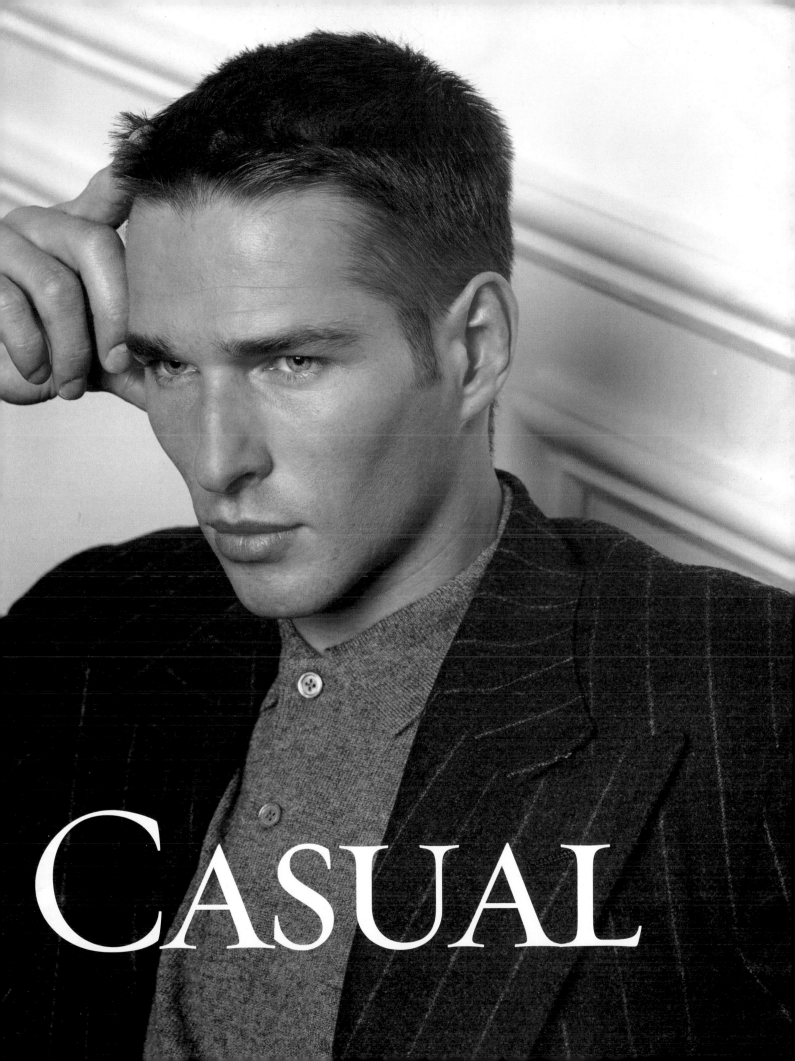

CASUAL

In the rush to change from the classic work paradigm to the new casual one, a dress-down free-for-all ensued, leaving many men struggling to find a style of office attire that didn't jeopardize their business credibility.

The emergence of cravatless attire in the executive office marks the single most important change in business fashion in our time. Except for blue-collar labor or taming the West, the collar, cravat, waistcoat, and dress coat have been the cornerstone of male business dress for nearly two hundred years. With the democratization of corporate dress codes taking on a life of its own, casual-Friday clothing has now replaced traditional business dress at least one day a week for 90 percent of American office workers.

Relaxing the corporate dress code was intended to diminish those hierarchical barriers that discouraged a more collegial working atmosphere. Either out of fear of appearing old-fashioned or not wanting to place themselves in the path of what seemed like a cultural tidal wave, management gurus eagerly jumped on the dress-down bandwagon. Having embraced the casual trend with such zeal, they neglected to analyze whether the Master of the Universe's new clothes made much sense.

Regardless of its virtues, business casual has complicated the lives of men who once thought themselves immune to fashion. While elevators are jammed with open-collar shirts and casual slacks, most executives keep a spare suit and a couple of neckties in their office for impromptu meetings. At most companies, old-economy clothes (meaning suits and ties) are still mandatory for meetings with old-economy clients. Trying to juggle two dress modes while mixing internal work with client-facing work has left many men with a sinking feeling that the old rules have been thrown out, with nothing to put in their place.

Although the initial evidence is largely anecdotal, the dress-down phenomenon appears to be slacking off. The tech-sector meltdown removed some of the motivation behind casual dress. There are growing indications that dressier clothes are creeping back into the workplace.

While cynics are still not convinced of a true uprising toward more polished dressing, one thing is certain: The dot-com craze that took off like a rocket and fell like a rock altered the landscape both culturally and sartorially. The onset of casual Friday followed shortly thereafter by corporate casual can be viewed as a business guy's grassroots movement, the outgrowth of his desire to look and feel comfortable. Consumer-driven style has come of age, modernizing the male closet with its message of function and comfort. With a new fashion vacuum to fill, casual clothes now hang next to suits, dressing each other up or down as the occasion demands. To believe that the comfy shirt is now about to succumb to the starchy one is a dream. In other words, it's going to be tough to turn back the clock.

The challenges posed by a casual corporate climate should not distract men from the larger goal of becoming more literate about what their business clothes mean. Because client expectations continue to set dress policy for most well-managed businesses, making one's daily dress more client-sensitive should be just as important as honing one's language and presentation skills, which many ambitious executives dedicate themselves to throughout their careers. Since clothes are the most powerful nonverbal tools of communication, why shouldn't they become an effective force in one's overall business strategy? And with the corporate-casual phenomenon helping to further remove any stigma from men putting more effort into what they wear, the time has never been more propitious.

In enlisting one's attire for the larger business mission, the ideal of "business-appropriate attire" should be extended to include the dress-down option. Whether matching the style of the client with a less-formal outfit to make him or her feel more at ease or calling out the pinstripes and brogues to commandeer the situation, "business-casual dressing" should be embraced rather than eschewed as one more weapon in the businessman's arsenal. The result should be a business-appropriate style of dress and a wardrobe capable of seamlessly seeing one from work to weekend to anything in between.

GUIDELINES FOR BUSINESS-APPROPRIATE DRESS

- The first measuring stick for business attire should be cleanliness. Clients prefer their professionals looking well groomed. Casual dressing is no excuse for looking sloppy, rumpled, or unwashed.

- When in doubt as to the correct attire for a specific business meeting, opt for a suit. Dress-down wear is still relatively new to the corporate arena and still not perceived as professional and powerful as the classic business ensemble.

- If unsure about an occasion's level of formality, overdressing is the safer bet. By dressing up, not only do you pay a compliment to your client, cohort, or company, but you always have the option of removing one or more articles of clothing.

- Dress in line with your superiors and never more casually than your subordinates. Be careful not to dress in such a relaxed manner that you no longer look like someone who can become an authority figure.

- Whatever clothes you choose to wear to work, make sure they have the same characteristics that you look for in a fine suit: good material, fine workmanship, and excellent fit. Buy the best quality you can afford. Like one's education, clothing is an investment in your future.

Business-casual attire is typically broken down into multiple categories denoting varying degrees of formality, such as active casual, sporty casual, or smart casual, as the trend is known in England. In the interest of simplicity and structure, I am going to divide the enterprise into two camps, dress-up business casual and dress-down business casual. The dress-up business category ranges from the dressed-down suit to an ensemble of separates formed around the tailored jacket exclusive of a necktie. With this jacket-driven option, the mission is to communicate the same degree of authority and professionalism as the traditional business uniform but on a less starchy wavelength.

Alternatively, dress-down business casual is that two-piece office attire ranking below the jacket-oriented outfit in dressiness but above the pressed-jeans and sport-shirt look. Contrary to what Wall Street or the Wharton School may have naively reasoned, by jettisoning the suit and necktie uniform, they elevated the khaki and polo shirt uniform into the new common dress-down denominator. While corporate casual attire was intended to be a more comfortable and less formal alternative to the classic suit and necktie regime, it was also supposed to convey an image of businesslike intention. But contrary to popular thinking, no combination of dress pant and shirt will ever tip the authority scale at any weight approaching that of the classic business suit ensemble.

With that noted, there are many ways to make the trouser-shirt paradigm more executive-looking and businesslike, which will be addressed later. However, dress-up business casual offers the higher probability of remaining both sartorially and socially relevant over the longer term, which is why it is emphasized in this chapter.

DRESS-UP BUSINESS CASUAL: THE THIRD WARDROBE

Before men's weekend dress stepped down to a pair of sneakers and jeans, if a guy were going out socially, he would usually step out in what used to be termed "tailored sportswear." If he didn't don a sport jacket and necktie, he usually showed up in a three-piece outfit composed of a sport coat or sweater with harmonizing dress pants and open-collared sport shirt. Dress-up business casual is really an updated version of that somewhat old-fashioned mix-and-match formula, with the added fillip of increased comfort and personal expression.

Today, most men's closets are stocked with somber suits for the workday and slob clothes for the weekend. In pulling from neither the pinstripe nor the jeans side of the closet, dress-up business casual demands a dressing style and a wardrobe that falls somewhere in between; one that incorporates softly constructed jackets and dress trousers with fine-quality sweaters and sport shirts. Unfortunately, trying to assemble outfits from unmatched separates requires dressing skills men never had to learn in an exclusively suit-oriented work environment.

COLORING UP YOUR DRESS-UP
BUSINESS WARDROBE

Dress-up business casual forces a man to coordinate tailored ensembles made from differing fabrics. The easiest way to pull together unmatched separates is through the medium of color. A good rule of thumb when harmonizing three different separates is to keep two pieces in the same color family. This approach simplifies the melding process and usually yields a more contemporary image. For example, pairing this navy corduroy sport coat and navy knit shirt strikes a more modern mood (*left*) than taking the same blue jacket and wearing a different-color shirt (*right*) with its gray trousers. Taking the concept one step further, wearing each piece in a different tonality tends to achieve a more traditional mood, as you can see from this beige jacket, peach knit polo, and dark brown slack ensemble (*far right*).

Should you want to accelerate the fashion tempo, keeping all three pieces in the same color family picks up the pace. As the *fashionistas* learned by acquiring a predominantly black

More modern.

Less modern.

More traditional.

wardrobe, swathing themselves head to foot in one color not only reduced their margin of error, it uniformed them in a kind of streamlined cool. Accessorizing a suit in a monotoned palette imbues it with instant sleekness and modernity, as evidenced by this charcoal mélange of gray turtleneck on gray flannel. What's changed in the new millennium is that men have learned how to embrace their existing wardrobe by stretching its fashionability.

A professional-looking outfit relies on a certain level of formality to convey authority, a prime point of concern when dressing down. The uniforms or robes of authority figures such as judges, law enforcement officers, or clergy are usually in dark, solid colors: navy or black, sometimes mixed with white. Business suits are typically relieved by lighter-tone dress shirts, while men's formalwear revolves around the classic black-and-white costume. Although psychologists consider black and white the most authoritarian of all color combinations, such high contrast does not flatter everyone's facial colorings.

As discussed earlier, a man's complexion and physique still constitute the main compass for his selection of clothing colors and their ideal coordination. Even though darker-hued harmonies happen to be in vogue, that is no reason for the fair-haired, light-skinned executive to show up mantled in a cacophony of dark colors. Likewise, trying to project a less ceremonial office image is no excuse to submerge a high-contrast visage in a sea of anemic-toned apparel.

On the architectural side, just as contrasting tops and bottoms can unnecessarily diminish shorter men, darker trousers will make sport jackets appear dressier. In evolving a corporate-casual style of dress that both flatters and projects professionalism, you must not stray too far from those individual guideposts that dictate one color strategy over another.

LEFT:
Here's how to fashion a successful transaction between a brown sport jacket and camel turtleneck using gold-hued hair and lighter-toned skin to help determine the ideal amount of contrast to show below.

OPPOSITE:
Keeping the color scheme monotone ratchets up the ensemble's—and in this case, the suit's—modernity.

PIECING TOGETHER THE DRESS-UP BUSINESS-CASUAL WARDROBE

The dress-up business-casual wardrobe revolves around two jacket-oriented scenarios, the three-piece separates ensemble and the nontie suit outfit. Since most men have less experience dressing down a suit than teaming up a sport jacket, let's start with the dark-colored sport jacket worn with a cut-and-sewn or collared knit shirt and a pair of well-pressed dress slacks.

Because it covers the largest portion of the body, the jacket sets the color direction for the rest of the team. As sport coats are appropriate in most casual business settings, a high-quality, well-tailored jacket is critical to the dress-up business-casual wardrobe. Start with a textured dark solid or subtle patterned sport coat in one of the power-neutral shades of navy, charcoal, dark brown, or taupe. Gimmicky jacketings are too memorable for multiple wearings, so stick with understated patterns at the beginning.

With the sport coat functioning as this capsule color family's centerpiece, surround it with related separates. Following the guideline of coordinating two of the three garments, begin by harmonizing the trouser with the jacket. The buttons of most sport jackets often come in a complementary contrast shade, so it's a fair guess that trousers chosen in the same tonality will match the jacket pretty well. With the jacket and trouser in a similar hue, the shirt can either be in a contrast or tonal relationship to both, its coordination dictated by your own complexion and personal taste. If the shirt is multicolored, one of its colors should echo that of the jacket and trouser. One way to boot up visual interest is to employ a pattern-on-pattern strategy, which comes with a certain risk but can produce handsome dividends.

Pattern-on-pattern dressing keeps outfits interesting.

One example of evolving such an initial capsule wardrobe might start with an unsolid, small-patterned, two-color jacket in a predominant charcoal shade, with tan as its secondary accent color. After acquiring basic gray components, such as charcoal flannel trousers, a gray long-sleeve collared knit shirt, and perhaps a small gray-and-tan patterned woven sport shirt, you will want to exploit the tan side of the jacket's color scheme. A pair of fawn covert trousers and matching-toned long-sleeve collared knit shirt would introduce it nicely to the gray color family. Add a V-neck sweater vest in charcoal gray or a cardigan in brown, and you're well down the dress-up casual road without being forced to make a blazer pit stop.

As far as other jacket-driven outfits go, the inherent classiness of the single- or double-breasted navy-blazer and gray-trouser coordination would certainly be high on the list. Next might follow a less stately rendition of the blazer look, perhaps a patterned or textured dark blue sport coat that could be paired with the blazer's navy and gray accessories, like this composition here. One alternative to the classic sport coat would be some version of the safari jacket, like the shirt-jacket, which can easily multitask to accommodate a broad spectrum of dressed-down alternatives, such as this modern assemblage of dark-hued separates.

Alternative blazer.

A shirt-jacket can be dressed up or down.

Another surrogate jacket look would be the shawl-collar or other button-front-model sweater. As it is a multi-ply wool garment, its weight tends to confine it to cooler climes, but as a long-sleeve cardigan with hip pockets, this knitwear classic can serve either as a jacket for a dressed-down necktie ensemble or as a finishing top over a turtleneck or woven sport shirt.

*Cardigan front jacket-sweaters
are another way to dress up the
dress-down look.*

THE BUSINESS-CASUAL SPORT JACKET

With comfort dictating office decorum, the classic sport coat must become more than a vessel of male respectability: it needs to combine sweaterlike comfort with businesslike protocol. Whereas you can update the traditional suit by pairing it with a turtleneck or T-shirt, trying to recycle those straitjackets from the seventies or eighties undermines the entire enterprise, because their padded formality belies today's modern casualness.

The most versatile and contemporary jacket style is the three-button, single-breasted model with soft-rolled fronts, lightly padded shoulders, and notch lapels. Because of its soft underpinnings and three-button front, it can be worn in various button configurations: one-buttoned at the waist, done up with it's two upper buttons, or left open, like a cardigan sweater, albeit with more form and structure. While most men are quick to remove their jackets upon settling into the office, this cloudlike garment might encourage them to keep them on.

And like the sinuous cardigan sweater, the softly contoured sport jacket can be worn incrementally longer. When mated with a variety of long-sleeve knits, such as turtlenecks or polos, its sleeve length can also drop slightly lower on the wrist. This additional sleeve length lines up better with the jacket's longer length, and together they promote a more relaxed body language.

While the older man tends to favor the classic two-button to the newer three-button jacket model (although the three-button jacket predated it, fashion-wise) either is perfectly acceptable. The double-breasted jacket is also an option; although, because it looks better buttoned up, it tends to convey a slightly dressier posture. While all three jacket models can be stylishly worn to convey a more casual business manner, it's usually "how" rather than "what" one wears that distinguishes both the apparel and the man.

The new sport coat needs to combine sweaterlike comfort with businesslike protocol.

UNHINGING TRADITION: DRESSING DOWN THE SUIT

Society's smart set has been sporting suits without ties for many years, as we observe both Cary Grant (*below*) and Jack Bouvier, Jacqueline Kennedy Onassis's father (*opposite*), acquitting themselves with characteristic aplomb. Such a vogue had previously been confined to the non-business arena of resort or spectator sportswear; however, once Italian designer Giorgio Armani unhitched the suit from its unbending box of a business uniform in the 1980s, wearing it without a tie became both a logical and permanent fashion.

While the Internet generation grew up not having to wear a suit to work, in eschewing Nikes and jeans for tucked-in shirts and clothes that fit true to size, many younger men have rediscovered the suit. The well-cut suit still has sex appeal. Traditional men can no longer afford to hide behind the suit—they need to reinvent it.

There are many new ways to wear a suit today, because it has undergone a makeover in both fabric and construction. Modern technology has produced fabrics lighter and more supple than would have been believed only a decade ago. Combined with a soft construction using lighter padding and thinner interfacings, this formerly hot and restrictive citadel of ruling-class authority has downloaded itself into the ultimate softwear.

Learning how to wear a suit without a tie affords the businessman one more opportunity to extend his range of corporate-casual options. Accessorizing the suit with something other than its customary fare leads it away from its roots; however, embracing such a style is not about abandoning the way men have dressed in the past. It's about opening up choices for the way they will dress in the future.

LEFT:
Here's Cary Grant stretching the suit's sartorial boundaries.

OPPOSITE:
Jack Bouvier and daughter Jacqueline in island fare.

Black cashmere turtleneck,
black-and-white plaid suit—
gray, but tan, Ralph Lauren.

Let's use the backdrop of the classic gray business suit to help illustrate some of the more practiced casual techniques. Without the closed shirt collar and necktie's ordered glamour to highlight the face and fill up the void under the chin, the dressed-down neckline must still frame the face without distracting from it. The button-down collar accomplishes such a mission, because of how its fastened-down points help it to stand up around the wearer's neck. When worn under a jacket, its in-place stability conveys a snappy élan, dressing up the face more than other sport shirt collars. Layering a dark T-shirt underneath adds visual interest while helping fill in the space left by the open collar.

As a general rule, closing a shirt's collar creates a dressier image, because its relative neatness helps the face to appear more important (see page 262). Camp-style collars should be avoided if the idea is for the shirt collar to add stature to the tailored jacket's open neckline. The absence of a collar band encourages their flat-lying collars to slide down the base of the neck, leaving the throat uncovered and the wearer looking disheveled.

Likewise, a knit shirt buttoned at the neck invariably exudes a tidier, less casual look. However, its soft knit collar can be easily overwhelmed by the jacket's sturdier collar—it usually ends up getting pushed out of position and falling down the neck, eroding the face's presence. This can be avoided by mating a sport coat with only those knit shirts made with the more substantive one-piece self-collar, which sits on the neck much like a woven sport shirt collar.

Along with the standard turtleneck or mock-turtle knit collars, here are several other seasoned ways to soften up the starchy environs of the classic gray two-piece. Modern casual business dressing elevates the concept of layering, cross-pollinating it with something not normally paired, like a T-shirt and a sport jacket, or a turtleneck and a suit. Donning a simple T-shirt, either by itself or leaving its neckline to peep out above a V-neck or round-neck sweater, has become standard operating procedure. One exceptionally stylish way to appoint the open-collar neckline is by tying an ascot or, in this case, a neckerscarf, around it.

The B.D. collar stands up the best.

Classic necklines of the round tee and V-neck sweater.

Dressing up the dressed-down neckline.

In the rush to expand the sartorial boundaries of the suit, certain guidelines get trampled upon. For instance, trying to make a suit jacket double as a sport jacket generally leaves you with neither. Suit coats tend to retain their dressy probity by virtue of their fabrics' smooth surfaces and their flatter, polished buttons. The exceptions to this rule would be the classic cotton gabardine or the larger-than-micro-scale check suit jacket, particularly if appointed with sportier horn-style buttons and patch-type pockets.

Open or flapped patch pockets can abet a jacket's casual aspirations. Jackets from a winter suit of corduroy or tweed would also probably make the cut. Like wearing a convertible single cuff with cuff links, sporting only the top half of a suit usually ends up falling short in both style and sophistication.

Patch and flap pockets permit this cotton suit jacket to assume the composure of a sport coat.

DRESS-DOWN BUSINESS CASUAL

While a dark sport jacket can make any man look more professional, dress-down business casual removes the protective wrapping of such tailored refuge to reveal what's underneath. Built on the foundation of the sport-shirt-and-trouser combination, this category varies in dressiness from a high-quality cotton dress or sport shirt atop dark wool trousers to a pair of well-pressed khakis or crisp jeans below a fine-gauge, long-sleeve, cut-and-sewn knit shirt. As long as classic fabrics and patterns are relied upon, arriving at a businesslike presentation should not test the coordinating skills of the average fashion-pressed male.

Taking a page out of the two-piece suit's story, the less contrast generated by colors found above and below the waistline, the dressier and more elongating the effect. In general, dark colors worn under the chin tilt the shirt-slack scheme toward the dressier side of the casual spectrum. Just as most shirt-and-trouser coordinations acquire an increased importance when anchored by a deeper-toned bottom, sequestering darker colors on the lower half of the body tends to produce a taller, slimmer outline.

Without a jacket as the top layer, the shirt takes center stage. As mentioned earlier, for the shirt component to command authority, it should be collared, preferably cut and sewn in either one piece or with a collar band. These two constructions help the collar to stand up around the neck, better presenting the face.

Ideally, the dress-down business-casual shirt should have long sleeves, since even rolled-up sleeves convey a more professional look than half sleeves. If favored, short sleeves that extend to just above the elbow give a slightly more dignified appearance than mid-biceps versions (see the Duke of Windsor, page 76). Although they still communicate an attitude of leisure, short-sleeve knits become slightly more business-appropriate when paired with dress trousers.

The fine-gauge, long-sleeve, collared knit pullover has recently become a stylish alternative to the conventional woven sport shirt. A deep-toned cashmere-and-silk pullover in a turtle-neck, mock turtle, or collared model can lend refinement to casual trousers. Although the level of sophistication depends on the fabric and finishing, lightweight knit tops wear well with all pants types, from dress trousers to jeans, corduroys to khakis. Like its woven colleague, the knit sport shirt should be tucked in the trousers for neatness and dressiness (see page 259).

One way to inject individuality into the business-casual ensemble is to mix patterns and textures. As for patterns, the most fail-safe approach is to mate a solid with a pattern. Plaid or striped sport shirts clamor for solid bottoms, the bonus being that by repeating one of the colors from the shirt's pattern in the solid bottom, you have an easy coordination.

Injecting texture into the two-piece is another means of increasing its visual mileage. While texture can add dimensional interest to a shirt-and-slack mélange, make sure to keep both halves different, such as shiny versus dull, flat versus raised, coarse versus smooth. If the same surface effect runs from top to bottom, the coordination can end up looking contrived

instead of sophisticated. In winter, matte-finished knits or finely brushed wovens can be paired with textured cords or flannel pants. Cotton is an excellent natural fabric for trousers, but it conveys a more casual attitude than wool. In the spring and summer, linen trousers can be added to the mix, although part of their chic is in their obligatory wrinkling. Dressed-down business bottoms should be pressed crisp to exude professionalism.

The patterned woven top and solid bottom are the bedrock of the dress-down business outfit; introducing another layer helps in diversifying the look. The neckline of the classic gray T-shirt peeking out from under a sport shirt's collar can add a subtle touch of individuality. Layering a V-neck or cardigan sleeveless vest on top is another technique. Repeating a color from the shirt's pattern would be the most direct way to integrate the third layer into the whole. While shirttails need to disappear beneath trouser tops for a business image, layer sweaters may be left untucked.

As mentioned, one undervalued but surprisingly useful addition to the stylish business-casual wardrobe would be the ascot or the neckerscarf. It substitutes for a necktie under a suit jacket or sport coat, transforming the most humdrum of two-pieces into an ensemble of considerable chic. With less practice and skill required to tie a bow tie, the neckerscarf folded in a four-in-hand knot adds a spot of flair to the unattended neckline, turning the typical dark but dressy business-casual outfit into something special, and elevating a simple shirt-and-trouser outfit into an ensemble of surprising stylishness.

OPPOSITE & RIGHT:
*Dressed-down business casual
can look distinguished.*

ACCESSORIZING THE DRESS-DOWN BUSINESS-CASUAL OUTFIT

With so few garments to help convey a dressed-up bearing, each accessory becomes that much more important. Because of the belted waistline's visibility, relating it in either mood, color, or texture to the footwear below immediately advances the outfit's overall harmony. Likewise, echoing one's hair tone in the choice of accessories can also promote the cause. Given clothing's role in leading the viewer to the observed's communications center, his face, reiterating one's hair color at the waistline and again at the foot is another highly recommended stratagem.

Dark brown leather belts and brown suede shoes raise the taste level of any casual outfit. For the Milanese and other clothing aficionados, no wearable better signifies one's standing than a pair of brown suede shoes. Worn with jeans or a suit, sport shirt or sport jacket, this former symbol of Windsordom has become a sign of everyday chic.

Mixing a black alligator belt with a pair of black slip-ons imposes a different sense of style, particularly if the wearer's hair happens to be in dark accord. However, unless the outfit's dominant color scheme contains a strong black motif (and sometimes even then), dress-down leather accessories are better kept in the warmer, earthier brown family, whether in tanned saddle leather, simple pin seal, or sybaritic lizard. Wearing top-quality brown leather enriches anything worn in close proximity.

The exception to this prescription would be those men trying to affect a more downtown demeanor. Although black belts and shoes would not be the classicist's choice to appoint his chinos, should the fashion acolyte be swathed in lower-rise, flat-fronted khakis, black leather resonates a more modernist mantra than brown.

Shoes should complement the outfit as a whole, and dress-down business footwear is no exception. A man's shoes reflect his taste more than any other item of clothing, and nothing reflects more poorly on a man's dressing style than unpolished or broken-down footwear. The state of one's shoes broadcasts how you manage details, especially items requiring maintenance.

The traditional distinction between dress and casual shoes used to be that the former laced up, while the latter slipped on. Today, some of the best-looking casual shoes are wing-tip or cap-toe lace-ups in brown suede with a lug sole. Chunkier soles change the tone of an outfit from dress-up to dress-down. Regardless of how dressy the upper shoe's design, if it cannot be

A dress-down version on a dressed-up classic.

polished like matte finishes or suede, it generally falls into the more casual shoe category (an exception, of course, being reverse calfskin shoes with leather soles).

As the shoe gets more substantial, so should the sock. The thicker the sock, the more casual its intentions. The thin black or navy dress variety have no place inside these larger-proportioned shoes. Like dress hosiery, casual hose must be long enough to cover bare skin when one's legs are crossed. In general, they should be in the same tone as the trouser. Multicolor patterned socks can either partner with the trouser and shoe tone or blend with a color above the waist.

DRESSING FOR THE JOB INTERVIEW

Job interviews do not permit a great deal of time to create the right impression. People tend to size you up in the first thirty seconds, which can influence how they choose to interact with you. In the process of gathering information, the interviewer consciously and unconsciously makes judgments based on your visual and verbal cues. The most compelling nonverbal indicators are your clothes and overall grooming.

Choosing the right clothes for a job interview has always been daunting. Showing up dressed appropriately has become even more of a challenge since corporate dress codes continue to be in flux. As business attire now allows for a broader range of personal expression, it also invites more margin for error. The candidate who shows up wearing the right clothes may gain a competitive advantage.

Any smart applicant prepares for a job interview by familiarizing himself with the company's business, its competition, and the marketplace. Today, investigating a prospective employer's workplace persona—meaning its dress code—should also be part of the preliminaries. Beyond dressing well and making a professional presentation, you want your choice of clothes to type with the prospective organization's culture. Although it is always preferable to err on the overdressed side, if a company's executives happen to be partial to jeans and turtlenecks, showing up in a three-piece suit and black lace-ups would not be putting your best foot forward.

Appropriate interview attire sends the message that here is an applicant who did his homework. Think about the way the person interviewing you may dress. Try to objectively see yourself through the eyes of a stranger; consider what your clothes may announce about you. And to the man trying to shimmy up the corporate career pole within his existing company: dress for the position you aspire to hold, not the one you currently have.

GLOSSARY

Cross-referenced definitions appear in SMALL CAPS.

ACCORDION PLEATS: A series of narrow folds in a fabric that resemble those of an accordion.

ALBERT SLIPPER: A laceless, pull-on, tab-front shoe originated by Prince Albert, Queen Victoria's Prince Consort. (*See* page 192.)

ALL-OVER: A design, such as polka dots, that repeats continuously and regularly over the entire surface of a tie. (*See* ties, page 71.)

ALPACA: A member of the camel species, similar to the llama, found in the Andean Highlands in Chile and Peru. It is a dappled animal whose undercoat is downy with very fine hair, very soft and lustrous. Its wool can be selected from a great variety of soft grays, russets, and browns, from pure white to a rusty black.

AMERICAN LOOK: As described by Brooks Brothers circa 1939: "This style is, above all, distinguished by its *naturalness*. Clothes should be worn for comfort and unconscious ease. The wearer should look like himself, and no other, no matter what the occasion or what he has on. This cannot be accomplished with clothes that have something about them that is foreign to the wearer's habit, disposition, or everyday appearance. Indeed, natural clothes, like natural people, are always the most pleasing." (*See* Dean Acheson, page 39.)

ANTIQUING: Also called "bootmaker's finish." A process of applying stain, wax, or oil to leather, allowing it to be absorbed or set, and then rubbing the leather with a cloth or brushing it. Beginning around 1936, antiquing produced a deliberately weathered patina, enriching a shoe's appearance while paving the way for the rich brown shoe's acceptance for town and business wear. (*See* page 191.)

APRON: The American term for the wide ends, front and back, of a long tie. Also, a raised or flat seam around a shoe's front or vamp. (*See* shoe, page 196.)

ARCH: The bottom curve of a shoe from the heel to the ball of the foot.

ARGYLE: A multicolored diamond pattern, sometimes with overplaid, usually in wool; originally knitted in England on hand frames, it is now made by machines and applied primarily to socks and sweaters. (*See* Frank Sinatra, page 177.)

ARMSCYE: A contraction of "arm's eye"; the lower side of the armhole to which the sleeve of a jacket or coat is sewn. If this area fits closely, it is known as a "high armhole"; if it fits loosely, it is known as a "low armhole."

ASCOT: A square-ended tie with each end of equal width, worn primarily for formal day wear. Deriving its name from Ascot Heath, the English racetrack where the tie was first worn, the ascot consists of two knots.

The first is a single knot, while the second is a Gordian knot with one end crossing over the other and held in place with a stickpin. Also, a throw-over neck scarf for sportswear. (*See* Cary Grant, page 169.)

AUBERGINE: A shade of purple resembling that of the eggplant.

BACK PLEATS: The two pleats in the topsides of trousers located between the front pleats and the side seams. (*See* pleated trouser illustration, top of page 61.)

BACK VENT: A single opening or slit at the back of a garment of varying lengths, depending on the styling of the jacket. (*See* page 89.)

BACKLESS WAISTCOAT: A modern kind of formal vest introduced in London in 1923 made without a back and held in place by means of bands, fastened with a buckle or button, across the back at the waistline. An innovation of the DRESS SOFT era popularized by the Prince of Wales allowing for more comfort and coolness for male formal wear. Hawes and Curtis, the Prince of Wales's shirtmaker, claims to have invented the garment.

BACKSTITCH: The tailor's stitch, a kind of lockstitch, differing from others by covering the whole of the surface between the stitches, with the thread exposed on the face of the material. A well-formed backstitch gives a perfect line of seam.

BAL COLLAR: A high military collar that may be worn flat or turned up and buttoned. The collar is a band of material about three and a half inches wide, on a raincoat or topcoat. The name derives from BALMACAAN.

BAL SHOE: A closed-throat shoe with a laced front, derived from Balmoral Castle in Scotland. (*See* Oxford shoe, page 193.)

BALANCE MARKS: Guides for the workman in sewing the various sections of clothing together correctly as well as indications to the cutter that this has been done. In trousers, instead of chalk marks, small V marks are cut at the knee and hip for the lining up of the respective parts. In this way, the BALANCE of the whole garment is preserved.

BALANCE: A term used to describe the hang of a garment.

BALL: The part of the shoe just behind the toes.

BALMACAAN: A loose-fitting coat based on the original military version worn by the Prussian Army. Named for Balmacaan, an estate near Inverness, Scotland, it features raglan shoulders and a narrow, turned-down collar; both collar and coat are called "bal" for short.

BALMORAL: A soft, peakless Scottish headgear for men named in the nineteenth century in honor of Queen

Victoria's great castle at Balmoral, where it was frequently worn. Also called "Tam 'o Shanter," or "Tammy," after a hero in one of Robert Burns's poems.

BANDANNA: A large, brightly colored handkerchief worn tied around the neck. Originally made of silk, they were imported from India in the early eighteenth century and worn by the American cowboy. Also, a Hindi word for tying and dyeing cloth.

BANDOLIER STRIPE: A diagonal stripe appearing only once below the tie's knot.

BARATHEA: A fine-textured worsted cloth of a broken FILLING effect, which produces a pebblelike surface. It is made primarily in wool for evening clothes and silk for neckwear.

BARBOUR COAT: A classic English hunting overcoat with a stand-up brown corduroy collar and throat latch detail, made from dark green oilskin of Egyptian cotton and lined in a durable bright cotton plaid. Its multiple pockets and weatherproof construction make it the squire's choice for country or city wear.

BARLEYCORN: All-over design of miniature proportions characterized by small, faint "corn" triangles used for tweed and other woolen fabrics. This twill-weave pattern is achieved by contrasting the WARP and WEFT threads. (See Humphrey Bogart, page 180.)

BARREL CUFF: A single cuff attached to a shirtsleeve and fastened with a button and a buttonhole.

BARRYMORE COLLAR: A low-set, attached dress-shirt collar with long points, first worn by John Barrymore in the late 1920s and then adopted by Hollywood stars and others in California; it later became known as the California collar.

BAR-SHAPED TIE: A four-in-hand tie in which the ends are of equal width and parallel.

BAR TACK: A stitch made in heavy yarn to reinforce the slip stitching that joins the body of the tie at the front blade end.

BASKET WEAVE: A variation of a plain-weave fabric in which two or more yarns are worked in the WARP and WEFT to produce a plaited cane-basket effect, hence the name. It is used mainly in shirtings and sport jacketings. Oxford cloth is a type of basket weave.

BASQUE BERET: A close-fitting, round-crowned cap with no visor or brim, as worn in the Basque country. (See the Prince of Wales, page 8, far left photograph.)

BASTE: To sew loosely together or fasten temporarily in place with long, easily removed stitches. In men's tailoring, it is usually used to temporarily hold the parts of a garment so that it can be tried on.

BASTED FITTING: The first fitting in the creation of a true custom-tailored jacket. A shell or "raw try-on" is prepared directly from a paper pattern created by the tailor. This skeleton coat has its canvases tacked in, seams basted, front edges turned in, collar basted on, and, sometimes, one sleeve tacked on, after which it is usually ripped apart to be made into the next, more advanced and permanent fitting.

BATISTE: A finely woven, sheer, textured fabric of fine cotton or other fibers used for shirtings. Named for Jean Baptiste, a French weaver of fine linen who lived in Cambrai and first produced the cloth. (See "Summer" in the "Shirt Fabrics" gatefold.)

BATTLE JACKET: A waist-length, single-breasted khaki woolen jacket, which was regulation for the U.S. Army in World War II. The style is used for civilian sportswear in a variety of fabrics.

BATWING: A name given to a bow tie whose straight square ends resemble that of a bat's wing before tying. Known as the club bow in America, it is an alternative shape to the butterfly bow. Narrower than a butterfly bow, it is tied with a larger knot as well. May be found in ribbed silk or satin for evening wear or in a patterned fabric for day wear. (See page 163.)

BEAVER: Fur fiber of a shiny, smooth, silklike texture used extensively in the manufacture of felt hats.

BEDFORD CORD: A sister cloth to piqué, it is a closely woven sturdy fabric in a rib weave with a raised or corded effect. It was first used to make breeches for the Bedford militia, hence the name. Its original color resembles COVERT CLOTH. Bedford cord comes in wool, cotton, or blends. (See the seated sportsman, page 115.)

BEETLE BACK: The back of a waistcoat with rounded corners whose length extends beyond the edge line of its foreparts.

BEIGE: A natural or undyed color; a very pale tone of tan.

BELL BOTTOMS: Flares, or pants with flared fullness, suggesting the shape of a bell. Originally the blue or white trousers worn by navy seaman; also known as sailor's pants.

BELLOWS PLEAT: A deep fold at the side of a jacket or coat to provide extra fullness for comfort. (See Henry Fonda, page 106.)

BELLOWS POCKET: Also termed "safari pocket." A patch-style pocket with three side pieces that permit the pocket to expand. These side pieces give the appearance of old English fire-lighting bellows. (See Clark Gable, page 107.)

BEMBERG: A trade name for Cupramonium rayon. Usually found in top-quality jackets, either as coat or sleeve linings.

BENCHMADE: A misleading term suggesting a 100 percent handcrafted shoe made on a bench by one craftsman. Today it means a 75 percent machine-made shoe hand-lasted with hand-welted soles.

BENGAL STRIPES: Alternating stripes of equal width, usually white and a color. They were originally shipped to world markets from Bengal, India, and are usually found in shirtings. (See "Fall" and "Summer" in the "Shirt Fabrics" gatefold.)

BERET: A brimless, unvisored, tam-effect cap of felt or fabric.

BERMUDA SHORTS: Walking shorts of the style worn in Bermuda. Extending to about the break in the knee, their side seams range from twenty to twenty-two inches. (*See* pages 182 and 183.)

BESOM: A tailoring term for an inset pocket made with a narrow welted edge above the pocket opening. It is called a double besom pocket if both top and bottom edges have welts, and called a flapped besom when a flap is added.

BESPOKE: Custom-made; a term applied in England to articles made to individual order.

BIAS CONSTRUCTION: *See* RESILIENT CONSTRUCTION.

BIKINI: Abbreviated-style swim shorts; adapted from women's underwear.

BILLY COCK: *See* DERBY.

BIRD'S EYE: All-over woven suiting or neckwear fabric made from a small geometric pattern with a dot, suggesting a bird's eye. This fancy-solid suit is a favorite of bespoke tailors and their more stylish patrons. (*See* "Winter" in the "Suit Fabrics" gatefold; folded arm, page 93.)

BISQUE: A pale tone of tan suggestive of the color of a slightly brown biscuit. (*See* page 253.)

BI-SWING BACK: The back of a jacket with a GUSSET or INVERTED PLEAT extending from shoulder to waistline on each side, usually with a stitched-on half-belt in back. (*See* page 106.)

BLACK WATCH: The Black Watch, or Black Guard, was originally a group of renegade Scots recruited by the king of England to check troublesome Highland clans. They wore a particular kind of TARTAN or PLAID. It is the uniform tartan of the British Army's 42nd Highland Regiment—the Campbell tartan minus the yellow-and-white overchecks. Popular in men's wear because it combines two classic blazer colors, navy and green, thereby serving as another blazer possibility.

BLADE: Or "British blade, this is extra fullness at the jacket's shoulder blades, a construction originating with custom tailors in the West End of London in the late 1920s. It is also the British term for the broader end of a FOUR-IN-HAND knot, which usually hangs to the front of the under-end of a necktie. Also, the ends of a BOW TIE.

BLAZER: The first blazers were bright scarlet jackets worn by student members of the Lady Margaret Boat Club at Cambridge University. A joking reference to a "blaze of color" was applied to brightly striped boating jackets, which became popular in the 1880s. This style sobered greatly in the 1930s with the modern blazer reflecting more similarity to the British Navy REEFER, but for some reason the name "blazer" stuck. (*See* page 109.)

BLEEDING: The term descriptive of a fabric in which the dye is not fast and comes out when wet.

BLIND STITCH: A concealed stitch.

BLOCK PRINTING: An old method of hand-printing fabrics from carved wood or metal blocks.

BLUCHER: A lace-up shoe with a low, open-throat front over the instep patterned after the military boots worn by General Gebhard Leberecht von Blücher, who led the Prussian army against Napoleon. Also known as a DERBY. (*See* pages 177, 195.)

BLUFF EDGE: An edge made up in usual way but finished without outside stitching.

BOAT NECK: A horizontal opening at the top of a knitted pullover.

BOATER: *See* SENNIT.

BOILED SHIRT: An inelegant term for a stiff-bosomed evening shirt. Originally, the fronts literally had to be boiled to remove the starch for washing.

BOLD LOOK: Introduced by *Esquire* magazine in the spring of 1948, the Bold Look was a reaction to the lack of new fashions during and just after WWII. Basing it on the appeal of the large WINDSOR knot and command spread-collar dress shirt, *Esquire*'s fashion department proposed a head-to-toe look of oversized apparel featuring fuller suit jackets with prominent shoulders, aggressive-patterned neckwear, massive jewelry, and thick BLUCHER footwear. Although the Bold Look lost momentum by the next decade, it unhitched American men's taste from its Brooks Brothers/Savile Row anchor, initiating America's downward spiral into the 1950s CONTINENTAL LOOK, the 1960s PEACOCK REVOLUTION, and the disposable fashions of the 1970s.

BOLO TIE: A cowboy-inspired string tie made of leather or heavy braided cord with metal tips fastened with a slide device.

BOLT: An entire length of wool cloth from the loom, rolled or folded. Bolts vary in length anywhere from fifty to seventy meters and width from thirty-two to sixty inches.

BOMBER JACKET: A waist-length jacket worn by U.S. Air Force pilots, adapted for civilian purposes in leather with sheepskin lining, or in a fabric with a pile-fabric lining.

BOOT: Footwear that extends any height above the ankle.

BORSALINO: The name of the great Italian hatmaker's contribution to the TRILBY hat family, with its characteristic triangle pitch to the crown. (*See* Milton Holden, page 130.)

BOTTLE GREEN: A deep shade of green resembling that of certain glass bottles.

BOTTLE-SHAPED TIE: A tie shape with a marked narrowing under the knot that widens down to resemble the shape of a bottle; permits a wider-bodied tie to make a normal-sized knot.

BOTTOM: The section of a shoe sole extending from its toe to the breast of the heel, not including the heel.

BOUCLÉ: From the French word *bouclé,* meaning a "buckle" or "ringlet." A novelty yarn and finish effect produced on cloths whereby very small, drawn-out curly loops in the individual thread appear on the surface of the material.

BOUND EDGES: Edges finished with braid or other kinds of covering.

BOUTONNIERE: Carnation, cornflower, or other flower worn on the lapel of a jacket or outercoat. (*See* pages 201, 231, 236.)

BOW TIE: *See* pages 160–64.

BOWLER: *See* DERBY.

BOX CLOTH: A heavy, coarse cloth, originally in buff or tan-colored MELTON, used in the overcoating trade. Also used for men's SUSPENDERS.

BOX PLEAT: A pleat with folded edges facing in opposite directions, used on pockets of shirts and jackets, or the back yoke of a shirt for fullness and ease of movement.

BOX TOE: The support used inside the shoe to hold the shape of the toe; usually rigid, but may be soft or flexible.

BRACE BUTTON: A specially shaped button domed on the side and attached to the waistband, permitting sufficient space for the suspender's loop to move freely from side to side. (*See* page 224.)

BRACES: British term for SUSPENDERS. (*See* page 222.)

BRADFORD SPINNING: One of three principle methods of spinning WORSTED YARNS. Originating in Yorkshire, England, this process of spinning wool into worsted yarn takes the wool and thoroughly oils it before it is combed, which produces a smooth, lustrous yarn used for worsted suitings. This differs from the French system, which is dry-spun.

BRAID: Woven, knitted, or plaited material used for trimming or binding. Often used for formalwear trousers. *See* pages 248, 251.

BREAK: The amount of folding, creasing, or "shiver" of the trouser bottom when it meets and sits on the top of the shoe. (*See* pages 48, 61.)

BREECH: An old-fashioned English word for buttocks—hence, "breeches" is what covers them. The word first appeared in England in the sixteenth century and originally referred to knee-length trousers with fancy buckles for decoration. Later, breeches were lengthened and came to mean pants.

BREEKS: Colloquialism for breeches; also a term for trousers implying trim lines.

BRIDLE: A bridle is actually controlling gear—like the bridle in a horse's mouth; its meaning here is as a jacket's principle source of support. Also, a term applied for padding a piece of material from the neck onto the canvas along the inside crease or roll of the lapel to hold or control the chest.

BRITISH WARM: DOUBLE-BREASTED outercoat of military origin, in knee- or above-knee length, with shaped body lines and a flare toward the bottom, often with epaulets. It is usually of MELTON.

BROADCLOTH: Closely woven fabric with the rib running weftwise, it contains twice as many WARP threads as the FILLING, producing excellent luster, all-cotton, or poly blends. It is used in shirts, undershorts, and sportswear. (*See* the "Shirt Fabrics" gatefold.)

BROCADE: From the Italian *broccare,* meaning "to prick," or "to figure." A heavy, large, and figured silk, usually in all-over designs, of raised figures or flowers made by WARP threads being raised in JACQUARD weaving to form the pattern.

BROGUE: Historically, a rough outdoor shoe of untanned leather with a thong closure, worn by Scots and Irish peasants (from Gaelic *bròg*—a shoe). Today a brogue is a heavy oxford shoe with a large perforated design on toe and border seams, usually WING TIP. (*See* page 194.)

BROLLY: A British term for umbrella.

BROWNSTONE: A combination of deep shades of earth-made rock set off with overtones of steel gray. Coined by *Esquire*'s "Apparel Arts" in 1941 as a new key fall color blending with all complexions and promoted as a new way to sell brown.

BRUMMEL, GEORGE BRYAN: Beau Brummel (1778–1840). An early-nineteenth-century English dandy whose dictates on male dress still endure as the essential code of the well-dressed gentleman. Prior to "The Beau," a gentleman's appearance depended on the richness of the material on his back, even though the clothes were often badly made, ill-fitting, and not always clean. With Brummel, male style became a matter of impeccable fit and cut, exquisite detail, and immaculate cleanliness. Even his preference for the color blue would endure to the extent that the navy suit became the uniform of millions through much of the twentieth century.

BRUSHING: Also called napping; a finishing process where circular brushes pull up the fiber ends to form a fuzzy surface thereby raising a NAP on knitted or woven fabrics.

BUCKSKIN: Soft napped leather of deer or elk for fine gloves or BESPOKE quality shoes. (*See* page 200.)

BUDAPEST: A well-known full-brogue DERBY style of shoe with a high toe cap.

BUGGY: The strip of an unlined jacket extending across the back neck that gives a finish to that part of the coat. (In custom tailoring, when the lining comes four to five inches below the armhole, it is referred to as "half-lined.")

BURBERRY: Thomas Burberry, a country draper in England, hit upon a method of chemically treating cotton fabric so that it repelled water while remaining porous. In 1904, he advertised "PROOF against the Heaviest Rains and Mist." Burberry's uniform department designed a rain-resistant cotton-gabardine trench coat that was issued to more than a half million men in the course of WWI. *See* TRENCH COAT.

BURGUNDY: A deep rich red shade suggestive of burgundy wine. (*See* velvet slipper, page 192.)

BUSHELING: Another term for repairing or altering suits, jackets, slacks, or outerwear.

BUSHEL MAN: A journeyman tailor who undertakes alterations and repairs.

BUSH JACKET: A belted, single-breasted shirt jacket with four PATCH POCKETS and flaps in tan cotton DRILL or GABARDINE. (*See* page 108.)

BUTTERFLY: A BOW TIE cut with thistle-shaped or flared ends, tied with a small knot and a wide bow with broad ends. Given its name in 1904 due to the success of the opera *Madama Butterfly*. Until that time, ties fashioned in a bow were simply called CRAVATS. (*See* pages 245, 247.)

BUTTERNUT: Descriptive of a brown color that was created with the dye of the bark of a butternut or walnut tree. Applied to a coarse, woolen homespun fabric once extensively worn in the Southern states of the U.S.

BUTTON-DOWN COLLAR: *See* page 134; Fred Astaire, page 140.

BUTTONHOLE GUARD: The loose strand of twisted thread sewn on the underside of the jacket's left lapel buttonhole to secure the BOUTONNIERE's stem.

BUTTON NECK: The thread allowance given to a button when sewn to a garment; aids in the use of the button as well as in promoting fewer wrinkles when the garment is buttoned.

BUTTON STANCE: The height, distance, and spacing of a coat's front buttons relative to its front edge and waist. (*See* pages 38, 84.)

BUTTON-THROUGH: Designating the closure of an outercoat or jacket in which buttons are fastened in buttonholes cut through the fabric and not covered with a fly front.

CABLE STITCH: An overlapping knitting stitch made by machine or by hand that resembles a cable; used in sweaters and socks. (*See* page 105.)

CALFSKIN: Leather made from the skin of a young calf a few days or weeks old, weighing sixteen pounds or less, processed for use in footwear and other leather goods.

CALIFORNIA COLLAR: *See* BARRYMORE COLLAR.

CAMBRIDGE GRAY: *See* OXFORD GRAY.

CAMEL: A light yellowish tan based on the color of the two-humped camel.

CAMEL HAIR: Fiber from a camel ranging in color from natural tan to brown. A very warm and lightweight wool, less delicate than cashmere. The finest camel hair comes from the undercoat of a Bactrian (two-humped) camel found in the Chinese highlands. Used either by itself or in combination with wool for coats, suits, and sweaters.

CANVAS: Originally a cloth made from hemp yarns, and named from the word *cannabis*. A general classification of strong, heavy, coarsely woven fabrics usually made of cotton. The terms canvas and duck are used interchangeably, but "canvas" generally relates to heavier constructions.

CAP: A visored fabric headpiece with a rounded crown, cut in either an eight-piece-top or a one-piece-top style. In 1571, the British Parliament passed a law requiring all English males over the age of six (but excluding nobility) to wear a woolen cap on Sundays. The law, intended to stimulate the wool trade, was repealed in 1597, but the cap with horizontal front brim of varying lengths has ever since been the headgear of leisure. (*See* page 66.)

CAPE: An outer garment without sleeves but with slits at sides for the arms.

CARDIGAN: A kind of knitting stitch. Also a knitted sweater without a collar or lapels, made with or without sleeves. Named for the seventh earl of Cardigan, who disliked disturbing his coiffeur but who did lead the Charge of the Light Brigade in the Crimean War. (*See* page 163.)

CARDING: A process for preparing wool yarn for spinning. The fibers are automatically placed in proper alignment and the impurities removed. The carded yarns are then put into a manageable form known as "sliver" that approximates the size of a man's thumb.

CARNABY STREET: The birthplace of the Peacock Revolution in swinging London. A two-block street parallel to Regent Street, London, where many shops in the 1960s introduced "mod" clothing and later, such styles as flared slacks, brightly patterned shirts, and adaptations of American Western clothes.

CASH POCKET: *See* TICKET POCKET.

CASHMERE: Fine wool from the undercoat of the long-haired Kashmir goat, which is woven or knitted into soft fabrics that are luxurious to the touch. Cashmere first won acclaim when the people of Kashmir wove it into exquisite shawls. In the nineteenth century, the English, Scottish, and French so coveted these shawls that they imitated them, especially in Paisley, Scotland. The bulk of the wool is a pale warm gray and takes dye better than any other of the rarer wools. WORSTED cashmere is finer and more expensive than woolen cashmere as the combed yarns cannot be spun with defective or imperfect fiber. Worsted cashmere yarn yields extremely light material that is more resistant to PILLING (the creation of little nubs of fuzz on surface of the fabric); used exclusively for suitings and sport jacketings. Woolen cashmere is slightly loftier, less secure, and balls easier than worsted cashmere. Woolen cashmere is used primarily for jacketings and sweaters.

CASUAL: A nonlaced, low-vamped shoe.

CAVALIER: A soft felt hat with a sharply pinched crown and a floppy brim turned up all around.

Modeled after a gloriously plumed affair from the sixteenth century worn by the Swedish cavalry, which found immediate favor with certain rakes in the British royalty. Initially sported with plumes on the left side and turned-up brim on the right in order to have more freedom wielding a sword, some courageous blade upped the third side and the soft cocked hat has been known as a Cavalier ever since. (*See* man in polka dot tie, page 158.)

CAVALRY TWILL: A sturdy-weave fabric made with a diagonal cord steep-set on a 63-degree twill weave for trousers and breeches; hence the association with British cavalry officers. Although cavalry twill is the original name, the U.S. government named it "elastique" because of its stretch quality and durability for riding clothes.

CHALK STRIPE: A stripe of ropelike effect similar to the mark made with a tailor's chalk; usually found in flannel cloths with a light- or white-color spaced-stripe setting. (*See* the "Suit Fabrics" gatefold; page 79.)

CHALLIS: A lightweight, fine-spun, plain-weave worsted wool fabric originating in England around 1830. Its name comes from a Hindi word meaning "soft to the touch." It was first used as a neckwear print cloth for small overall patterns of a sport or paisley nature and then adapted by the natural shoulder set in the 1950s for odd vests, trousers, and jackets. (*See* page 159.)

CHAMBRAY: A fine, plain-woven fabric with a soft finish utilizing a white cotton WARP and colored FILLING and found primarily in shirtings. Originated in Cambrai, France. (*See* "Fall" and "Spring" in the "Shirt Fabrics" gatefold.)

CHAMOIS: A pale yellow suede color from the tanned skin of the European goat of the same name.

CHANNEL: A slanted groove cut around the under edge of a shoe to conceal the sole's stitching.

CHARMEUSE: A lightweight, rich-looking, soft satin with a subdued luster and a dull backing. It is a registered name of Bianchini, Ferrier, and Company.

CHARVET: A weave technically known as *regence*, a name given it during its first era of popularity, from about 1715 to 1723, during the regency of Philippe, Duke of Orleans. Made from a diagonal rib weave, this soft, dull tie silk drapes very well. Charvet et Fils, the famed Paris shirtmaker, made skillful use of this fabric, as well as bold-figured, spaced-print neckties, which the name "Charvet" came to denote. (*See* page 157.)

CHELSEA BOOT: A plain-toed, side-elasticated ankle boot, similar to the JODHPUR BOOT but strapless. Popular in the 1950s and 1960s when very narrow trousers were in vogue.

CHENILLE: A yarn with a cut pile protruding all round at right angles; from the French word for "caterpillar."

CHESTERFIELD: A plain-back, slightly shaped overcoat in either single-breasted fly-front or double-breasted style. In dark gray, blue, or black, it may have a matching velvet or self-collar. The coat is named for a nineteenth-century Earl of Chesterfield. (*See* page 130.)

CHEVIOT: A tweedy woolen fabric (pronounced *chee-vee-ot*) made from the coarse yarn of the shaggy wool of the sheep found in the Cheviot hills of Scotland. Its traditional weave is a fish-bone pattern on a four-harness twill intersected by bright color silk decoration yarns. As a grainy, rough-napped tweed, the Cheviot's character is quintessentially English. (*See* page 39.)

CHEVRON WEAVE: An up-and-down zigzag effect formed by reversing the direction of the twill at regular intervals. Resembling a herringbone, this broken-twill pattern is found in topcoats and suitings. (*See* pages 72 and 73.)

CHINO: A durable, close-woven cotton fabric originally made in Manchester, England, exported to India, then exported again to China, from where it was bought for use by the U.S. Army stationed in the Philippines before WWI. The name "chino" was apparently derived from the fact that the fabric was purchased in China. Dyed in khaki, it was the only fabric and dye that would withstand the abuse of military wear. Also, the name of a men's washable sport pant made of chino cloth.

CHROME TANNING: The tanning of leather by action of chromium salts; a less expensive and less desirable method than vegetable tanning.

CHUKKA BOOT: *See* page 204.

CLASSIC: Any wearable of enduring value and interest, usually characterized by understated design and simple detailing. It used to be said that if an item of apparel remained fashionable for seven years, it could be considered a "classic."

CLEAR-FACED WORSTED: A closely woven fabric of twisted yarns, with the nap removed and thoroughly scoured so the weave is clearly visible. Used for suitings.

CLIPPED FIGURES: Small embroidered figures on the face of a fabric from which the "floats" between the figures have been clipped. An old and expensive process for weaving fine-patterned broadcloth shirting; now almost exclusively produced in Switzerland.

CLOCK: A knitted or embroidered vertical design on the outside side of the sock. (*See* page 172.)

CLUB TIE: A tie printed in the chosen colors or emblem of a club or group. The first club tie is credited to the members of the 1880 Exeter College rowing team at Oxford University who took the striped bands off their rowing hats and tied them around their necks in 1880.

CLUB BOW: BATWING BOW. The American name given to a batwing-shape bow tie. White when worn with TAILCOAT; black or midnight blue with dinner jacket. (*See* Le Corbusier, top of page 161; Philippe Noiret, page 163.)

COAT: An outer garment with sleeves, worn for warmth; style, fabric, and length vary with fashion.

COAT LENGTH: The distance as measured from the collar seam under the center of the back of the neck of a jacket's collar, down to the hem of the jacket's center bottom. (*See* page 40.)

COLLAR-ATTACHED SHIRT: Popularized after WWI, this is a standard shirt with lined, fused, or starched collar attached to a neck band.

COLLAR STAND: The vertical dimension of a collar band in front.

COLLAR STAYS: *See* SLOTTED COLLAR.

COMBINATION LAST: A LAST or form of a shoe with standard width and length measurements, but with narrower-fitting heel. For example, a D-width shoe with C-width heel.

COMBING: An advanced form of carding, the process of arranging fibers in parallel alignment and removing any fibers shorter than the desired length. The result is a smooth yarn for spinning and weaving.

CONTINENTAL LOOK: In counterpoint to America's IVY LEAGUE fashions, this 1950s American interpretation of a pseudo-Italian look featured a short, shapely, side-vented suit jacket and tapered, cuffless trousers.

CONVERTIBLE CUFFS: Cuffs that can button or take cuff links.

COPENHAGEN BLUE: A soft, medium shade of grayish blue.

CORDED STRIPE: A type of shirting fabric in which raised threads are bunched at evenly spaced intervals on the fabric's surface, giving a textured dimension.

CORDOVAN: A kind of leather for footwear made from split-horsehide or from the inner hide of the horse's rump. Named for Cordoba, Spain, where it was first made. Tanned with vegetable materials, it is durable but nonporous.

CORDUROY: A hard-wearing, cut-FILLING pile fabric made of cotton with sunken lines running lengthwise. So called because it was originally made and exclusively worn by the huntsmen of a certain Bourbon king of France, thus a corruption of the French name of the king's cloth, *cord du roi*. (*See* page 115.)

CORRESPONDENT: A spectator shoe. (*See* page 207.)

COSSACK COLLAR: A style of collar featuring a high neck band with a side closure, worn by Russian Cossack troops.

COTTON: Soft, fluffy white fibers from the seedpods of the cotton plant. First known of in India around 3000 B.C., cotton was considered very rare and precious. The longer its fiber, the better the cotton quality.

COTTON FLANNEL: A twill sport-shirt fabric in which the slack-twist FILLING threads are napped to create a woolly effect, like Viyella. In solid colors, stripes, or plaids. (*See* "Winter" in the "Shirt Fabrics" gatefold.)

COTTON GABARDINE: A durable, silky, smooth suiting or bottoms fabric with a preponderance of WARP threads in a woven twill effect showing pronounced diagonal lines or wales.

COTTON TWILL: A fabric with a diagonally steep-waled surface caused by the interlacing of the WARP and WEFT threads. TWILL is one of the three basic weaves.

COUNT SYSTEM: A scale for evaluating the quality of wool, with grades ranging from 80s or higher for merino wool to lower for tweeds, etc. The thicker the yarn, the lower the grade number; the higher the grade number, the finer the yarn.

COUNTER: A piece of stiffening material or leather inserted around the back part of the shoe to support the outer leather.

COURSE: One of the horizontal rows of loops in a knitted fabric or sweater. Courses are similar to FILLING in a woven fabric.

COVERT CLOTH: A midweight overcoating constructed from two yarns of different colors in WARP and single color in FILLING, giving a twilled, mottled appearance. Derived from the French *couvert* and associated with the riding coats worn by horsemen going into the thickets or "couvert" where the pursued game takes refuge. Covert cloth's classic shade is a tan with a drab olive cast. Used today in its original 16- to 18-ounce weight for TOPCOATS as well as lighter-weight versions for dress or sport trousers.

AS A RULE OF THUMB:
Clothes don't make the man any more than a man can demand respect. He can, however, do much to command it. —*Brooks Brothers*

COVERT COAT: A knee-length, shower-proof fly-fronted topcoat in VENETIAN TWILL, generally of a pale stone color and often with toning velvet collar and detailed with three or four rows of stitches three-eighths of an inch apart at its sleeve cuff and bottom hem. The stitchings are holdovers from the time when reinforcement was needed to protect the coat's edges from wear in the thicket.

COW HEEL: An old expression for a rounded corner shirt cuff.

CRAVAT: A term for a necktie derived from the French *cravate*. In the seventeenth century, Croatian mercenary soldiers employed by the French government wore linen scarves around their necks. Frenchwomen took up this kind of neckwear, which men later adopted. The fashion spread to England where the scarf was called a "cravate." It was the origin of the modern necktie.

CREPE: From the French verb *creper*, meaning "to fuzz and curl," derived from the Latin *crispus*. Wool crepe's crinkly matte-surface effect is obtained with a high-twist yarn known as crepe-twist yarn and alternately right-hand and left-hand twisted yarns in the FILLING.

It was popularized for menswear in the 1980s by Italian designer Giorgio Armani. Whether in a twill or plain weave, crepe cloths are dry, light, and drapey. Even though the yarns are worsted, if not of the best quality, wool crepe can be coarse to the touch.

CREPE DE CHINE: A very fine, lightweight silk made with a crepe weave, usually constructed with a raw-silk WARP and crepe-twist silk FILLING.

CREWNECK: Pullover sweater with a round rib-knit neck. Named for knit shirts worn by members of college rowing teams or "crews." (*See* Cary Grant, page 169.)

CRIMP: The natural waviness found in wool fibers. Uniformity of waviness indicates a superior wool. The more the crimp, the finer the wool.

CRIMSON: A deep to vivid purplish red to a vivid red color.

CROCHET: A material handmade or machine-knit by hooks. From the French word meaning "to hook."

CROCKING: An excess dye that rubs off on an article of apparel of which the material is said to "crock."

CROSS-STITCH: A needlework stitch sometimes used for ornamentation, or as a substitute for FELLING thin materials or those liable to fray on the edge.

CROTCH: The fork of a pair of trousers; the angle formed by the parting of two legs or branches.

CROTCH LINING: A piece of lining placed at the trousers' fork to cover the junction of its four seams.

CROTCH PIECE: A piece of self-fabric sewn on to the trousers' undersides at the fork, when the material is not wide enough.

CROWN: The rounded section of the topside head of the sleeve.

CROW'S FOOT TWILL: A satin weave with a broken twill effect.

CRUSHED BEETLES: English slang for "badly made buttonholes."

CUBAN HEEL: A broad low or medium-high heel with a straight breast and a curved back line.

CUFFS: The turn-up of trouser bottoms, which were often turned up in wet and muddy weather. King Edward VII (then Prince of Wales) started the fashion for permanently turning them up in the 1890s. PTUs (Permanent Turn-Ups) is the SAVILE ROW term for trouser turn-ups.

CUMMERBUND: A waistband of solid or patterned silk made with or without upward-facing pleats in place of a formal waistcoat with a single-breasted dinner jacket. Originally a sash worn in India (Hindi *kamarband*), brought to the West by the British Raj. In 1933, the cummerbund came to the fore as an accessory for the white mess jacket. While the mess jacket's popularity was short-lived, it did open the door for the white dinner jacket and helped make Americans cummerbund-conscious. (*See* page 246.)

CURTAIN: A hanging strip of lining from the trousers' waistband, usually of the same fabric as the waistband lining, to give a clean finish to the trousers' insides.

CUSTOM-MADE: The term applied to shoes and other apparel made to conform to the measurements of an individual customer's feet or body. The English term for this is "BESPOKE."

CUT: A term used principally in circular knitting, which indicates the number of needles per inch on the knitting machine. Thus, a machine having 34 needles per inch is a 34-cut machine and the resulting fabric is a 34-cut cloth.

CUT AND SEWN: The term applied to apparel cut from woven or knitted fabric and sewn to size by hand or machine.

CUTAWAY: In formal day wear, a coat cut away in front with tails extending to the break of the knees in back and a one-button, single-breasted front with notched or peaked lapels. The coat is cut away on a slanting line from the waist in front to the rear. It may be black or oxford gray worsted, with braided or plain edges, and is worn with a matching pale gray, white, or buff waistcoat.

CUTAWAY COLLAR: The formal day-wear shirt with widespread points that accompanied the formal cutaway ensemble. Today, the term is a generic description for any shirt collar whose points are extremely spread or open. (*See* page 26, right photograph.)

"D" POCKET TACK: A practically invisible *D*-shaped, pricked side-stitch tack running from seam to seam of a jetted pocket to reinforce its ends from breaking. Such a tailoring detail is emblematic of the finest quality in handmade clothing. (*See* Douglas Fairbanks's suit pocket, page 86.)

DB LAPELS: A pointed style of lapels, usually seen in double-breasted coats, suit jackets, or topcoats, sometimes styled in single-breasted suit coats. (*See* illustration, pages 84 and 85.)

DAKS WAISTBAND: The first self-supporting, beltless trouser, invented in 1932 by Alec Simpson. He eventually named it "Daks," the acronym combining "dad" and "slacks," in memory of his father. (*See* page 117.)

DANDYISM: Popularly thought to mean "display" or "exhibitionism," but, in fact, it only means perfectionism. In the time of Beau Brummel, dandyism was a stern reaction against the beaux and macaronis of the eighteenth century who had been foppish beyond all bounds. Brummel produced a dressing style of such severity that it renunciated excess replacing it with neatness, simplicity, and, at all times, correctness.

DART: A short seam used to give required shape to a particular part of garment. A cut or "fish" in tailor's parlance, owing its name to its rough resemblance to a fish, being wider in the middle than at either end.

DEERSTALKER: A stiff-brimmed, soft-tweed cap with ear flaps that are tied up on the crown when not in use.

Popularized during Queen Victoria's reign on Scottish estates where deer stalking was popular.

DEMI-BOSOM: A short, starched, plain or pleated bosom of a shirt. Designed primarily for formal and semiformal wear. (*See* page 238.)

DENIM: A sturdy twill-weave fabric in cotton or a blend of fibers, with a solid WARP and white FILLING. Denim was first made about two hundred years ago in Nîmes, France, and its name is a corruption of *"de Nîmes."* The word "jeans" is another corruption, of *"Genoese,"* Italian sailors from the port of Genoa being the first to wear the type.

DERBY: A bowler. A hard-finish felt hat with a rounded crown and a stiff, curled-edge brim. Taking its name from the Derby, a horse race established at Epsom Downs in 1780, it was custom to wear a bowler at this and other races in England. In the United States, the stiff hat also had associations with horse races, particularly the Kentucky Derby. In 1850, Norfolk landowner William Coke (hence the name "Billy Coke" or "Billy cock") commissioned James Lock, the venerable London hatter, to devise something rugged for his gamekeepers, whose toppers kept getting knocked off when they were chasing poachers. Lock adopted one of their own eighteenth-century riding hats and had the prototype made up by a Southwark felt maker named Bowler. The French like to point out that it should be rightly called a "Beaulieu," since that was the name of the felt maker who built the Lock prototype, before he anglicized it to Bowler. Lock, London still calls it a Coke. (*See* page 88.)

DIAGONAL WEAVE: A steep twill weave with noticeable lines that appears in many fabrics such as woolen tweed and worsted suitings. When a "diagonal" is spoken of in the trade, it is understood to mean a worsted cloth with a well-defined right-hand twill face such as the standard SERGE.

DIAMOND: A twill weave that progresses just so far and then reverses, and then reverses the reversion to make diamonds join on each other. This weave can make many different sorts of diamondlike designs, such as the pheasant's eye; for suitings and jacketings.

DICKEY: A detachable bosom that could be slipped over the body of the shirt that became an essential part of a waiter's uniform in the 1930s.

DIMPLE: The vertical groove formed under the four-in-hand or Windsor knots when tied knowledgeably. (*See* pages 167, 212.)

DINNER JACKET: *See* TUXEDO.

DISCHARGE PRINTING: The process of imprinting a pattern on a previously dyed fabric with bleaching chemicals. The chemicals discharge the dye, thus creating the pattern.

DOBBY LOOM: A loom with special attachments that make it possible to weave all-over designs, dots, and stripes in raised woven or self-color effects.

DOESKIN: The SUEDE side of the skin of a doe, lamb, or sheep, used for gloves or other leather goods. Also, a closely woven fabric with a slightly napped surface, used for slacks or sportswear.

DOLMAN SLEEVE: A full-cut sleeve that is very wide at the armhole.

DONEGAL TWEED: A hand-scoured, homespun tweed originally handwoven by crofters in County Donegal, Ireland. Now woven by machine, a characteristic of the fabric is its colorful nubs.

DOUBLE-BREASTED: A double-chested jacket, waistcoat, or outercoat cut to allow overlapping at front closing, with two vertical rows of buttons and a single row of buttonholes, with usually a single button on the underside to secure the fabric on the other side.

DOUBLE COLLAR: An old term for a turned-down or folded collar, as opposed to the upturned single wing-collar style.

DOUBLE CUFF: *See* FRENCH CUFF.

DOUBLE KNIT: Double-faced fabric that has the appearance of twice-knitted jersey fabric. Double-knit fabric by reason of its two-needle construction is a more dimensionally stable cloth than single-needle or conventional jersey fabric. Made on circular machines.

DOUBLE-VENTED. *See* page 89.

DOUBLE WARP: This closely textured twill construction for neckwear produces very full-bodied, luxurious silk that provides the ground for many spaced and all-over figures.

DRAPE: The manner in which a garment hangs from the shoulder or waist. For example, the English drape (or English lounge) is an intended style feature of men's jackets or outercoats pioneered in the early 1920s by the Prince of Wales's maverick tailor Frederick Scholte, inspired by the GUARDS COAT; it is characterized by fullness across chest and over the shoulder blades to form flat vertical wrinkles for form, comfort, and the impression of muscularity. The draped silhouette dominated men's tailored fashions throughout the 1920s and 1930s. The word derives from the French *drap,* meaning "cloth." (*See* Douglas Fairbanks and Gary Cooper, page 38.)

DRAWING-IN: A trade expression describing a necessary tightening at a part of a garment where looseness exists; a running stitch drawn tight so as to gather the material more or less upon itself.

DRESS: Refers to that side of the crotch fork of a pair of trousers where the male genitalia are placed. Before briefs, when most men wore boxers, suspenders pulled the trouser high up into the crotch, necessitating that the upper thigh area of a slim-fitting trouser be designed to accommodate the "right-" or "left-dressed man. (Most men dress on the left.)

DRESS SOFT: Edward VIII rescued men's style from its Victorian straight-jacket mentality by promoting what he termed "dress soft"—soft-collar shirts with lounge suits; pleated-front, soft, double-collar formal shirts instead of starched front ones with stiff wing collars; dinner jackets over tailcoats; backless waistcoats to replace full-backed ones, etc.

DRILL: A durable, coarse material with a twill weave extending upward toward the left SELVAGE. The name probably derives from its use for the drilling uniforms of the British army in tropical climates.

DROP: The difference in inches between the measurement of a suit jacket's chest and the suit trousers' waist. Most American men's suits are designed to accommodate a six-inch drop (for example, a 42-inch coat chest and a 36-inch trouser waist); athletic cuts feature a drop of seven inches or more.

DUCK: The most durable fabric construction, so called because it sheds water, like a duck does. Originally a plain, closely woven fabric resembling the lightweight canvas used for sails. Used for slacks, sportswear, and work clothes.

DUFFEL COAT: A three-quarter-length, loose-fitting coat with a hood fastened with loops and toggles of wood or horn. In a heavy woolen fabric, it was dubbed by the Royal Navy the "convoy coat" and became the signature wear of Field Marshal Montgomery in WWII. In the 1950s, the IVY LEAGUE set adopted it as a campus fashion. The name comes from the Belgian seaport town of Duffel.

DUKE OF WINDSOR: PRINCE OF WALES. See pages 64 and 65.

DUNGAREE: A coarse twill cotton, originally made in Bombay and taken up for wear aboard ship by sailors in the eighteenth century. The word now refers to a pair of work bottoms or jeans in blue denim.

DUPIONI: A luxurious shantung-type silk fabric made from a double silk fiber from two cocoons nested together. (See "Summer" in the "Suit Fabrics" gatefold; page 99.)

EBONY; EBON: A black color, like that of ebony wood.

ECRU: A beige or pale tan shade of unbleached silk or linen.

EDWARDIAN: Descriptive of fashions favored by King Edward VII (reigned 1901–1910) and of subsequent fashions based on the originals, such as long jackets and drainpipe pants.

EGGSHELL: An off-white, the shade of an eggshell.

EISENHOWER JACKET: Waist-length jacket of olive-drab wool worn by General Dwight D. Eisenhower and others in military service in WWII. Later, various versions of this style were adapted for civilian wear.

END: See WARP.

END-ON-END SHIRTING: A term applied to a weave of alternating white and colored WARP yarns that form a minuscule check effect; used in CHAMBRAY, BROADCLOTH, and OXFORD dress shirtings.

ENGINEERED MOTIF: A motif that appears in a particular position on a tie, usually only once.

ENGLISH BACK: The high-waisted trouser designed to be worn exclusively with suspenders and whose waistband curves upward in the back finishing into a notch at the center back seam. The ideal cut of a man's trouser when wearing a waistcoat.

ENSIGN BLUE: A dark navy blue, associated with the color of an ensign's uniform.

ENVELOPE: The outer shell of the necktie that is visible into which the interlining is inserted.

EPAULET: A strap or ornament stitched or buttoned onto the shoulder of a garment, borrowed from military uniforms. (See safari jacket, page 108.)

ERECT: An upright stance requiring a shortening of the coat's back length and a lengthening of its front. The opposite of STOOPING.

ESPADRILLE: A sandal with a canvas upper and a rope sole for beachwear. It was originally worn by dockworkers in Spain and France.

ETON COLLAR: A rounded "club" collar required as part of the Eton school uniform. (See page 130.)

EXTENSION WAISTBAND: A beltless style of trouser top where the left front of the waistband extends two to four inches across the middle to fasten with either a buttonhole and button or hook and eye onto the opposite side of the waistband's front. (See illustration, page 61, top; page 268.)

EYELET: A small hole or perforation made to receive a lace or tape, as in a shoe.

EYELET COLLAR: A dressy collar style where small holes are situated near the edge, midway up the collar, to accommodate a gold or silver collar bar that unscrews at one end. These ends are usually in the form of tiny squares or balls, which can be garnished with a small stone, such as a cabochon ruby or sapphire.

FABRIC: The most comprehensive term in the textile trade. Any kind of article made from a combination of textile yarns. Cloth, which ranks next to fabric in its descriptive broadness, cannot be used to denote lace, carpet, or knitted goods, but all of these are fabrics—that is, materials made with textile fibers or yarns.

FACE: The better-looking or intended upper side of cloth.

FACING: The lining or covering at the edge or other part of a garment, like the covering on the lapel of a dinner jacket. (See page 242.)

FAILLE: A rib-weave fabric with a cordlike effect, achieved by using heavier yarns in the FILLING than in the WARP. The opposite of REP, faille is used for lapel facings on formal evening clothes, other trimmings, and neckwear. It was originally a hood worn by nuns, a term later describing actual veiling. (See page 247.)

FAIR ISLE: Both a place and a design. The place is a small, rugged island tucked off the coast of Scotland. The design is a colorful knitting pattern with crossbands of color in a jigsaw type of configuration against a sandy background. Sweaters bearing this pattern were first made by the island's crofters or tenant farmers. Hearing that the Hebrian farmers were in economic trouble, the Duke of Windsor donned one as the captain of the Royal and Ancient Golf Club in Saint Andrews in 1922, catapulting the sweater and the island's economy into fast-forward. (*See* Prince of Wales, page 8, bottom right.)

FASHION MARKS: Small indentations around the collar and shoulders of a full-fashioned garment showing that it was knitted in one piece and then stitched. Fashioning means the process of increasing or decreasing the width of knitted fabric by controlling the movement of the needles. *See* FULL-FASHIONED.

FAST: The term applied to a color that retains its original shade after exposure to sunlight, water, bleaching, pressing, heat, etc.

FEDORA: A men's soft felt hat with a center crease and a rolled brim. It takes its name from the drama *Fédora* (1882), by Victorien Sardou. (*See* Biddle, page 3.)

FELLING: Sewing one piece of material, by its edge, upon another, the sewn edge being either raw or turned in, according to the material or the purpose to be accomplished.

FELTING: The process of combing fur particles or other fibers by kneading, then shrinking these into one solid piece of material. Three ounces of fur make a hat. Beaver was once used, but now mostly nutria has taken its place.

FILLING: *See* WEFT. In weaving, the yarn running at right angles to the length, or WARP yarn.

FINE: The term applied to grades of wool or cotton in weaving, such as 100s, 120s, 150s.

FINGERTIP LENGTH: The length of a coat that extends to the tips of the fingers, or midway between the hips and knees.

FINISHING: Treating a fabric by covering the surface to improve its appearance, by bleaching, dyeing, printing, or waterproofing it. It is said that textile fabrics are "made in the finishing," as no yard of cloth is completely free from defects.

FISHERMAN KNIT: Bulky, hand-knit sweater made of natural-color, water-repellent wool in fancy stitches characteristic of Aran Islands off the Bay of Galway in Ireland. Originally from Irish fishermen who wore handknit sweaters in a pattern indicating where they lived.

FLAIR: A surplus of width put in below the waist of a garment to give an intentional appearance of looseness at sides. Produces an A-line shape from the waist down. (*See* hacking jacket, page 108.)

FLANNEL: From the Welsh *gwlanen,* a loosely woven cloth of woolen or worsted yarns in plain or twill weave with a napped surface to conceal the weave.

FLAP: A covering for the mouth of a pocket.

FLARES: *See* BELL BOTTOMS.

FLAT SEAT: A seat with less fullness than average, causing the garment to appear too big in seat area.

FLIGHT JACKET: Waist-length jacket of leather or other material with a sheepskin lining and trimming, fastened with a slide fastener or with buttons.

FLOATS: WARP threads that are not mechanically tucked into the back side of jacquarded design that must "cross " or "float" over the WEFT threads on the back surface of a woven fabric.

FLY FRONT: A closure in which a placket or piece of fabric covers the buttons or zipper; used on coats, jackets, and trousers.

FOB: A chain or ribbon hanging from a pocket watch, connecting it with an ornament. It is worn on the man's left side (the same side of which a man carried his sword, since the watch was easier to locate with his right hand than with his left). (*See* pages 84 and 91.)

FOOTWEAR LEGEND: The reason why an old boot or shoe is tied to a honeymoon car is a reminder of an ancient custom: In Anglo-Saxon times, the shoe had the importance that a wedding ring does in modern times. The bride would pass her shoe to the groom during the ceremony, and he would strike her head with it as a sign of his future authority—a warning to his spouse to watch her "steppe!"

FORK: *See* CROTCH.

FORMAL: The term applied to clothes and accessories for wear on full-dress, or formal, occasions; tailcoats or dinner jackets for evening; cutaway coats or oxford jackets with striped trousers for daytime.

FORWARD PLEAT: A trouser pleat that folds facing the fly; associated with English tailoring, as opposed to the reversed pleat, originally called the Continental pleat, which faces toward the pockets. (*See* Errol Flynn, page 118.)

FOULARD: To a Frenchman, a *foulard* is a silk handkerchief. Today, foulard is a twill cloth for neckwear or scarves, usually made in a light silk fabric for printing multicolored patterns and often shaped like teardrops or abstract motifs. Introduced to America in 1890 by the senior partner of Brooks Brothers, Mr. Francis Lloyd. (*See* pocket square, page 218.)

FOUR-IN-HAND: One of several names for the "slip knot" (the "sailors knot" being another), used to knot the "long tie" at the end of the nineteenth century and early twentieth centuries. The four-in-hand is thought to be a reference to the Four-in-Hand Club, founded in England in the nineteenth century by young men who indulged in carriage racing and who adopted this kind of knot for their ties. Alternatively, it could refer to the type of knot used by the driver when he held the reins of a carriage pulled by four horses in a manner that resembled a knot with two long trailing ends. (*See* pages 166 and 167.)

FOXING: The leather used in the lower part of the quarter or back portion of the shoe's UPPER.

FRENCH BOTTOMS: A tailoring trick of giving trousers the appearance of normal-size cuffs that do not have enough length to make the cuff width's properly.

FRENCH CUFF: The double-length, turned-back cuff of a dress shirt; fastened with cufflinks.

FRENCH TIPPING: The finishing of the inside ends of a necktie with the same material as the shell of the tie, instead of a lining; a more expensive and skilled finish to a tie.

FRESCO: Many summer suitings in the 1920s were fashioned of a loosely woven, crisp, woolen fabric called "fresco." As it weighed almost 13 ounces to the yard, it was scarcely lightweight, but it's porousity accounted for its coolness. Today, milled in 8- to 10-ounce worsteds, this father of the modern high-twist cloth makes a perfect antidote to wrinkle-prone tropical-weight suitings.

FRONT PLEATS: The pleats in the topsides of trousers that run in line with trousers' front creases. (See page 61.)

FULL-CARDIGAN STITCH: A basic loop structure in bulky rib knitting is produced by plain needles knitting while the rib needles tuck. At the next course, the reverse occurs. The fabric has the same appearance on both sides, there being an equal number of loops on the face and the reverse of the fabric.

FULL-FASHIONED: A term applied to sweaters and other garments completely knitted to their finished shape on the machine. Shaping is done by adding or subtracting stitches to widen or narrow the fabric in desired areas. The process is used for socks, sweaters, underwear, and other sportswear.

FUSED COLLAR: A collar stiffened by an interlining laminated through heat and pressure to the top and/or the underside fabric to prevent wilting and wrinkles.

FUSING: Bonding the inner and outer shell of a garment by welding the two layers together. The most common method of tailoring coat fronts today, the interlining is coated with a bonding agent and "fused" to the underside of the surface fabric with heat and pressure, giving the cloth more shape and stability. In expensive clothes, these two sections would be sewn together by hand.

GABARDINE: A twill weave in single- or two-ply combed yarn; sometimes a three-harness weave. Characterized by diagonal twill lines in either a 45- or 63-degree obtained with more WARP threads than WEFT threads, tightly woven as to make it almost waterproof. Usually in solid colors, in wool, cotton, or wool blend, this delicate but luxuriously silky cloth is popular for midweight suitings or trousers. (See David Niven, page 114.)

GALOSH: Overshoe of rubber or rubberized fabric with a rubber sole, closed in front by a zipper or buckles.

GARNET: A dark red; a precious mineral used in a gem that is compared in color to the fruit of a pomegranate. (See boutonnierre, page 201.)

GAUGE: The spacing of the needles of a knitting machine, which determines the thickness or fineness of the knitted fabric. The higher the gauge or number of needles per given area, the thinner the fabric.

GAUNTLET BUTTON: Button on sleeve placket to close the opening made by the cuff's attachment to the tapering shirt sleeve.

GILLIE/GHILLIE: A low court shoe with corded lacings that pass through leather loops instead of eyelets and cross backward and forward across the instep, sometimes also around the ankle. A Scottish creation, they are usually made without a tongue. However, if a tongue is used, it is usually fringed. The present ghillie is named after the highland servants who wore them.

GIMP THREAD: A special twisted thread suitable for making raised edges around handmade buttonholes.

GIMPING: Trimming and simultaneously decorating the edges of leather pieces. The shoemaker does this with a gimping machine in which steel tools with various patterns and designs can be fitted.

GINGHAM: From the Malaya word *genggang,* which became the French *guingan.* A dyed-in-the-yarn fabric, an exact replica of the madras construction, or as many threads in WEFT as in the WARP. Generally shown in checks or plaids. (See David Niven, page 209.)

GLEN PLAID: A four-by-four and two-by-two color effect in both the WARP and FILLING directions; the fancy overplaid of the GLENURQUHART PLAID is missing in a glen plaid. (See page 268.)

GLENURQUHART PLAID: A woolen or worsted suiting or coating material made with the ever popular glen plaid with an overplaid effect weave in both WARP and FILLING directions. This is one of the "district checks" originally adopted for livery wear by nineteenth-century Scottish landowners. It was a favorite of Edward VIII when he was the Prince of Wales. (See the "Suit Fabrics" gatefold.)

GOING NATIVE: An expression coined in England during the 1920s and 1930s, meaning to adopt the indigenous dress of any local culture. For the European, it meant wearing the espadrille of the Mediterranean fisherman, the beret of the Basque local, or the seaward chic of the Riviera; for Americans, it translated into dressing like the Caribbean islanders of Bermuda and Jamaica.

GORGE: Seam that joins the jacket's collar to its lapel. (See pages 42 and 43.)

GRAIN: The markings that are left on the finished surface of a leather after the removal of hair; leather with a patterned surface, produced by printing or embossing for footwear.

GRANITE GRAY: A darkish shade of gray suggestive of granite.

GREIGE (GRAY) GOODS: The state of cloth as it comes from loom prior to bleaching, dying, or finishing. The name comes from the French word *greige*, which used to refer to natural silk cloth before finishing—later anglicized to "gray."

GRENADINE: A neckwear fabric with a gauzelike quality made on a jacquard loom with threads crossing from side to side. Originally a black silk lace worn in France during the eighteenth century. First woven exclusively in Italy on hand looms, the sumptuousness of its open texture has established this solid-color tie as a staple in the lightweight wardrobes of the world's sartorial cognoscenti.

GROSGRAIN: This dulled, rib-silk facing is used as an alternative to the shinier satin for trimming on formal evening clothes, neckwear, and accessories. It originated in the Middle Ages and gained popularity in France when silk yarn was used to make fabric, and is noted for its pronounced FILLING rib effect. Like FAILLE, the term implies a heavy or thick grain line in the crosswise direction of the goods. (*See* page 247.)

GUARDS COAT: A civilian overcoat patterned after the long coat worn by the grenadier guards in England. It is a dark-color, double-breasted coat with a half-belt, an inverted pleat extending from between the shoulder blades to the bottom hem, and deep folds at the sides.

GUM TWILL: A name sometimes applied to a FOULARD. Raw silk is left slightly harsh by a certain gum exuded by the silkworm. As its removal lessens weight, a gum twill is woven with part of the gum intact to be boiled off after weaving. This process produces a velvet textured surface similar to the feel of ancient madder.

GUMMIES: An old-fashioned term for casual shoes with thick crepe-rubber soles.

GUN CLUB CHECK: This check was originally The Coigach from the Ullapool area in the west of Scotland. At around 1874, it was adopted by an American shooting club as their livery and the name changed. Its WARP and WEFT are generally arranged in three colors and woven in a two-up, two-down twill. An even check pattern with rows of alternating colors and, usually, a white background. Used for suitings, sports jackets, and trousers. (*See* Jimmy Stewart, page 159.)

GUN FLAP: Originally an extra thickness of fabric added to neutralize the impact of a shotgun's recoil on the shooting jacket's shoulder. Nowadays it is added as simply as a decorative feature.

GUNMETAL: A dark gray shade, similar to the shade of the metal of a gun barrel.

GUSSET: A fabric section inserted at the seam of a garment to allow extra fullness for easy movement and to serve as a reinforcement. Also, an extra layer or piece of cloth inserted at the bottom joining of a shirt's side seams for reinforcement. The use of the gusset is a symbol of higher-quality shirt making. Also, the center section of a well-made necktie that goes around the back of the neck and underneath the collar joining the front blade to the small end.

HACKING JACKET: "Hack" is short for "hackney," designating a saddle horse for ordinary road or bridle path riding rather than for racing or hunting. A longer-than-regular-length tweed jacket for riding a horse, with a waist line raised a three-quarter inch for more "spring" or flair at the hip to allow for width when sitting astride a horse, a deep center vent to open over the horse (the originals had waterproofed tail lining), three- or four-button front with short lapels and slanted side flap pockets (with or without a slanted ticket pocket) for easy access. The hacking silhouette greatly influenced the cut of high-class English tailoring. (*See* page 108.)

HACKING POCKET: A hip-level flap pocket at the side of a sport jacket that is slanted or cut on a an angle, as with the flap pockets on a hacking jacket. (*See* page 88, top.)

HAIRCLOTH: A stiff, wiry fabric usually made of a cotton or linen in the WARP and formerly horsehair (as in the horse's mane) in the FILLING as an interlining or stiffening material. Today, mohair or forms of horsehair are used in the filling.

HAIRLINE STRIPES: Very narrow stripes in one-thread thickness that resemble hair made by weaving single threads in color to contrast with the background of worsted wool or cotton shirting. More dimensional than a solid, the fine fancy lines set off the wearer as well as giving him a slightly elongated effect. (*See* "Shirt Fabrics" gatefold; page 155, bottom.)

HALF-BACK: A measurement across the widest part of the jacket's blade from the back center seam to the point where the sleeve's back seam intersects the armhole.

HALF-SLEEVE: The sleeve of a shirt or other garment extending approximately to the elbow. (*See* the Duke of Windsor, page 76.)

HALF-WAIST: A measurement taken at the waistline from the jacket's back center seam to the coat's front edge.

HALF-WINDSOR: A knot larger than the four-in-hand but smaller than a full Windsor; tied in the manner of a lock knot or a partial full-Windsor knot.

HAND; HANDLE: The touch or feel of a fabric. An experienced individual can determine the quality and character of a fabric by handling, pulling, stroking, or squeezing it.

HAND-BLOCKED: The term applied to material printed by hand with a wooden or a wood-and-metal block.

HANDPICKED: The term applied to hand-stitching at the edges of a jacket, lapel, vent, pocket, or trouser seams. The expected finishing for top-quality tailored clothes. (*See* page 213.)

HAND-ROLLED HEM: The edge of a handkerchief or other article rolled and stitched by hand. In a necktie, the ends are folded under about a quarter inch and stitched by hand, producing a soft roll of fabric held by irregular stitches; found only on high-quality neckties.

HANDWOVEN: Woven on a loom operated by hand and foot. The finished fabric, such as a tweed or homespun, has irregularities that enhance its authenticity, adding character and appeal.

HARMONY: The pleasing effect achieved by the proper relationship between and coordination of colors, fashion details, and accessories in the assemblage of one's attire.

HARNESS: The frame on a loom that is raised to separate the WARP from the FILLING yarns to allow the shuttle to pass between them. There are at least two harnesses on a loom. More elaborate weaves require more harnesses, for example, a bird's-eye loom requires four harnesses.

HARRIS TWEED: The trademark of woolen material spun, dyed, and woven by hand by the crofters of Harris and Lewis and other islands of the Outer Hebrides islands of Scotland.

HAT BOWS: Today, the feathery-like bow on the hat's inside, a holdover from the ancient drawstring that used to fit the hat tight on the head. Men's hat bows are always worn on the left side of the hat—a reminder of the days when the plume or love token was worn on the heart side for love, and away from the sword side for safety.

AS A RULE OF THUMB:

Clothes that are too trendy are destined to become old before their time. Today's peacock is tomorrow's feather duster. — Brooks Brothers

---

HEAD FORWARD: When a human figure's head is carried forward slightly from the normal. This usually requires an alteration of shortening the jacket's collar and a slight increase in its back length.

HEM: The finish produced by turning back the raw edge of a material and sewing it by hand or machine.

HERRINGBONE: A ribbed twill weave in which an equal number of threads slant right and left to form a zigzag pattern similar to that of a fish's skeleton (North American *Herring*). A popular design for clothing and accessories. (*See* Bobby Short, page 154.)

HIGH-RISE: *See* RISE.

HIGH SHOULDERS: A figure with shoulders whose squareness is greater than the norm.

HIGH-WATER PANTS: Pants that reach only to a point slightly above the ankles.

HOMBURG: A formal-looking soft felt hat with a tapered crown and a rolled, bound-edge brim. In black or dark blue, it may be worn with a dinner jacket; in

other colors, with a business suit as well. Introduced by King Edward VII, who brought it back from Germany to London as an alternative formal town hat. Later popularized in the 1930s by British foreign secretary (later prime minister) Anthony Eden. (*See* page 91.)

HOPSACKING: Originally, a loosely woven burlap carried by the pickers of hops; a general description of a coarse, loosely woven fabric made in a basket- or hopsack weave. Two threads of both WEFT and WARP rise together instead of only one, using rough-textured yarns. Found in suitings, jacketings, and other sportswear.

HOUNDSTOOTH CHECK: A medium-size check pattern with jagged edges resembling those of a dog's tooth and is not perfectly square. (*See* page 11.)

HUDDERSFIELD: A town in Yorkshire, England, that is the center of the better British worsted-weaving industry.

HUDSON BAY COAT: A double-breasted, woolen outercoat in white or off-white, with two or three wide, colorful horizontal stripes around the lower part.

HUNTER GREEN: A deep shade of green with a faint yellowish cast.

HUNTING PINK: Not actually "pink" but a softer shade of scarlet. Originally all English hunting rights belonged to the king and those taking part in a hunt had to wear the king's livery, which was scarlet. The authentic hunting pink dye is said to come from a paste made up of male cactus beetles mixed with tin in acid.

INLAYS: The extra cloth left in seams, which enable enlargement. Sometimes called outlets.

INSEAM: The distance in inches from the crotch, or fork, to the bottom of the trousers. Also, a seam on a glove that is sewn inside out.

INSOLE: The foundation of the shoe; a piece of leather between one-tenth and one-seventh of an inch thick, cut to conform exactly to the size and shape of the bottom of the LAST of the shoe. Also, the part of the shoe between the WELT and the outsole.

INSTEP: The bridge over the top of the foot.

INTARSIA: From the Italian term for *intarsiare*, meaning "inlay." A knitted design that gives the effect of being inlaid in the fabric with its pattern in solid colors showing on both sides of the fabric.

INTERLINING: A cloth or material sewn between the body fabric of a garment and the exposed lining inside, for stiffness, shape, or buoyancy. Also, the piece of material—most often wool or a wool blend—found inside the envelope of the tie to give it bulk and firmness.

INTERLOCK: A term applied to a closely knitted fabric produced on a circular knitting machine fitted with long and short needles.

INVERNESS: A town in northwest Scotland where temperatures demand warm garments. The coat of that name is a single-breasted, sleeveless coat with peaked or notched lapels and an attached cape extending to the elbows as protection to the arms and upper body. In tweeds, it was a favorite of the Victorian traveler. In dark, smooth fabrics, it metamorphoses into an elegant formal coat. Like the DEERSTALKER, it is also apocryphally associated with Sherlock Holmes.

INVERTED PLEAT: A pleat with fullness on the inside; the reverse of a box pleat. (*See* G. Fitzpatrick's breast pocket, page 107.)

IRIDESCENCE: The interplay or reflection of multiple colors attained by using a variety of colors in the WARP and FILLING of a fabric. (*See* Gary Cooper's tie, page 38.)

IVY LEAGUE: Another term for America's natural-shoulder fashion, circa 1950, as popularized by Brooks Brothers and found on America's Ivy League college campuses. A kind of suit in which the jacket has natural-width shoulders, is straight-hanging, and has a center vent. The trousers are plain-front and straight-hanging, made without PLEATS at the WAISTBAND.

JABOT: Originally a ruffle on the bosom of a man's shirt; a style of neckwear for formalwear with a neckband and ruffles below it.

JACQUARD: Named after Joseph Marie Jacquard, a Frenchman born in Lyons, who, in 1801, invented a loom that used punched cards to weave patterns in cloth. Napoleon invited him to Paris to demonstrate it, and by 1806 the loom was patented. Today jacquard is a term used to describe any motif pattern or intricately woven fabric, from tapestry and brocade to damask and knits.

JAMAICA SHORTS: Shorts ending at mid-thigh, shorter than BERMUDA SHORTS. Named for the style of shorts found on the island of Jamaica in the 1920s.

JASPE. A neckwear fabric with an arrangement of fine stripes formed by light, medium, and dark shades of a given color.

JEAN JACKET: A waist-length jacket of denim or other twill cotton with panel stitching and chest-height patch pockets.

JERSEY STITCH: A knitted fabric made from loops that intermesh in one direction with the result that the fabric has one appearance on the face side and a wholly different one on the reverse side; made of wool, cotton, or blends of fibers for shirts, sportswear, and underwear. It derives its name from the island of Jersey, where sailors first wore sweaters made of this fabric.

JETTING: *See* BESOM. From the French *jeter,* "to shoot forth" or "to throw out." The tailor's word "jetting" means to bead or pipe cloth or other material at pockets as in "showing" their edges. Jettings may be placed at top as well at bottom of pocket mouths. When jetted on both sides, the pocket is termed "double-besom" or "double-jetted." (*See* page 86.)

JIGGER BUTTON: A name given by tailors to the button placed inside the left forepart of a man's double-breasted coat or waistcoat, so as to keep the underneath wrap from dropping downward.

JIPIJAPA: Synonym for *toquilla:* palmlike trees the leaves of which yield fibers that are plaited into hats known as Panama hats. Also, a broad-brimmed planter's style of hat.

JIVY IVY: A narrow-shouldered, single-breasted jacket with a four-button front and snug fitting pant; any garment or dressing style tending to parody by exaggeration the Ivy League look.

JODHPUR BOOT: A low leather boot with a strap-and-buckle fastener or elastic side for wear especially with JODHPURS. (*See* page 4.)

JODHPURS: Long riding trousers flared over the hips and narrow from knee to ankle. First seen in England where they were appropriated from the state of Jodhpur, India, whose locals favored them over the smarter, but more effort-consuming, breeches and polished leather riding boots. (*See* page 4, upper right picture.)

KHAKI: A Hindi-Urdu word meaning "dusty" or "earth-colored." The first khaki-colored cloth was soaked in mud and ironed dry. Khaki has come to refer to brown tones and olive tints, which military forces have found useful in reducing visibility against ground and foliage. In the nineteenth century, the British in India wore the first khaki uniforms.

KILTIE: A shawl tongue of fringed leather that is draped over the instep of a shoe, covering the laces and eyelet.

KIPPER: A wide-width necktie that became fashionable in the sixties thanks to Michael Fish, the buyer of the famous Jermyn Street shirtmaker in London, Turnbull and Asser. The question is whether the moniker came from Mr. Fish's name or the tie's shape, which resembled a "kipper" fish

KNEE: The knee measurement of a trouser, which is determined by halving its inseam and then measuring two inches above the resulting fold line.

KNICKERS; KNICKERBOCKERS: Loose pants draped over the knee and fastened with a band and buckle above the calf, originally worn for golf and then other sports. The name comes from Diedrich Knickerbocker, fictitious author of *A History of New York* (actually written by Washington Irving). Plus-fours are full-cut knickers that pouched four inches below the knee; plus-twos and plus-eights were described accordingly. (*See* page 66.)

LA COSTE STITCH: A cross-tuck construction with alternate plain jersey courses produced on a fine cut machine. Used primarily for knit sport shirts of mercerized cotton yarn.

LAMB'S WOOL: The material made of fibers shorn from lambs up to seven months old. The fibers are soft and have superior spinning properties.

LAPEL: The facing of a jacket or coat front; that part of a jacket or coat front joined with the collar that is worn turned back.

LAPPED SEAM: A swelled seam. The pronounced seam made by pressing the seam to one side, its two edges being lapped over each other and finished by a row of top stitches of varying width, sewn either by hand or machine. If the lap seam is left open and not stitched down, it's called an "open lap seam." This seam detailing renders the odd jacket or trouser more sporty. (*See* Henry Fonda, page 106; Humphrey Bogart, page 180.)

LAST: A form of wood or metal shaped like a foot, over which a shoe is fashioned. In BESPOKE shoemaking, a pair of individual lasts is hand-carved by a special last-maker from beech, maple, or beam wood into a precisely contoured facsimile of the customer's feet—protrusions, indentations, and all. The title chosen for the book written on the life of John Lobb, the legendary English bootmaker bears a pun: *The Last Comes First*.

LAWN: Originally from the city of Laon, France, a fabric used for garments worn by the clergy. The present-day lawn is a lightweight cotton or linen fabric of the better grade, usually made of combed cotton yarn and given a polished surface.

LE SMOKING: *See* TUXEDO.

LIBA: A semiautomatic machine that reproduces hand slip-stitching in necktie manufacture.

LIGNE: Unit of French origin, equal to $^1/_{11}$ inch, used in measuring the width of hat bands and bindings of hats.

LINE: The standard for measuring buttons; the twelfth part of an inch. (*See also* LIGNE.)

LINEN: A strong, lustrous yarn or fabric of smooth-surfaced flax fabrics that wrinkles easily. The fiber is actually flax. Mentioned in the Bible, linen was woven more than four thousand years ago.

LININGS (SHOE): Used to reinforce and absorb perspiration, afford a smooth fit to the inside of the shoe and to help it retain its shape. Materials for linings are leather on all better grades of footwear.

LINKS-AND-LINKS: The term applied to a pattern of purl or fancy-knitting stitches produced on a special machine known as a links-and-links machine that knits vertically rather than horizontally. This is the stitch used for alpaca golf-type sweaters. (*See* alpaca vest, page 163.)

LISLE: A fine quality of tightly twisted, long staple-cotton yarn that is passed near a gas flame to remove the fuzz and give it a sleek surface. Originally used in hosiery, now used for fine knit shirts. It is so called because it was first made in Lisle (now Lille), France.

LOAFER: A brand name of a moccasin-style slip-on shoe with a broad flat heel registered by Nettleton Shops, Inc. (*See* page 203.)

LODEN: The olive green of the Austrian Tyrol, which originated in the sixteenth century. The peasants, who first made this green shade of cloth in the mountainous district were called Loderers, looming the material from the rough and oily wool of the area's mountain sheep. Better loden cloth often has some camel hair in it and is waterproof without being treated chemically.

LODEN COAT: The favorite coat of the European "Ivy League." A single-breasted coat with a button-through front, military collar, chest yoke, slash pockets, deep inverted pleat in back and a specially stitched set-in shoulder design featuring an opening in the lower part of the armhole for ventilation and maneuver. It was made from a soft fleece fabric originating in Austria of warm, shower-proof, lightweight forest green loden cloth. Worn by sportsmen from the Tyrol for years for walking, shooting, and driving.

LONDON-SHRUNK: The shrinkage of cloth by the cold-water method in order to prevent shrinkage and readied to be cut up. The dry cloth to be shrunk is folded between an upper and lower layer of wet cloth, then dried naturally and afterward pressed by cold hydraulic power. Originally all Yorkshire cloth was sent down to London merchants to be submitted to a consistent method of shrinkage control. Nowadays the technique is applied usually at the seat of production, but the term "London shrunk" remains a widely accepted standard.

LONG FRONT BALANCE: An excess of length in the front balance of garment; causes garment to appear full at front-crease edge when buttoned, a defect common on clothes worn by stooping figures.

LONG NECK: A neckline that requires a higher placement of collar. (*See* page 125.)

LONG-ROLL COLLAR: A shirt collar set low in front with points four inches long and adequate fullness to permit a rolled effect.

LOOPING: The hand-fastening of sweater seams in high-quality sweaters; also done on a looping machine to simulate a handmade appearance.

LOUNGE SUIT: The early name given to a SACK SUIT with single- or double-breasted jacket in soft fabric for business wear.

LOVAT: Named after Lord Lovat of Scotland who preferred blends of hazy blue, soft green, and tan and gray, suggesting the heathered tones found in the landscape of the Highlands.

LOW-SLOPE COLLAR: The upper line of an attached collar that has a forward slope and a low neck band. (*See* shirt collar in illustration, page 49.)

MACCLESFIELD: *See* pages 147–49.

MACKINAW: A type of heavy-napped wool blanket in big stripes or checks, used to barter with the Native American Indians around Fort Mackinaw, Michigan. The blanket material was also turned into coats for lumberjacks. The typical coat was double-breasted in a fingertip length with shawl collar and an all-around belt that became known as the "Mackinaw."

MACKINTOSH: The term used in England today for a raincoat, called a "Mac," for short. Years ago it was a term often applied to any shiny, black waterproof raincoat. In 1823, Charles Mackintosh, a Glasgow chemist, patented a method of bonding rubber between two layers of cloth to make the first waterproof fabric.

MAD AS A HATTER: A phrase first applied in 1830 to William Henry Miller, a famous English hatter who suffered sunstroke and went insane after being carried bareheaded through the streets of London on his election to the House of Commons.

MADDER: A plant from Eurasia, the root of which was used as a type of vegetable dyestuff for soft-tone printed fabrics for neckwear, known as madder prints. Madder neckties are characterized by deep, muted colors and a soft, suedelike texture. (*See* James Stewart, page 159.)

MADRAS: Plain weave cotton or blended material for strongly colored stripes, checks, and plaids; used for shirts and sportswear. It is named for Madras, India, an early source of such textiles. (*See* "Summer" in the "Shirt Fabrics" gatefold.)

MAGENTA: A shade of red with a tinge of purple, named for the Battle of Majenta (1859), in which much blood was spilled.

MANDARIN: The term applied to a pajama top with a stand-up collar about an inch high and a front closed with buttons or frogs; inspired from styles of Chinese Mandarin costume.

MAO JACKET: A button-front jacket or tunic with a standing collar an inch or slightly higher, so called because it was worn for most of his life by Mao Tse-tung, chairman of the People's Republic of China.

MARCELLA: A double-twill cotton material (PIQUÉ), usually having a diamond pattern used for formal waistcoats and formal shirt bosoms. Also, a semiformal evening shirt promoted by London's Bond Street shirtmakers in the 1930s as an alternative to the soft-collar, pleated-front dinner shirt for wear with a dinner jacket. The marcella's turndown collar, demi-bosom front, and French cuffs are in white piqué, with the body and sleeves in white voile or broadcloth.

MARL: A blend of two or more colors in a yarn used primarily in knitted articles such as socks and sweaters, but also used in woven fabrics such as tweeds.

MEDALLION: The perforated pattern punched in center of shoe tips. (*See* page 197.)

MELTON: A compact, heavily felted woolen fabric, usually of a plain weave with short, napped surface, primarily used for overcoats. Melton cloth is named after the town of Melton Mowbray, a hunting area of England where it was first worn.

MERCERIZED COTTON: A smooth, lustrous knitted fabric resulting from the treatment of cotton yarn or fabric under a tension with a solution of caustic soda; named after John Mercer, an English calico printer, who perfected the process in 1844. Mercerizing lusterizes cotton by strengthening the yarn, adding absorptive qualities, and improving dye penetration.

MERINO: An Australian breed of sheep descended from the original Spanish breed whose fleece is dense and uniformly high in quality, yielding the whitest wool with a softness resembling that of cashmere. Developed in Spain by the Romans and Arabs, the merino sheep is the forebearer of all the world's leading wool-producing sheep. The first wool produced from this breed was shipped to England in 1808; wools of 1960s quality and finer.

MESS JACKET: A semiformal, waist-length dress-white military jacket adapted for civilian wear that was the progenitor of the white summer dinner jacket. (*See* page 252.)

MILL FINISH: The finish of a worsted fabric with a slightly napped surface.

MILLE STRIPE: A single-thread dress shirt design that looks like a fancy solid. Its name derives from the French term for a "thousand tiny stripes."

MOCCASIN: The true moccasin has a single unseamed piece of leather that extends all the way under the bottom of the foot and upward to form the back, sides, and toe section. The forepart of the foot is covered by a piece of leather called a "plug." (*See* page 203.)

MOCHA: A dark, grayish-brown shade.

MOCK-TURTLE: A type of knit collar with a separate neckband stitched down to simulate a low turtleneck collar.

MOGADORE: Although a closely woven fine-corded fabric with an extremely firm texture, Mogadore is really a FAILLE. Frequently used for stripe neckwear featuring a repeat of a wide stripe surrounded by many smaller contrasting stripes. Originally a plain woven silk treated with an Arabic gum that at one time made its principal entrance to commerce through the port of Mogadore.

MOHAIR: This sleek, lustrous material is made from the long, silky hair of the angora goat. Its crisp, dry feel makes it ideal for summer formal wear and suitings. Today, mohair is sometimes blended with a fine worsted wool, producing a cloth with less sheen, but more softness and drape. From the Arabic word for goat hair, *mukhayyar,* later called, in medieval times, "mockhaire." (*See* Sir Anthony Eden, page 98.)

MOIRÉ: An all-over watered appearance of silk, velvet, or other fabrics, mostly in FAILLE or TAFFETA weaves, achieved with engraved rollers. The word was originally applied to fabrics of great value, as mentioned in fifteenth- and sixteenth-century French documents. When watered silks became fashionable in eighteenth-century France, the word *moiré* was applied to them. (*See* Cecil Beaton, page 245.)

MOLESKIN: A rugged, one-WARP, two-FILLING cotton fabric in which there are two picks of face filling and one pick of back filling. Made in a satin construction, the cloth is given a thick, soft nap on the back to simulate mole fur. Used for trousers for men in usually a drab olive or brown shade. (*See* sportsman's trousers, page 204.) Also, the term used to describe the grayish-brown color resembling the skin tone of a mole.

MOMME: A Japanese formula used in the silk industry to measure the weight of a silk cloth. One *momme* cloth equals 4.33 grams per square meter, or .127 ounces per square yard.

MONK STRAP SHOE: *See* page 198.

NAILHEAD: Small dotted design, suggestive of the head of a nail, used for worsted suiting cloths in a sharkskin weave. Also found as micro-nailhead (*See*

"Spring" in the "Suit Fabrics" gatefold; Ralph Lauren, page 93.)

NAP: The fibrous surface given to a cloth in finishing, such as flannel and doeskin. Surface fibers are raised by revolving cylinders covered with metal points or teased burrs.

NAPPING: *See* BRUSHING.

NATTE: A basket weave of heavier construction, employing several colors to achieve a pebbled effect, used in neckwear. The word is French and means "braided."

NATURAL SHOULDER: *See* IVY LEAGUE, and page 39.

NAVY BLUE: As worn in the British Navy, this color is virtually black.

NEAT: A term used in the neckwear trade for referring to a conservative tie pattern with small regular figuration. (*See* page 139.)

NECKBAND SHIRT: A shirt with a narrow band circling the neck and buttonholes at the ends designed to be attached to a separate collar.

NECKERCHIEF: A square knotted or draped in ascot fashion around the neck, usually made of cotton, silk, linen, or a wool-blend. (*See* page 169.)

NECKERTIE: A square folded and draped around the neck with the ends tied in a FOUR-IN-HAND or other knot and worn with an open-necked sport shirt. It is usually made of cotton, silk, linen, or a wool-blend. (*See* page 169.)

NECKTIE: The standard term used for male neckwear from around 1840 onward, superseding the word "neckcloth." Two or more thicknesses of fabric sewn in a shaped scarf or band for wear under the collar fold or around the neck and knotted in front.

NEHRU JACKET: A single-breasted jacket of shapely lines buttoned high to a standing-band collar, named for India's former prime minister Jawaharlal Nehru.

NEUTRAL: The term applied to color that contains none of the primary colors. Undyed linen is one example.

NORFOLK JACKET: An informal jacket with a box pleat at each side in front, yoked, two similar box pleats in back, and an all-around belt. Considered the first sport jacket.

NORWEGIAN: First popularized by Londoners as a casual shoe, this footwear was later adopted by visiting Americans in the mid-thirties. Two models became popular: a slip-on moccasin-toe casual that was called "WEEJUNS," and a laced model with a split-toe design and moccasin front that became known as the Norwegian. Originally, Norwegian shoes were hand-sewn by Norwegian fisherman during their off-season. (*See* page 202.)

NOTCH LAPEL: Step collar; a lapel style for single-breasted coats, featuring an angle-shaped opening, or "step effect," at the point where the collar of a jacket or coat meets the lapel. (*See* page 23, bottom.)

NUB: A knot or tangle in yarn planned by a series of increases or decreases of tension during the spinning process; nubbed yarn gives an irregular texture to fabric's surface.

OILSKIN: Originally a garment made waterproof by Scottish fishermen with several coatings of crude linseed oil. Today, a raincoat made of a cotton fabric processed with coatings of oil. (*See* SLICKER.)

OLIVE: A soft tone of green with a slight yellowish cast, like that of an unripe olive.

OMBRE: A French term (meaning "shadow") applied to a fabric dyed or woven in a gradation of shades. (*See* Randolph Scott's tie, page 91.)

OPERA HAT: A collapsible high hat with a firm curled brim for formal evening wear, covered with dull silk or other material.

OPERA PUMP: *See* page 251.

OPTIMA: The shape of a PANAMA or other straw hat with a full crown and a ridge extending from front to back. (*See* page 182.)

OTTOMAN: Of Turkish origin, a textured, closely woven fabric of raised crosswise ribs, made of silk or other fabrics; used for neckwear and formalwear facings.

OUNCES PER YARD: One of two accepted designations for the weight of a cloth. It should really read as "ounces per linear yard," not per square yard.

OUTSEAM: The trouser-length measurement taken from the top of the waistband to the trouser bottom.

OVERCOAT: Warm outer garment in single- or double-breasted style heavier than a topcoat. This coat can be traced back to the seventeenth century, when ancient Britons made do with a piece of wool cloth that doubled as a mantle by day and a blanket by night.

OVERPLAID: A pattern in which a block figure plaid is superimposed upon a smaller plaid or other type of design. (*See* Luciano Barbera's jacket, page 77.)

OXFORD BAG: In reaction against the drainpipe trouser leg worn by Edwardians, Oxford University students widened their trouser legs so that they resembled a pair of elephant's legs. Although the fashion for "Oxford bags" gradually died out, they were worn for some time on the golf course for comfort, and probably played a role in the eventual demise of plus-fours in favor of trousers for golf. (*See* Fred Buchanan, page 112.)

OXFORD: Named for Oxford University, a low shoe with two or more sets of eyelets for laces, made in BAL, BLUCHER, or GILLIE styles (see page 193). Also, a plain or basket-weave shirting in cotton first produced by Flemish weavers who had migrated to England at the time of the revocation of the Edict of Nantes, in 1685. The cloth simulates a type of basket weave with a two-ply WARP and a bulky, rounded, or flat single-FILLING yarn of equal size to the WARP yarn. Brooks Brothers popularized the fabric in its button-down collar model, becoming one of the sartorial icons of the twentieth century (see Fred Astaire, page 140).

OXFORD GRAY: A dark-gray shade of color effected by blending certain properties of bleached white (5 to 15 percent) and black dyed wools (95 to 85 percent). A lighter gray was given the name of Cambridge, by way of distinguishing it from Oxford, suggested by the fact that the university colors of Cambridge are light (blue), while those of Oxford are dark (blue). (*See* the "Suit Fabrics" gatefold.)

OYSTER: A very pale shade, just off white.

PADDOCK MODEL: The term applied to a two-button jacket with the lower button placed above the waistline and the upper button set high, worn by the horsey set in the 1930s. (*See* page 54.)

PADDING: An additional piece of fabric or stitch intended to give or fix a particular shape to parts of a garment.

PAISLEY: An intricate allover design suggesting a swirling pine-cone pattern, woven or printed, resembling the patterns of woolen shawls made in Paisley, Scotland (the town so named in Victorian times for its legendary product). These Scottish shawls were, in turn, adaptations of cashmere shawls of Persian derivation originally made in Kashmir, India. In the late 1920s, the paisley was adapted as print designs for men's neckwear. (*See* necktie, page 39.)

PAJAMAS: The late-nineteenth-century replacement for the nightshirt; a suit consisting of a button-front or pullover top with a drawstring or elastic waistband trousers, made of cotton, silk, or other fabrics primarily for sleeping but also for lounging. The word is of Hindi origin, as the garments were brought back to England by returning members of the British Raj.

PALM BEACH CLOTH: A brand of cloth registered by the Palm Beach Company. Originally a summer suiting material ranging in weight from 7 to 8 ounces in a plain weave with a cotton WARP and MOHAIR FILLING.

PANAMA CLOTH: A summer suiting material that ranges from 8 to 10 ounces in a plain weave, originally made with a cotton WARP and worsted FILLING. (*See* "Summer" in the "Suit Fabrics" gatefold.)

PANAMA HAT: A type of unlined and unshaped straw hat first bought by sailors and visitors in the ports of Panama. It is hand-plaited from fibers of the long-stalked *jipijapa* (toquilla) plant. (Jipijapa is the old Spanish name for Ecuador.) Originating in Ecuador, Colombia, and Peru, the raw material does not come from Panama, but Panama marketed the hats and got the credit.

PANTS: The word "pants" is short for "pantaloons," which is derived from "Pantalone," a character in the Comedie dell'arte whose leg covering looked somewhat like present-day TROUSERS. Originally a tight-fitting garment extending from waist over feet.

PAPILLON: Used in Europe to describe the shape of a bow tie; from the French word for "butterfly."

PARFAIT COLORS: Pale, whitish colors that bring to mind the shades of mixtures of ice cream and berries.

PARKA: A hooded coat derived from the Eskimo parka. Originally a wind breaker–like garment cut to hang loosely from the shoulder and slip over the head, with a zipper at the throat and a drawstring hood; initially made of a lightweight material.

PASTEL: A very pale tone of a color.

PATCH POCKET: A pocket made by stitching a piece of material on the outside of a garment with or without a flap. This pocket design conveys a sporty, casual mien. (*See* page 86.)

PEA JACKET: A heavy, double-breasted dark blue woolen jacket worn by sailors. It derives its name from the Dutch word *pij* for a heavy, coarse, woolen material. In the early part of the nineteenth century, Count Alfred d'Orsay, a fashion personality, got caught in the rain without a coat and bought such a reefer jacket from a sailor. By the 1850s, it had become popular in the United States and Great Britain.

PEACOCK REVOLUTION: *See* CARNABY STREET. The name given to the exotic colors and eccentric clothes of the 1960s that made men look like peacocks. As the popularity for this dandified display grew, it became known as the Peacock Revolution.

PEAKED LAPEL: A lapel cut on an upward slant, coming to a point and leaving only a narrow space between the collar and lapel. Usually found on double-breasted coats, but sometimes in single-breasted coats. This style of tailcoat lapel gives suits or sport jackets a more formal, dressy look. (*See* page 84.)

PEAU DE SOIE: A French phrase meaning "skin of silk," defining a fine, even grain, or leatherlike surface. Soft, dull, satiny fabric woven like a FAILLE but with a rib so fine an almost smooth face is produced.

PEBBLE WEAVE: A cloth with a roughened surface formed by either a special weave or highly twisted yarns that shrink when wet.

PEG: A description for that section of a TROUSERS' outer leg line extending from the middle of the hip pocket down to the knee. Peg-top trousers are cut full and wide over the hips and taper to narrow bottoms.

PEN POCKET: A special division within a larger pocket, or a separate narrow pocket, usually inside a man's jacket, to house one or more pens.

PENCIL STRIPES: Very fine stripes, two or three WARPS wide, suggesting those drawn by a pencil in men's suit fabric, in a color to blend or contrast with the background. (*See* the "Shirt Fabrics" gatefold; Ralph Lauren, page 94.)

PERMEABILITY: The performance characteristic of cloth, which permits air, water, and gasses to pass through its interstices.

PICK: *See* FILLING.

PICK-AND-PICK: A term applied to a neat-patterned weave with single FILLING threads in different colors. (*See* "Summer" in the "Suit Fabrics" gatefold.)

PIECE-DYED: The term applied to a fabric that has been dyed after it has been woven; the opposite of YARN-DYED.

PIECE GOODS: Materials sold in various lengths by the yard.

PILLING: The formation of groups of short or broken fibers on the surface of a fabric that are tangled together in the shape of a tiny ball called a "pill." Pills are formed when the ends of a hairy or woolly fiber break from the fabric surface usually from wear.

PIMA COTTON: A long-staple cotton grown in the American Southwest named after Pima County, Arizona. Created by crossbreeding Egyptian and American varieties, Pima cotton is only found in finer-quality shirtings.

PIN CHECK: A check size approaching that of a pinhead, smaller than a shepherd's check produced by the end-to-end weave of alternating colored threads; used for suitings, sportswear, and shirtings. (*See* suiting, page 71, bottom.)

PIN DOT: Like a BIRD'S EYE pattern but smaller; a small dot approximately the size of a pinhead, usually found in worsted suitings. (*See* suiting, page 145.)

PINPOINT OXFORD: A type of shirting that is lighter in weight and finer in bead than standard oxford cloth.

PIN WALE: Corduroy with a very narrow wale or rib. (*See* navy jacket, page 259.)

PINK: A soft shade of red.

PINKING: The cutting of the edge of a material in a zigzag, saw-tooth design to prevent fraying.

PINNED COLLAR: Any shirt collar such as a round or straight-point collar whose points are designed to be held in place with a safety-style pin. If the collar has a natural fiber lining, rather than fusing, the pin's holes will close up in the washing process. (*See* pages 133, 229.)

PINSTRIPES: Fine stripes the width of a pin scratch resulting from the use of white, gray, or other yarns in series in the WARP of a WORSTED FABRIC. (*See* "Fall" in the "Suit Fabrics" gatefold.)

PIPING: A narrow cord, braid, or fold used to finish or decorate the edges or pockets of a garment.

PIQUÉ: A cord, rib, or wale fabric achieving its raised surface crosswise from selvage to selvage. Sometimes woven to form a honeycomb or waffle effect, it is used for bosoms of formal shirts and formal waistcoats. The word is derived from the French and refers to "a pike" or "that which pierces."

PLACKET: A separate strip of fabric sewn onto a shirt front or sleeve gauntlet to secure the buttonholes and provide structure and finish. (*See* shirt, page 272.)

PLAID: A boxlike design formed by stripes of various widths running vertically and horizontally on a fabric. Originally the "plaid" was a long rectangular cloth with tartan (usually in black-and-white shepherd check) worn over the left shoulder by day; at night, the

Scottish shepherds wrapped themselves with it. The term is from the Gaelic word *plaide.*

PLAIN BOTTOMS: Trouser bottoms without cuffs.

PLAIN WEAVE: The simplest, most important, and most common of all weaves in textile making, in which the FILLING yarns pass over the one WARP yarn and under the next, continuing alternately across each row.

PLEAT: A fold of material pressed or stitched so that it is held in place. As the narrow stovepipe legs of the Edwardian suit trouser widened, pleats or folds were inserted below the waistband to enhance their neater management. Pleated trousers facilitate the natural widening of the hip when seated, while restoring the vertical line when standing. (*See* page 118.)

PLEATED BOSOM: A soft-shirt bosom formed by one-quarter- to three-quarter-inch folds running vertically whose length stops short of the wearer's dress trouser and whose width does not extend under the suspenders. (*See* page 246.)

PLUGGING: The process of making a hole in the cloth, forcing the shank of the button through, and securing it on the other side with a plug of LINEN, SILESIA, or other material. Used with military, dress, or blazer buttons with metal shanks that, if not plugged into a hole, will not lie flat on the surface of the jacket.

PLUS-FOURS: *See* KNICKERBOCKERS.

PLY: A strand of a yarn in which two or more strands are twisted together. The term is used as a system of classification; for example, single ply, two ply, six ply, etc.

POCKET: A bag made of cloth inserted into a garment.

POINT-TO-POINT: A measurement of jacket shoulder width. The distance between the two shoulder points, which is defined as that point where the top shoulder seam meets the top sleeve at the neck seam then running behind the back of the collar across to the other shoulder; along with the halfback measurement, these two measurements control the width of the jacket's shoulders.

POLKA DOT: The earliest design known to be used on neckwear; originally reputed to be a tribute to the Sun God. (*See* page 158.)

POLO COAT: A double- or single-breasted overcoat of camel's hair or soft fleece with set-in or raglan sleeves, patch pockets with flaps, sleeve cuffs, and a half- or all-around belt. This American classic's ancestry can be traced to Britain's Edwardian polo fields, when sporting society gentlemen had their tailors come up with something to throw over their shoulders, a "wait coat" between "chukkas" and sets of tennis. Brooks Brothers is largely credited with introducing the polo coat for wear away from the playing fields. (*See* page 3.)

PONGEE: A lightweight, slightly textured, plain-weave silk fabric in a natural shade, for summer suits and tailored sportswear. Pongee is said to be either a corruption of the Chinese *punchi,* "home-woven," or of *pun-shi,* "native or wild silk."

POOR-BOY SWEATER: Loose-fit, ribbed-knit sweater made with a high, round neck or turtleneck. Revived in 1960s from a type of sweater worn by newsboys of the early twentieth century.

POPLIN: A plain, tightly woven fabric with pronounced ribs produced by using heavier and courser WARP yarns than WEFT. Usually MERCERIZED for higher luster, poplin has a heavier texture than broadcloth. It was originally a silk fabric for church vestments, and the term is derived from the French *papeline,* from when the fabric was made in Avignon, a papal city. (*See* "Summer" in the "Shirt Fabrics" gatefold.)

PORK PIE: A sport hat in felt or fabric having a flat-topped crown resembling a pork pie in shape. "A Head of its Time," so termed *Esquire* magazine, which introduced it in the 1930s. Initially, the hat's low lines drew mostly scoffs; however, it evolved into an established fashion for town and campus in a variety of colors, and later becoming a generic term in the hat business.

PRINCE OF WALES CHECK: The name widely, but incorrectly, applied to the GLENURQUHART check and similar checks with a colored overcheck. The authentic Prince of Wales check was designed by King Edward VII, grandfather of the famous Duke of Windsor, when he was Prince of Wales, as livery for his shootings at Abergeldie House on Scotland's Deeside. It is of similar pattern to the glenurquhart but nearly twice its size, on repeat with colors of red-brown on a white ground, with a slate gray overcheck.

PRINCE OF WALES COAT: A short, loose-fitting, raglan-sleeved, single-breasted fly-front topcoat with a stubby peak lapel and slash pockets. The story of this coat is that the Prince of Wales saw the original in a window of a department store in Edinburgh, liked it, and went inside and bought it.

PRINT: Patterns applied to fabric by means of screens, rollers, or other impressions.

PROMINENT SEAT: A person with a larger seat than average; a cause of seat tightness on coats and trousers.

PRUNELLA: A fine material made from a two-up and two-down WARP-faced twill weave. An eighteenth-century English worsted fabric made in a three-harness twill and usually dyed a dark purple or plum shade. The term is derived from the French word *prunello,* which means "plum."

PUFFS: An old tailor's term for side slits in waistcoats.

PUGGAREE: A pleated, woven fabric, in a solid or pattern, for the band of a straw or felt hat. A similar fabric was worn originally in India. (*See* page 102.)

PUMP: The standard male footwear for formal occasions, grand receptions, and balls. No one is quite sure how name "pump" originated. The term was first used during the Elizabethan era when footmen and other male servants, called "pumps," wore thin-soled leather shoes. It has been suggested that their loose-fitting house shoes, flapping up and down as they walked across the marble floors, sounded like a water

pump. Although the pump began as a peasant's shoe, it was adopted by the uniformed manservant. By the late 1700s, the low-heeled slip-on with flat bow finally entered society as a smart slipper for the fashionably dressed ladyship of London. Later, it became standard wear for men for grand affairs and worn with breeches. (*See* pages 208, 251.)

PUNCHINGS: Perforations to create an ornamental effect on shoes. (*See* page 191.)

PURL: A stitch in knitting in which the yarn is pulled from the face of the fabric toward the back as the new loops are formed. The reverse of the plain knit stitch, it produces horizontal rows. In machine knitting, purl stitches are produced on a links-and-links machine.

PURPLE: A color halfway between blue and red. The color that is associated with the garments worn by emperors of ancient Rome was actually crimson.

QUARTER: The complete back and upper part of a shoe that joins the VAMP.

AS A RULE OF THUMB:
The most expensive clothes you'll ever buy are the clothes you never wear. —*Brooks Brothers*

RAGLAN: A loose-fitting topcoat with full-cut sleeves extending at an angle from each armhole to the collar in front and back, generally single-breasted with a button-through front, notched lapels, and turn-back cuffs. Named for Lord Raglan, an English general in the Crimean War who was reputed to have suggested that his troops cut holes in their blankets and then stitch the hanging folds into cylindrical shapes for their arms to protect them from the bitter Balaclava cold. Another story goes that Lord Raglan had his tailor design a coat sleeve that disguised the loss of one of his arms in battle.

RAYON: A textile fiber made from regenerated cellulose by the viscose or cuprammonium process. The word "rayon" was invented in 1924 by Kenneth Lord, who thought the fiber had luster.

REEFER: A short, double-breasted overcoat or jacket usually made of a heavy cloth worn by seaman. Originally, it fastened at the sides so centrally placed buttons would not be caught in rigging lines when aloft, "reefing" sail. Today it is the basic British Royal Navy officer's jacket and the forebear of the double-breasted blazer model. (*See* Prince Charles, page 111.) Also, a single- or double-breasted fitted, tailored overcoat. Also, a muffler.

REGIMENTAL STRIPE: *See* page 152.

REP; REPP: A closely woven ribbed fabric with a transverse cord effect formed by the FILLING covering the WARP in regular rows of floats. Particularly adapted to stripes with the rib running across the fabric in weaving. It is used primarily for neckwear and accessories. The term originated in eighteenth-century France, corrupted from *rib*.

REPEAT: A design that appears again and again in a fabric; also the number of threads or inches required to complete one design.

REPROCESSED WOOL: Wool fibers that have previously been fabricated but never worn, they are then unraveled, restored to fiber form, spun, and woven again into material.

RESILIENT CONSTRUCTION: A method of manufacturing a necktie, invented in the early 1920s by Jessie Langsdorf, in which the bias-cut shell and the bias-cut interlining are held together by a resilient slip stitch so that the finished tie stretches and recovers when knotted. All fine ties are cut on the bias, helping them to knot properly, to not twist when hung from the neck, and to retain their resiliency after untying.

REVERS: Another name for lapels, actually the facing of the lapels, which folds back to show the *reverse* side of the collar and lapels.

REVERSE PLEAT: A TROUSER PLEAT that folds or faces out toward the pocket; originally called the Continental pleat as opposed to the English forward pleat. The reverse pleat produces a flatter trouser front than the forward pleat. (*See* page 118, two bottom photographs.)

RIDING BOOT: A high leather boot shaped to fit the leg, designed especially for horseback riding.

RISE: The distance from the crotch to the top of the TROUSERS' WAISTBAND, as in low-rise slacks and high-rise trousers; or the difference between the trouser leg's OUTSEAM and INSEAM.

ROLL COLLAR: *See* SHAWL LAPEL.

ROPE SOLE: A shoe sole made of hemp or braided fibers and held together with thread or adhesive.

ROYAL OXFORD: A lustrous, high-count, originally English dress-shirting cloth constructed in a BASKET WEAVE design of fine two-ply yarns. (*See* "Winter" in the "Shirt Fabrics" gatefold.)

RULE OF THUMB: "The term 'rule of thumb' is derived from the ancient practice of using the thumb as a measuring device. In more modern times, it has come to be known as a guiding principle with wide application, once again not intended to be taken as gospel. While much fuss has been made about the rules that govern proper dress, little has been said about the less tangible covenants that influence plain, old-fashioned good judgment."—Brooks Brothers, 1939.

RUSSET: A cloth dyed with bark to a dark brown.

SACK SUIT: A softly tailored coat (rather than a suit) with straight-hanging lines, lightly-padded natural shoulders, and undarted fronts (which means the coat has little shaping at the waist). First popularized by the

Ivy Leaguers in the early 1920s, this silhouette was the basis of Brooks Brothers' "natural" American fashion for the next sixty years.

SADDLE SHOE: A laced oxford shoe with a strip of leather over the instep in the same color as the rest of the shoe or in a contrasting color such as brown or black on white. (*See* page 206.)

SAFARI JACKET: *See* BUSH JACKET.

SALT AND PEPPER: The speckled effect in tweeds or other fabrics produced by flecks of black and white, brown and white, etc.

SANDAL: Footwear consisting of a sole with a strapped upper in front and a buckled strap extending from the back over the instep. Sometimes there are crossover or toe straps in front.

SANDUNE: A soft, tannish-yellow shade, first appearing on the fashion scene as a new gabardine shade for sport slacks; coined by *Esquire*'s "Apparel Arts" around 1940.

SANFORIZED: The patented process of compressive shrinkage that guarantees that a fabric's residual further shrinkage will be less than 1 percent; used primarily for dress shirts. The brand name is owned by the Sanforized Company, which is a subsidiary of Cluett, Peabody.

SATIN: A closely woven, shiny fabric produced by a weave that permits as many of the WARP ends as possible to float on the face of the goods, resulting in glossy face and dull-finish back. Made of silk or synthetic fiber, satin is used for neckwear and as trimming for formalwear as an alternative to the duller ribbed grosgrain. (*See* neckties of James Mason, page 94, and Lucius Beebe, page 220.)

SAVILE ROW: The famous fashion establishment built by the Earl of Burlington and named after his wife, Dorothy Savile. Today a street in the West End of London on which many custom tailors are located. Not until Beau Brummel created a vogue for BESPOKE wool tailoring in the latter part of the eighteenth century did Savile Row became a mecca for the well-tailored, maintaining such a reputation to this day.

SAXONY: A cloth that derives its name from the very high-grade wool raised in Saxony, Germany, which the heirs to the English thrown, such as Edward VII, liked to wear on their country estates. The name is also applied to soft-finished woolen fabrics of similarly fine stock, in fancy yarn effects on the order of tweeds; used for suitings, jacketings, and trousers.

SCHAPPE: A type of waste silk that received its name from *hacher,* which means "to chop or cut up." Schappe silk is cut into short lengths and mixed with other fibers in the spun-silk method of making yarn; it is strong but evinces irregular luster.

SCOTCH GRAIN: A peeble grain that comes from a heavy chrome-tanned side leather with a deeply embossed pebblelike surface that is retained even after the shoe has been LASTED; originally made in Scotland and England for shoes of the sturdy BROGUE type. Its textured surface lends the shoe a sporting look.

SCOTCH TWEEDS: Tweeds made in a two-up and two-down twill in plain white with a FILLING of stock-dyed yarns; they are shaggy and irregular in appearance.

SCREEN PRINTING: Printing fabrics by means of a fine mesh screen of which specific areas are treated to avoid coloring matter. The coloring material is forced through the screen to the part of the fabric under the untreated areas. Each color in the design requires a separate screen.

SEA ISLAND COTTON: The very finest long-staple cotton, lustrous and strong, grown originally in British colonial islands in the Caribbean. Today it is raised on islands off the southern coast of Georgia, in South Carolina, and in the West Indies. Sea Island cotton is available only in the highest-quality shirtings.

SEAM: That part of a garment where the edges of two pieces of material are sewn together.

SEAT ALLOWANCE: Generally two to three inches of additional material for trousers allowing for the expansion of seat when wearer is seated.

SEERSUCKER: A washable fabric of cotton or other blends, with crinkled stripes made by altering the tension of the WARP threads. First discovered by the British in India as a silk fabric, the word is derived from the Hindi *sírsakar* (Persian *shir-o-shakar,* meaning "milk and sugar"). (*See* Anthony Drexel Biddle, page 105.)

SELF-LOOP: A loop made from the same shell fabric as that of the NECKTIE situated under its top blade through which the tie's small end can be slid to hold it in place. In the absence of a self-loop, the tie's label often serves the same purpose. Top-quality handmade ties reinforce their self-loops by securing their underside to the tie's center back seam.

SELF-PATTERN: A woven design in the same shade as the background of the fabric.

SELF-TIPPING: *See* FRENCH TIPPING.

SELVAGE: Either of the edges of a fabric, woven of heavier, special yarns, usually in bright colors for reinforcement or to prevent unraveling. The selvage was formerly marked in weaving to indicate the character or grade of those commonly used fabrics whose construction was fixed by law. Some firms mark their name or trademark at frequent intervals on the selvage. Originally the word was "self-edge."

SEMIFORMAL: The term denoting black-tie rather than white-tie formalwear. *See* TUXEDO.

SENNIT: A stiff straw hat with flat brim, in sailor style, popularized in 1880s, which enjoyed the privileged summertime right to be worn with a dinner jacket as well as with sportswear and blazers. (*See* page 10, bottom.)

SERGE: A mill-weave worsted fabric with a smooth surface and a diagonal rib on both sides of fabric. Also, a wool mixed with silk. Originally from the Latin word for silk, *serica.*

SERGING: A stitch that casts the thread over a material to prevent its seams from unraveling. Serging is also the joining of two pieces of fabric together for neatness to make for a flat surface, such as in the serging of a cuff to a sleeve.

SET-IN SLEEVE: A coat, shirt, or other garment sleeve sewn in at the armhole.

SEVENFOLD TIE: Unlined neckwear made with seven folds of fabric; the most skilled and costly tie construction.

SHADE: The tone of a color approaching the dark end of the value scale.

SHADOW STRIPES: An indistinct, shadowy stripe effect produced by employing alternating stripes of right- and left-hand twist yarn in the WARP. (*See* "Fall" in the "Shirt Fabrics" gatefold; page 155, bottom.)

SHADOW WEAVE: The effect on cloths in stripes or plaids produced by the immediate duplication of the weave formation after a definite repeat in darker tones or shades of yarn that give the appearance of reflected shadows being cast upon the lighter parts of the fabric.

SHAKER KNIT: A sweater knitted of heavy wool yarn in a plain ribbed stitch, so called because members of the Shaker sect originated it.

SHAM BUTTONHOLE: A finish having the appearance of a buttonhole, but not cut through.

SHANK: The steel plate or leather reinforcement in a shoe extending from the heel forward to support the arch.

SHAPER: A pattern guide or curved ruler used as a guide in giving the desired contour to the front of a garment. Also, a worker who performs this function by trimming the front with shears.

SHARKSKIN: A clear-faced, dressy worsted fabric in two tones of yarn of twill weave that simulates the skin of a shark. (*See* "Fall" in the "Suit Fabrics" gatefold.)

SHAWL LAPEL: A lapel cut in one piece, or with seam in center back, that follows the front opening of the single- or double-breasted jacket and rolls back without notches or peaks for a man's dinner jacket. The only alternative to the peaked lapel design for the classic dinner jacket. (*See* Nöel Coward, page 242.)

SHEARLING COAT: A very warm man's outercoat in lamb or sheepskin that has been tanned with its wool still adhering to the skin.

SHEPHERD'S CHECK; Shepherd's plaid: The foundation upon which the entire series of Scottish Border District checks rests. The origin of the pattern dates back to the seventeenth century, when it was used by the shepherds for their plaids in the lowlands. In the Great Exhibition of 1851, the pattern created a sensation and was adopted for men's TROUSERS. An evenly proportioned check pattern on a twill weave where the warping and wefting is usually four of black and four of white, or contrasting colors in wool, for suitings and trousers. (*See* "Summer" in the "Suit Fabrics" gatefold; the Prince of Wales, page 66.)

SHETLAND: A wool prized for its lightness and warmth, from sheep raised off the northern coast of Scotland, in the Shetland isles. Shetland sheep, like Shetland ponies, Shetland cows, and Shetland collie dogs, are the smallest of their species. Resembling tweed in appearance but softer in feel, "odd jackets" in Shetland wool became a staple of the society sportsman and IVY LEAGUE set in the early 1920s, courtesy of Brooks Brothers. (*See* striped jacket, page 108.)

SHIRRING: A series of close, parallel runnings of wool that are drawn up so as to make the material between them set full by gatherings. (*See* Clark Gable, page 106.)

SHORT BACK-BALANCE: In a tailored jacket, a lack of back-length over the shoulder blades to the back of the neck and shoulders, causing a collar to drag down from back of the neck and/or a coat to hang outward and away from the seat.

SHORT FRONT-BALANCE: In a tailored jacket, a lack of front length in the balance of the garment, causing the garment to pull forward from the figure and to appear shorter in front. A defect common to erect figures causing a back center vent to open.

SHORT NECK: A neckline that requires a lower placement of collar.

SHOULDER LINE: The finished outline of the shoulder run on a garment; that is, square, natural, etc.

SHUTTLE: An implement that moves FILLING yarns between WARP yarns to produce a woven fabric.

SIDE SEAM: The seam running from the armhole to the bottom of the coat, joining the front to the back of coat.

SIDE VENTS: *See* page 89.

SILESIA: A lightweight cotton TWILL material with a calenderized glaze finish; used for pocket linings, etc.

SILHOUETTE: The outline of a garment or outfit as worn by an individual, such as shapely or flowing lines.

SILK: A fiber extruded by the silkworm in forming a cocoon, which is processed and woven into fabric. The silk thread is almost as strong as one of equal diameter in steel. Silk is also extremely resilient and resists wrinkles. A three-foot length stretched to three and a half feet will subsequently revert to its original length.

SILK HAT; TOP HAT; TOPPER: A stiff, high-crowned hat with a rolled-edge brim, made of lustrous silk plush; used for white tie formal wear. Reputed to have originated in China around 1775, when a Cantonese hatter produced a silk topper for a Monsieur Betta, who carried the style with him back to France.

SINGLE-BREASTED: The term applied to a jacket, waistcoat, or outercoat with a single set of buttons sewn a short distance from the edge of one side of the front, and buttonholes sewn to the corresponding positions on the other side.

SINGLE CUFF: The cuff of a shirt, either soft or starched, of one thickness. It may be fastened with cuff links or buttons.

SIZING (HATS): Hat size is determined by dividing the head circumference in centimeters. The American system uses eighths—6 $\frac{7}{8}$, 7, 7 $\frac{1}{8}$, etc. The English use the same system with quarters instead of eighths, while French hats are sized by halves.

SIZING (SHOES): Shoes sizes are measured by thirds of an inch and widths by sixths of an inch.

SKIMMER: *See* SENNIT.

SLASH POCKET: A pocket set into a jacket with either a vertical or diagonal position that permits the hand to go through to the next layer of clothing inside. Often found on raincoats or outerwear.

SLEEVE PITCH: The position of the hang of a tailored jacket's sleeve. To "forward sleeve pitch" is to make the sleeve hang more forward, to run more in line with the natural hang of the wearer's arm. A normal sleeve pitch is where the arm hangs so that its front bisects the middle of the jacket's hip pocket.

SLEEVELESS CARDIGAN: A knitted, collarless, open-fronted VEST with button closure without sleeves, sometimes substituting for a woven vest under a sport jacket or even suit, usually in wool, cotton, or blend. (*See* page 163.)

SLICKER: A raincoat of oiled cotton or other treated fabric with snap fasteners or buttons and a corduroy-lined standing collar.

SLIP-ON: A nonlaced shoe, either elasticized or loafer-style.

SLIPPER: Any footwear (except a rubber) without a fastening that is slipped on the foot and held in place, without any fastening, from the tension around the top.

SLIP STITCH: A method of sewing together the shell and blanket of a necktie that permits maximum stretch and recovery, characterized by the presence of a "spring" or exposed loop of thread found at the blade's end. This loop of thread is drawn up into the length of the tie during wear, preventing the seam from splitting, adding elasticity to the tie and helping it to keep its shape. Superior neckties are hand slip-stitched.

SLOPING SHOULDERS: A person with shoulders having more than average slope to them.

SLOTTED COLLAR: A shirt collar with a small strip of linen, plastic, or metal put in the underside pocket of each collar point to "stay" or stiffen it, thus preventing it from curling up or down. Better shirts have removable stays for laundering.

SLUBS: A cloth defect caused by an abruptly thickened place in a yarn.

SMOKING JACKET: *See* TUXEDO.

SNAP-BRIM HAT: Felt, straw, or fabric hat with a soft brim designed to be turned down in front or on one side and up in back.

SNEAKER: A laced or slip-on shoe with a canvas upper and a rubber sole; used for sport and casual wear.

SNUFFED GRAIN: A process of finishing leather by buffing the grain side of the skin to give it a short-pile appearance somewhat like suede.

SOLARI: An iridescent, red-backed gabardine, originally favored by the English colonials because its red underside was supposed to ward off the sun's rays. In appearance, a greenish-sheen is also present on the fabric's face, explained by the prismatic law that green is red's complementary color. Favored today in a wool-gabardine broken-twill suiting by savvy Italians.

SPATS: An ankle covering in box cloth, linen, or other material. Spats extend above the ankle, are fastened at the sides with buckles or buttons, and are held under the shank of the shoe with straps and buckles. The word is an abbreviation of "Spatterdashes" (knee-high leg coverings formerly used against mud and water).

SPECTRUM: Colors visible when rays of light pass through a prism; arranged in order of their wave lengths: violet, indigo, blue, green, yellow, orange, red.

SPENCER: Similar to a MESS JACKET, a tailcoat without its tails. In the eighteenth century, Lord Spencer stood with his back to the fire and caught his tail alight. The burned parts were cut away and Spencer liked the resulting style. Vulgarly known back then as the "bum-freezer."

SPITALSFIELD: A heavy silk in small all-over patterns used for neckwear. It was originally woven in the Spitalsfield district of the East End of London, where the Huguenot weavers, expelled from France, settled. From 1727 to 1750, this area rivaled Lyons as a silk-producing center. (*See* page 152.)

SPLIT RAGLAN: A type of outercoat shoulder design with the sleeves set in at the front but forming a raglan sleeve in the rear, the seams extending at an angle from the neck to the armholes.

SPONGING: A shrinking process usually applied to woolens and worsteds before they are cut up. It calls for dampening the fabric with a wet sponge or steam emanating from a perforated cylinder.

SPREAD COLLAR: A collar whose points are more spread than a STRAIGHT-POINT COLLAR but less open than a CUTAWAY COLLAR. (*See* pages 128, 210.)

SPRING: *See* SLIP STITCH.

SPUN SILK: Waste or short fibers of silk spun into yarn and woven into fabric.

SQUARE SHOULDERS: *See* HIGH SHOULDERS.

STARCHED BOSOM: Set-in shirt front of two or more thicknesses of fabric, laundered with starch to achieve a stiff, smooth surface for formal evening dress. The term also applies to a pleated or piqué bosom that has been starched and pressed. (*See* Fred Astaire, page 236.)

STEINKIRK: In 1693, when the French and English were at war, a surprise night attack caught the French unprepared. Dressing hurriedly, the French troops, normally very fussy about the drape of their clothes, merely secured their neckwear by slipping the ends of their cravats through rings, and went off to the Battle of Steinkirk, where they won a great victory. Returning to Paris with their ties still pulled casually through their rings, they created a new NECKTIE fashion, which was promptly called the Steinkirk. The official Boy Scout uniform today still includes this kind of tie.

STEP COLLAR: *See* NOTCH LAPEL.

STOOPING: A leaning-forward posture that requires the coat to have a shorter front balance and longer back length. The opposite of an erect posture.

STRAIGHT-POINT COLLAR: *See* pages 126 and 139.

STUD: A fastener with a pin or button back for the bosom of a formal shirt. It can be made of tooled metal, pearl, a colored stone, or enamel. (*See* Fred Astaire, page 236.)

SUEDE: Leather that has been buffed to a fine nap or velvet finish on the flesh, or inner side of the skin. The word is derived from *Suède,* the French name for "Sweden," where the process originated.

SUNSHOT: *See* SOLARI.

SUPPRESS WAIST: An alteration by adding more shape at the waistline of a garment.

SURGEON'S CUFF: A Canadian expression for jacket cuffs with working buttonholes.

SUSPENDERS: *See* page 222.

SWALLOWTAIL COAT: The old-fashioned name for a TAILCOAT.

SWELLED EDGES: *See* LAPPED SEAM.

TAB COLLAR: *See* page 131.

TAFFETA: It is a plain and closely woven, smooth fabric. WARP and FILLING are almost of the same count. Taffeta is from the Persian word *taftah,* meaning "twisted," "woven."

TAILCOAT; TAILS; SWALLOWTAIL COAT: *See* page 234.

TARTAN: The Japanese have worn "plaids" for centuries, but only the Scottish Highland Clans wore colorful cross-checked plaids as a means of identification. The word, formerly spelled *"tartanem,"* was borrowed from the English, who took it from the Spanish term *tiritana.* The Spanish gave this name to tartan cloths as far back as the thirteenth century. The Scottish wore tartan by day and slept under them by night. In ancient Caledonia (now known as Scotland), the colors of tartan served to distinguish the thirty-three clans of the Scottish Highlands.

TATTERSALL: A checked pattern formed by vertical and horizontal lines usually in two colors on a light background. In 1766 Richard Tattersall founded a horse market in London, Tattersall's, which eventually became a rendezvous for gamblers. The horse blankets had a characteristic plaid of thin lines bisecting at right angles, which became known as "tattersall." It was first used by sportsmen for riding waistcoats; today the pattern is found in almost every type of wearing apparel. (*See* odd vest, page 119; "Winter" and "Summer" in the "Shirt Fabrics" gatefold.)

TELESCOPE CROWN: The crown of a felt or straw hat creased with a flat top and an even height at the sides. *See* PORK PIE.

TENSILE STRENGTH: The force, measured in pounds per square inch, or other units, that a fabric or a fiber can withstand without breaking.

TEXTURE: The surface of a fabric, whether smooth, rough, or irregular. Originally, a woven fabric (the word derived from the Latin *textura,* meaning "web").

THICK-AND-THIN: A fabric woven with uneven-textured yarns to create the effect of a homespun cloth.

THROAT: The part of the shoe at the INSTEP where the VAMP opens.

THROAT LATCH: A four- or five-inch strip of cloth attached to the left under-collar with a buttonhole at one end that can be strapped across the neck to fasten to a button on the opposite under-collar when the jacket's collar is turned up. Found on rugged sport jackets and intended to protect the neck from rain or cold. (*See* jacket, page 261.)

TICKET POCKET: British tailoring term for a small pocket, usually flapped, placed above the regular pocket on the right side of a man's suit coat or overcoat. Introduced in the late 1850s for a railroad ticket and used at intervals ever since. Also known as a "cash pocket." (*See* pages 87, 130.)

TIE CLIP: A spring-loaded fastener used to clip the two pendant ends of the tie to the shirt. Intermittently fashionable since the 1920s. (*See* page 228.)

TIE SPACE: *See* page 121 and copy on the bottom of page 122.

TIE TACK: A fastening device consisting of two parts: an outer decorative head backed by a pin that pierces through the necktie and top layer of shirt placket connecting to a pinch-type fastener underneath.

TIPPING: The inside lining seen on the blade and under-end of a tie often matching the shade of the tie itself. Top-draw NECKTIES use silk tipping instead of a synthetic. Also, tipping one's hat: You tip your hat today because in the days of chivalry, the knight removed his helmet or raised his visor as acknowledgment that he was among friends.

TOE BOX: A stiff, shell-shaped piece of leather placed between a shoe's lining and tip to maintain its contour and permanent shape.

TOE SPRING: The distance from the ground to the tread surface of the sole at the extreme tip of the toe, which gives the toe its slightly turned-up effect.

TONE: The quality or value of a color lightened with the addition of white or darkened by the addition of black or gray.

TONGUE: A leather flap attached to the inside or outside of a shoe's upper to protect the lacing area from friction, pressure, and penetration by extraneous objects.

TOPCOAT: An outercoat made of fabric lighter than that of an overcoat. The maximum weight fabric for this coat used to be 18 ounces per square yard or less.

TOPEE: Like the Derby to an Englishman, this Singaporean headpiece is a helmetlike affair of cork with a cloth covering, originally worn in India as protection from the sun. When the inner layer is made of pith, it is known as a pith helmet.

TOP HAT: *See* SILK HAT.

TOPPER: *See* SILK HAT.

TRENCH COAT: A double-breasted coat in tightly woven cotton gabardine with most of its authentic details present in the civilian version. Originally it was a waterproof military coat invented by Burberry's uniform department at the request of the British War Office for wear in the trenches by the British army officers in WWI. Overcoats soaked with rain and mud were too heavy and uncomfortable, while normal raincoats were inadequate. Tested against hose-pipes, the proofed material was double-thickness across the back; high storm collars buttoned tight across the front with special flaps. Various metal hooks and D-rings allowed the hanging of equipment, and so a tradition was born. Hollywood made it the garment of heroes and secret agents.

TRIAL SHOE: The most expensive method of creating custom-made shoes. A test pair of medium-grade leather shoes is done up from the individual's LAST to walk about in so that final adjustments can be made to the LAST prior to creating the first finished pair of shoes.

TRILBY: A slouchy felt hat with a wide rolled brim, originally worn in England by a heroine in a famous George du Maurier play about a hypnotist named Svengali, which was adapted from his novel named *Trilby.* (*See* page 159.)

TROLLEY: A cord or string around the crown of a hat, ending in a button. The blade of the Gay Nineties would anchor the button in his coat lapels to keep the hat from sailing off when bicycling or riding.

TROPICAL WORSTED: A sturdy but air-circulating worsted suiting material weighing usually 6 to 9.5 ounces per yard made in a variety of plain or open weaves with a two-ply or single-ply yarn in the WARP and FILLING. (*See* "Spring" and "Summer" in the "Suit Fabrics" gatefold.)

TROUSER: Pant; a garment from the waist to the feet, but not covering the foot. A term used in eighteenth and early nineteenth century for loose fitting pants worn particularly by sailors, soldiers, and town workers. After the War of 1812, "trousers" were widely worn in the United States instead of silk breeches and stockings, which seemed too British. From French *troussér,* meaning "tucked up."

TROUSER CREASE: Originally trousers were creased down the side (as in the old navy style), until 1886, when an elegantly frock-coated Edward VII appeared at the Derby horse race in a pair of gray trousers with sharply ironed front creases.

TURKEY RED: A bright scarlet dye formerly derived from the madder plant and now made chemically.

TURN-UPS: The English term for trouser cuffs. *See* CUFFS.

TURTLENECK: A knitted pullover with a long end that is slipped over the head and then rolled to fit closely around the neck; made in wool, cotton, or blended fabrics. Introduced in the 1860s for men, popular in the late 1920s and 1930s, revived in the 1960s for men, and even tried for formal wear. (*See* page 263.)

TUXEDO: In 1886 a notable group of upstate New Yorkers founded the private club Tuxedo Park. That spring, James Brown Potter and his wife, Cora, journeyed to England, where they met the Prince of Wales at a court ball. The Prince, always fond of pretty women, invited the Potters to Sandringham, his Norfolk hunting estate. When Mr. Potter inquired about what to wear, the Prince spoke of a short garment that he had adopted in place of the tailcoat, inspired by the jacket that one of his cronies, Lord Dupplin, had worn to dinner one night.

The Prince recommended that Potter go to his tailor in London and get one for himself. Potter did just that, and upon returning to Tuxedo Park that fall, Pierre Lorillard and other club members were impressed by Potter's visit and copied the new jacket, deeming it more appropriate than "tails" for informal dinners. One evening, some of the Tuxedo locals were seen sporting their Tuxedos at a bachelor dinner at Delmonico's restaurant, the only public establishment where gentlemen didn't have to dress for dinner. The other diners at "Del's" were astonished, and when told that that was how the men up in Tuxedo dressed for dinner, they naturally started referring to the jacket by its new moniker.

Pierre Lorillard, Griswold's son and confirmed prankster, attended Tuxedo's first Autumn Ball attired in a "tail-less dress coat." Shorter than a dinner jacket and probably some version of a MESS JACKET, this coat made "Grizzy" look like a "royal footman," according to the society gossip sheet. Although ceremoniously asked to leave, from then on, the shorter formal jacket and black tie accouterments grew steadily popular, with the appellation "Tuxedo" sticking for good. Other names are "dinner jacket"; "smoking jacket"; "*le smoking*." (*See* page 240.)

TWEED: A rough-surfaced woolen material with a homespun surface effect in plain or twill weave and many different patterns. Tweed caught the fancy of the London gentry who came upon it on their shooting and fishing trips up north. The royal association with Balmoral, the Royal Castle, did the rest. It was originally made by hand at home by crofters near the Tweed River in Scotland. Lore has it that tweed was not named for its place of origin, as it comes from *tweel*, the Scottish word for "twill." However, in 1826, when a London clerk drafted an order for "tweels," he accidentally wrote "tweeds," and the name stuck.

TWILL: One of the three basic weaves, characterized by diagonal lines on the surface of the fabric.

TWIST: The turning of the yarn, either to the left (S-twist) or to the right (Z-twist), to prepare it for weaving into a fabric. Also, woolens or worsteds of which the yarns are made of two colors, doubled, or twisted together to pattern a mottled appearance.

TYROLEON HAT: A rough-textured felt or velour hat with a sharply tapered CROWN, a narrow brim turned up in back and down in front, and a cord type of band decorated with a feather/brush mount; associated with the Austrian Tyrol. (*See* page 204.)

ULSTER: Double-breasted long OVERCOAT in heavy TWEED or MELTON with a big convertible collar, wide lapels, and a half- or all-around belt. It was introduced by a Belfast firm in the 1860s. By the turn of the century, English fashion deemed that no man could be well dressed without at least one Ulster in his wardrobe.

UNCONSTRUCTED: A term used by the menswear industry to describe a soft, unpadded, not fully lined tailored jacket; a term often misunderstood to mean "inexpensive" or "lacking in tailoring." In fact, because there is no lining to cover up its insides, its open interior often requires more exacting finishing and, thus, expense than a fully lined jacket.

UNION SUIT: Underwear consisting of a shirt and shorts or pants in one piece.

UPPER: The top most part of the shoe; depending on shoe type, consisting of one or more parts: linen lining, eyelet facing with underlay, collar, lining leather.

VAMP: The section of the upper part of a shoe extending forward to the toe cap and part or all the way to the rear seam.

VEGETABLE TANNING: The oldest and most costly type of shoe-leather tanning, which uses natural bark or extracts, sometimes combined with synthetic vegetable tannins.

VELVETEEN: A short pile fabric with a cotton FILLING that resembles velvet; used for smoking jackets and sportswear. (*See* page 245.)

VENETIAN: A fine worsted twill cloth where the WARP is almost all on the surface of the cloth, and the WEFT goes to the back. The name is taken from the resemblance noted to silk venetian, a cloth of real artistic value that was made in Venice. The cloth is smooth-textured dress worsted and made of wool or cotton. In wool it is used for suits, TROUSERS, and TOPCOATS.

VENT: *See* SIDE VENT. Term used since the fifteenth century to indicate a vertical slit in a garment, usually from the hem upward. (*See* page 88.)

VEST: A sleeveless garment for the upper body, extending to the waist, usually worn under a suit jacket or coat. Also known as a "waistcoat." First worn by England's King Charles II (recorded in *Pepys's Diary*, October 8, 1666) as one of the new fashions he introduced as a breakaway snub to the fashion lead of France, with whom England was at war.

VEST POCKET: A WELT pocket placed on the side chest of a waistcoat or a VEST, originally used to carry a pocket watch. In the age of Louis XV, men carried two pocket watches, therefore a pocket was made on either side of garment. (*See* page 91.)

VICUNA: The Rolls-Royce of wool fibers, from the undercoat of the vicuna, a rare llamalike type of animal that lives twelve hundred feet above sea level and the clouds in almost inaccessible regions of the Andes. Vicuna are about three feet high, have a life span of twelve years, and produce a clip of wool whose natural color is a rich tobacco shade.

VIRGIN WOOL: Wool used for the first time after being clipped from sheep; in other words, wool that has not previously been made into yarn or fabric.

VOILE: Woven from fine hard twisted yarns with reverse twist WARP threads, this plain fabric is lightweight, cool, and dry. Because of its sheerness, voile dress shirts are made with double-layer fronts and worn primarily for warm weather. A corruption of the Latin *vela,* which implies a "covering," "curtain," or "sail."

WAIST: The narrowest part of the torso.

WAIST SUPPRESSION: The addition of shape at the waistline of a garment.

QUALITY:

"There is hardly anything in the world that some man cannot make a little worse and sell a little cheaper, and the people who consider price alone are this man's lawful prey." —*Ruskin*

WAISTBAND: The strip of material running around the top of the TROUSER and forming a finish to trouser tops; usually faced and interfaced and then seamed to the waistline of trousers.

WAISTCOAT: *See* VEST.

WAISTLINE: An invisible fitting line where waist suppression is made.

WARP: Yarn that runs lengthwise in a loom and crossed by the WEFT. The warp yarn generally runs vertically in a cloth or garment as opposed to the FILLING yarn, or weft, which runs crossways from selvage to selvage.

WATCH POCKET: A small pocket in the side front of a man's trousers, usually of the welt style, used to carry a watch. Also called a "fob pocket."

WEAVING: The intercrossing of two sets of yarns, the WARP, which runs down the length of the cloth, and the WEFT, which runs across the width. In knitting,

only one set of threads is used; hence the difference between knitting and weaving. There are three basic weaves, of which two dominate in garment cloth; plain and twill weave.

WEDDING TIE: *See* MACCLESFIELD.

WEEJUN: *See* page 203.

WEFT: A FILLING thread or yarn that runs crosswise in a loom or in a circle. *See* FILLING; WARP.

WEIGHTED SILK: Silk treated with a metallic solution to add to its weight and to give a rich look.

WELLINGTON BOOT: Waterproofed rubber boots for work or leisure that are either worn under the trousers or with the trousers tucked in, usually in green. "Wellys," as they are known to the English, were originally leather with a soft upper extending above the knee, and were named after the military commander Arthur Wellesley, who became the 1st Duke of Wellington.

WELT: A narrow strip of leather stitched to the upper and to the edge of the insole of a shoe. The edge of the strip is then stitched to the outside. Also, that which being sewn or otherwise fastened to an edge, pocket, or border to guard, strengthen, or adorn it. The outside breast and waistcoat pockets are usually finished in this style. (*See* pages 90, 236.)

WEST OF ENGLAND FLANNEL: Woolen cloth of high reputation made in western districts of England, strictly associated with the Cotswold district, centering in and around Stroud and Trowbridge; characterized by its high and low shadings that produces richer grays with more dimension to the cloth than other flat plain gray flannels. (*See* Gary Cooper, page 43.)

WHIPCORD: This hard-twisted, worsted TWILL fabric has diagonal ribs so prominent that the twills stand up boldly in a kind of rolled effect, suggesting the plaited lash of a whip from which it derives its name. Weight ranges from 12 to 20 ounces.

WHITE: A chromatic color at the light end of the black-to-white scale. White is the combination of all colors of the spectrum, ranging in wavelength from the longest to the shortest.

WHITE-ON-WHITE: The term applied to a pattern of white figures or stripes on a white broadcloth or other shirting weave raised above the level of the background.

WHITE TIE: The term for formal dress. (*See* page 236.)

WICKING: The ability of a fiber to transfer moisture from one section of the garment to another. Body perspiration is transported along the fiber surface to the outer surface of the cloth, then evaporates into the atmosphere.

WINDOWPANE: *See* "Winter" and "Spring" in the "Suit Fabrics" gatefold; page 96.

WINDSOR COLLAR: An attached or separate collar with points that are more spread than a semi-spread collar but less open than a full cutaway. Supposedly first worn by the Duke of Windsor.

WINDSOR KNOT: A large necktie knot tied in a special manner with extra loops. It is inspired by but falsely attributed to the Duke of Windsor. (*See* Douglas Fairbanks, page 129; page 250.)

WING COLLAR: *See* page 239.

WING TIP: *See* page 194.

WOOL: Fibers from the covering coat of sheep and other animals; also woven, knitted, or felted fabric produced from the fiber.

WOOLEN SYSTEM: Process of sorting, scouring, blending, oiling, cording, and spinning yarn of short stables, waste, and reworked wool. Yarns that have been carded and spun from wool in which anything but a parallel position of the fibers is noticeable, as distinct from worsted yarn in which the wool fibers are markedly paralleled.

WORKING BUTTONHOLES: Jacket-sleeve buttonholes that actually unbutton. (*See* page 134.)

WORSTED FABRIC: Clear, smooth-handed fabric in which the structure and color are clearly defined, owing to the clearness and smoothness of both the yarns and interlacing.

WORSTED SYSTEM: Process of carding, combing, drawing, and spinning worsted fibers into yarn for manufacture into worsted cloths.

WORSTED YARNS: Made from combing the woolen fibers so that they lie parallel to each other, then drawing and tightly twisting the smooth yarn, the name comes from a little village in Norfolk, Worstead.

WOVEN TIE: A class of neckwear fabric in which the pattern is part of the weave—as opposed to prints, embroideries, and hand paints where the pattern is applied after the fabric is woven. As a result of the woven pattern's more textured and thicker fabric, this necktie has more body, thus making a better knot than the printed tie, which must rely on its inner armature for its form and stature. (*See* page 146.)

WRAP COAT: A loose-fitting, casually-belted bathrobe-like coat with turned-up collar introduced in London and Hollywood during the early 1930s; usually in CAMEL HAIR or soft fleece.

YARD: Unit of measure equal to thirty-six inches in America; the English yard is a standard established by the government, indicated by two marks on a metal rod embedded in the masonry in the House of Parliament, or 0.914 meter.

YARN-DYED: A fabric woven with yarns that have already been dyed, as opposed to piece-dyed, where the fabric is first woven and then dyed.

YOKE: The fabric fitted over the shoulders and joined to the lower part of the garment by a visible seam across the chest or back. (*See* Clark Gable, page 106.)

ZEPHYR: A yarn of lightweight WORSTED, often blended with other fibers; also applies to a sheer, soft, woolen fabric. The name is from *Zephyrus,* classical god of the west wind.

ZOOT SUIT: Outrageous suit worn by some young hipsters in the late 1930s, 1940s, and early 1950s, referred to as "the badge of the hoodlums." The jacket had heavily padded, square shoulders, a tapered waist, and extended almost to the knees. Its baggy-legged trouser, measuring almost thirty-two inches at the knee and tapering down to twelve to fifteen inches at bottom, was jacked up almost to the chest by suspenders. Worn with equally bizarre accessories— like six-foot key chains, snake ties, roll-collared shirts, and wide-brimmed head wear—this colorful costume represented an early rebellion of America's less fortunate youths against the conformist order.

SELECTED BIBLIOGRAPHY

American Fabrics Magazine, eds. *AF Encyclopedia of Textiles*. Prentice Hall, 1960.

Amies, Hardy. *The Englishman's Suit*. Quartet Books, 1994.

Angeloni, Umberto. *The Boutonniere: Style in One's Lapel*. Universe Publishing, 2000.

Bachrach, Bert. *Right Dress*. A. S. Barnes, 1955.

Baker, William Henry. *A Dictionary of Men's Wear*. W. H. Baker, 1908.

Berendt, John, and the editors of Esquire Magazine. *Fashions for Men*. Harper & Row, 1966.

Boyer, G. Bruce. *Elegance: A Guide to Quality in Menswear*. Norton, 1985.

———. *Eminently Suitable: The Elements of Style in Business Attire*. Norton, 1990.

Bridgland, A. S., ed. *The Modern Tailor: Outfitter, Clothier*, 3 volumes. Caxton Publishing, 1936.

Buzzaccarini, Vittoria de. *Elegance and Style: Two Hundred Years of Men's Fashions*. Lupetti & Co., 1992.

———. *Men's Coats*. Zanfi Editori, 1988.

Byrde, Penelope. *The Male Image: Men's Fashions in Britain, 1300–1970*. B. T. Batsford, 1979.

Chaille, François. *The Book of Ties*. Abbeville, 1994.

Chenoune, Farid. *A History of Men's Fashions*. Flammarion, 1993.

Donner, Jane. *Fashion in the Twenties and Thirties*. Ian Allan, 1973.

Flusser, Alan. *Clothes and the Man: The Principles of Fine Men's Dress*. Villard, 1985.

———. *Making the Man*. Wallaby, 1981.

———. *Style and the Man: How and Where to Buy Fine Men's Clothes*. HarperCollins, 1996.

Folledore, Guiliano. *Mens Hats*. Zanfi Editoni, 1996.

Gibbings, Sarah. *The Tie: Trends and Traditions*. Barron's, 1990.

Giorgetti, Cristina. *Brioni: 50 Years of Style*. Octavo, 1995.

Gold, Annalee. *Seventy-five Years of Fashion*. Fairchild Books, 1975.

Hart, Avril. *Ties*. V&A Publications, 1998.

Hochswender, Woody. *Men in Style*. Rizzoli, 1993.

Hollander, Anne. *Sex and Suits: The Evolution of Modern Dress*. Knopf, 1994.

Keers, Paul. *A Gentlemen's Wardrobe*. Harmony, 1987.

Kybalova, Ludmila, Olga Herbenova, and Milina Laniarova. *The Pictorial Encyclopedia of Fashion*. Hamlyn, 1968.

Laver, James. *The Book of School, University, Navy, Army, Air Force and Club Ties*. Seeley Service &Co., 1968.

———. *Dandies*. Weidenfeld & Nicolson, 1968.

Lenius, Oscar. *A Well-Dressed Gentleman's Pocket Guide*. Prion, 1998.

Lester, Katherine Morris and Bess Viola Oerke. *Accessories of Dress*. Charles A. Bennett Publications, 1940.

Lurie, Alison. *The Language of Clothes*. Owl Books, 1992.

McDowell, Colin. *Hats*. Rizzoli, 1992.

———. *The Man of Fashion*. Thames & Hudson, 1977.

Malossi, Giannino. *One Hundred Years of Italian Male Elegance*. Elemond Electra, 1999.

Martin, Richard, and Harold Korda. *Jocks and Nerds: Men's Style in the Twentieth Century*. Rizzoli, 1989.

Maysonave, Sherry. *Casual Power*. Bright Books, 2000.

Molloy, John T. *Dress for Success*. Warner, 1976.

Pifferi, Enzo. *Miss Cravatta*. Editrice E.P.I., 1998.

Schoeffler, O. E., and William Gale. *Esquire's Encyclopedia of 20th-Century Men's Fashions*. McGraw-Hill, 1973.

Stote, Dorothy. *Men Too Wear Clothes*. Lippincott, 1950.

Vass, Laszlo, and Magda Molnar. *Handmade Shoes for Men*. Konemann, 1999.

Villarosa, Riccardo, and Giulano Angeli. *The Elegant Man: How to Construct the Ideal Wardrobe*. Random House, 1992.

Walker, Richard. *Savile Row: An Illustrated History*. Rizzoli, 1989.

Waller, Jane. *A Man's Book*. Duckworth, 1977.

ACKNOWLEDGMENTS

For those individuals who deserve special thanks for their significant contributions to this book:

Joseph Montebello, coconspirator and aficionado, whose ambition is the book's birthright.

Al Zuckerman, agent and advocate, for his wise representation.

Henry Ferris, editorial tailor and champion, keeper of the tome, chaperon of the creative process.

Woody Hochswender, dear friend and editor-at-large extraordinaire; few combine his sartorial knowledge and literary craft.

David Croland, illustrator and muse, for his elegance of line and spirit.

James Murray, master photographer and digital doyen, for his iconic images.

Maison Avirom: Joel, Meghan, and Jason, architects who mold manuscripts into monuments. *The Look of the Book* could be their motto.

Eve Lederman, for her editorial skills and unflagging focus. John Jusino, for his meticulous attention to the minutia of the manuscript. And Roni Axelrod, for actually getting the entire enterprise produced.

Sincere thanks to the following for their time and support: Garrick Anderson, Eric Barsky, Sarah Beam, Robert Beauchamps, Tom Beebe, G. Bruce Boyer, John Carnera, Michael F. Coady, Lisa Cohen, Angus Cundley, Norman Currie, Hunter Demos, Philip Ferrante, Steve Florio, Robert Gilotte, Tom Graf, Jay Greenfield, Martin Greenfield, Tod Greenfield, John Hitchcock, John Hsultik, Tom Keatley, Ralph Lauren, Marion Maneker, Mario Manerino, Michael Mathews, Wayne Meichner, Richard Merkin, Philip Miller, Jim Moore, Derrill Osborn, Mark Rykken, Jay Stein, Luigi Turconi, Jon Vizzone, and Ken Williams

Grateful acknowledgment is made to the following for the illustrations on the pages noted:

Adam Magazine: Pages 17, 23 (right), 40 (left), 70 (bottom), 113 (lower), 173, 211, 217 (left), 251 (top).

Alan Flusser: Pages 86, 88, 105, 130, 133, 149, 183, 185, 205, 213, 225, 228, 237 (bottom), 244 (top).

Archive Photos: Pages 6, 7, 38 (right), 55, 126.

Archive Photos, Richard and Bert Morgan: Pages 243, 267.

Apparel Arts, courtesy of Conde Nast Publications, Inc.: Pages 4, 8,19, 23 (left), 31 (a, b, upper right), 42, 44, 45, 48, 49, 54, 73, 74, 75 (lower), 83 (lower right), 87, 88, 89 (lower), 90, 91 (lower), 93, 96, 97, 103, 108 (middle), 115 (upper), 119, 133, 134, 147, 156, 158, 159 (bottom), 168 (top), 169 (bottom), 178, 181, 182, 189, 191, 200, 201 (top), 204 (bottom), 212, 217 (right), 242 (top), 246, 247, 252, 253.

Bergdorf Goodman: Page 265.

Bettmann/Corbis: Pages 10 (top and bottom), 39, 43, 66 (left), 67, 112, 130, 151, 152 (top), 171, 172, 207 (bottom), 208.

Brooks Brothers: Pages 14, 102, 106 (upper right), 108, 113.

Black Enterprise Magazine: Page 124.

Borelli Shirts: Page 128 (lower).

Camera Press, London: Pages 64, 66 (right), 75 (middle), 76 (bottom), 99, 111, 115 (lower), 136 (lower), 184, 226, 245 (right).

Cigar Aficionado Magazine: Pages 20 (left), 33 (top), 68 (bottom), 263.

Culver Pictures: Pages 12, 20 (right), 38 (left), 68, 72, 75 (top right), 76 (top), 85 (upper), 94 (left), 107 (top right), 114, 118, 149 (bottom left), 127, 131, 139, 141, 153, 154 (upper), 157, 175, 177, 187, 206, 209, 220, 236, 238, 242.

Daks Simpson: Page 117.

Departures Magazine: Pages 22 (right), 33 (bottom), 260, 270, 274.

Gamma Presse Images: Page 128 (upper).

Getty Images, Archive Photos: Pages 6, 7, 38 (right), 55, 126, 243, 267. Hulton Getty: Pages 13 (top, bottom), 65, 84, 85 (lower), 86 (lower), 95, 98 (lower), 109, 121, 140 (middle), 199, 229, 244 (bottom), 245 (left). Roger Viollet: Pages 83 (bottom left), 140 (bottom).

Gentleman's Quarterly: Pages 5, 21.

Gentry Magazine: Pages 9, 108 (bottom right), 110, 118 (bottom right), 152 (bottom), 169 (top), 198, 201, 203 (bottom).

Grazie Neri, Italy: Pages 69 (top right), 140 (top), 155 (top), 166 (bottom), 230.

Henry Poole & Co., London: Page 241.

Holland & Holland: Page 218.

Illustrated News, London: Pages 25, 214 (upper left), 215 (bottom).

James Murray Photography: Pages 26, 27, 28, 29, 30, 31, 46, 155 (bottom), 215 (top), 259, 262, 269, 272, 273.

John Lobb, London: Pages 192, 207 (top), 251 (bottom).

John Weitz Photographer: Page 125.

Kobal Collection, London: Pages 11, 20 (left), 76 (middle), 91 (upper), 106 (top left, bottom right), 129, 136 (upper), 150, 159 (top), 214 (upper right, bottom left), 224, 233, 266.

Louis, Boston: Page 63.

Luciano Barbera: Pages 77, 134, 145, 219.

Magnum: Page 227.

New Yorker Collection: Mike Twohy: Page 78 (© The New Yorker Collection 1996, Mike Twohy, from cartoonbank.com). Leo Cullum: Pages 120 (© 2002 Leo Cullum from cartoonbank.com; all rights reserved), 144 (© 2002 Leo Cullum, from cartoonbank.com; all rights reserved), 186 (© The New Yorker Collection 1992, Leo Cullum from cartoonbank.com; all rights reserved).

Paul Stuart, New York: Pages 71 (top and bottom), 264.

Patrick Demarchelier, Inc.: Page 132.

Photofest: Pages 24, 79, 93 (middle right), 97 (top), 101, 143, 179, 180, 203, 214 (bottom right).

Polo Ralph Lauren: Pages 32, 69 (top left), 93, 94 (Bruce Weber), 255 (Bruce Weber), 261 (Bruce Weber), 268 (Bruce Weber).

Rapho, Paris: Pages 47, 163, 174, 250.

Retna Ltd. NYC: Page 154 (bottom).

Samuelson: Page 35.

Sipa Press: Page 161 (top).

Topham, Image Works: Pages 118 (top), 161 (bottom), 176.

Underwood & Underwood/Corbis: Pages 3, 104.